The Healthy SlowCooker

More than 100 Recipes for Health and Wellness

Judith Finlayson

Robert
ROSE

For complete cataloguing information, see page 282.

Disclaimer
The recipes in this book have been carefully tested by our kitchen and our tasters. To the best of our knowledge, they are safe and nutritious for ordinary use and users. For those people with food or other allergies, or who have special food requirements or health issues, please read the suggested contents of each recipe carefully and determine whether or not they may create a problem for you. All recipes are used at the risk of the consumer.

We cannot be responsible for any hazards, loss or damage that may occur as a result of any recipe use.

For those with special needs, allergies, requirements or health problems, in the event of any doubt, please contact your medical adviser prior to the use of any recipe.

Design & Production: PageWave Graphics Inc.
Editor: Carol Sherman
Recipe Tester: Jennifer MacKenzie
Copy Editor: Karen Campbell-Sheviak
Photography: Colin Erricson and Mark T. Shapiro
Food Styling: Kate Bush
Prop Styling: Charlene Erricson

Cover image: Mixed Vegetables in Spicy Peanut Sauce (page 216)

We acknowledge the financial support of the Government of Canada through the Book Publishing Industry Development Program (BPIDP) for our publishing activities.

Published by Robert Rose Inc.
120 Eglinton Avenue East, Suite 800, Toronto, Ontario, Canada M4P 1E2
Tel: (416) 322-6552 Fax: (416) 322-6936

Printed in Canada
5 6 7 8 9 TCP 14 13 12 11 10 09

Contents

Acknowledgments

ONCE AGAIN, MY THANKS to the great creative team who work behind the scenes to ensure that my books achieve the highest degree of excellence in editing, photography, styling and design. All the folks at PageWave Graphics — Andrew Smith, Joseph Gisini, Kevin Cockburn and Daniella Zanchetta — for their great design work; my editor Carol Sherman, who is always on top of my shortcomings, yet consistently tactful and fun to work with; Karen Campbell-Sheviak for her keen copy-editing eye; Kate Bush and Charlene Ericson for their talented styling; and last, but certainly not least, Mark Shapiro and Colin Ericson for their beautiful photographs, which make my recipes look delicious.

Special thanks to Audrey King and Jennifer MacKenzie for their diligent help with recipe testing and to all my friends and neighbors, who gallantly tuck in to my culinary creations, even those that miss the mark, and provide thoughtful comments that are always useful in fine-tuning the end result.

I'd also like to thank Bob Dees and Marian Jarkovich at Robert Rose for their consistent commitment to ensuring that my books are well received in the marketplace.

Nutrient Analysis

The nutrient analyses for all the recipes were prepared by Info Access (1988) Inc, Don Mills, Ontario. This also includes the evaluation of recipe servings as sources of nutrients.

The nutrient analyses were based on:

- Imperial measures and weights (except for food typically packaged and used in metric).
- The larger number of servings when there was a range. The smaller amount of ingredients when there was a range.
- The first ingredient listed when there was a choice. The exclusion of "optional" ingredients.
- The exclusion of ingredients with "non-specified" or "to taste" amounts. The analyses were done on the regular recipes, not the "Make Ahead" versions, which might vary slightly in the ingredients used.

The evaluation of recipe servings as sources of nutrients combined U.S. and Canadian regulations. Bearing in mind that the two countries have different reporting standards, the highest standard was always used. As a result, some recipes that would have been identified as an excellent source of a particular nutrient in one country may not contain any reference to the nutrient because the standard is so much higher in the other country.

Introduction

THIS IS MY FOURTH slow cooker cookbook. The more I use my slow cooker, the more ideas I have for using this versatile appliance. It fits so well with how I like to cook that I'm constantly seeing new ways to incorporate its services into my life. So perhaps not surprisingly, I became interested in finding a way to combine the burgeoning interest in health and nutrition with the convenience of using a slow cooker.

Like most people, I'm becoming increasingly aware of the important role diet plays in health. And while most of the recipes in my previous books could be described as nutritious, I gradually came to realize that they didn't maximize the advantages of all the exciting new developments occurring in the field of nutrition. Groundbreaking research is proving that food can provide much more than daily sustenance; it also has the power to prevent, and possibly even cure, many illnesses, from cardiovascular disease and type-2 diabetes to certain kinds of cancer. Integrating some of this information into slow cooker recipes that people can regularly use to make convenient and delicious meals seemed like an excellent idea.

The food we eat contains vitamins and minerals, plus a multitude of compounds known as phytonutrients, some of which you may be familiar with — for instance, antioxidants such as lycopene and beta-carotene, and phytoestrogens such as isoflavones and lignans. All these substances work together to keep us healthy in ways that scientists are only beginning to understand. What we do know, however, is that over the long term we can dramatically influence our health status by eating smarter to get the most out of food. Along with maintaining a healthy weight, being physically active, monitoring alcohol consumption and not smoking, eating a nutritious diet plays a key role in keeping us well.

Current strategies for healthy eating emphasize consuming a wide variety of whole foods, particularly fruits, vegetables and whole grains. By habitually eating an assortment of foods from all the food groups, you're making sure you get the broad mix of essential nutrients that make up a healthy diet: vitamins, minerals and dietary fiber. But more than that, you're tapping into the healing power of food. Emerging evidence indicates that all the nutrients in foods work together to create synergy in the health benefits they produce. A kaleidoscope of colors on your plate signals a host of phytonutrients that team up to keep you healthy. For instance, studies show that the lycopene in red tomatoes and the glucosinolates in green broccoli are far more formidable cancer fighters when combined than either component is on its own.

Making good food choices from every food group also means avoiding junk foods and those that are highly refined. Such foods tend to be high in calories and low in nutrients. Instead, choose foods that are "nutrient dense," those that deliver optimum nutrition for the calories they provide. These include red and orange vegetables, dark leafy greens, unrefined whole grains and deeply colored berries, among others.

Striving to achieve a balance among the intake of good fats, protein and carbohydrates is another objective. Each of these nutrients, which interact with one another in complex ways, plays an important role in helping the body stay well and defend itself against disease. Contrary to conventional wisdom and still a bit controversial, there do not appear to be any links between a low-fat diet and good health. It is the kind of fat that matters. Commercially produced trans fats, which have a well-documented adverse effect on cardiovascular health, should be avoided, and, whenever possible, saturated fats should be replaced with unsaturated fats, which have numerous health benefits. To help you get the most out of this book, in addition to the total amount of fat per serving, the nutritional analysis that accompanies each recipe also specifies the quantities of saturated, monounsaturated and polyunsaturated fat.

In writing this book I've tried to do several things. As in my previous books, I've included a wide range of recipes, from hearty soups to elegant desserts, accompanied, wherever appropriate, by "Make Ahead" information to help you take full advantage of the convenience provided by a slow cooker. But this time I've also focused on making the results as nutritious as possible, without sacrificing one iota of lip-smacking taste. Although this is not a vegetarian cookbook, vegetarian and vegan recipes have been noted. Also, in keeping with the latest research, the recipes emphasize healthy servings of fruits, vegetables and whole grains, and I've kept the proportion of animal protein relatively low. In addition, I've treated every recipe as a focal point for sharing valuable information about nutrition. Every recipe includes:

- a nutritional analysis. This lists the number of calories, and the amount of protein, fat (saturated, monounsaturated and polyunsaturated as well as the total amount), carbohydrates, dietary fiber, sodium and cholesterol per serving;

- an evaluation of the standard nutrients provided by a serving of the recipe. This identifies each serving as an "excellent source," "good source" or "source" of specific vitamins and minerals as well as dietary fiber, based on criteria defined by the USDA and *Canada's Guide to Food Labelling and Advertising*. For more information on how the nutritional analyses and evaluations were determined, see page 4; and

- two other sections, Mindful Morsels and Natural Wonders, which contain additional information on aspects of nutrition to help you make more informed choices about what you eat and to help you develop a pattern of healthy eating.

I hope you will find this book helpful. More importantly, I hope you will use it often to get the most out of the convenience your slow cooker provides by preparing delicious and nutritious meals that help to keep you and yours happy and well.

– Judith Finlayson

Using Your Slow Cooker

An Effective Time Manager

In addition to producing great-tasting food, a slow cooker is one of the most effective time-management tools available. Most recipes can be at least partially prepared up to two days before you intend to cook. (For detailed instructions look for the Make Ahead that accompanies appropriate recipes.) Once the ingredients have been assembled in the stoneware and the appliance is turned on, you can pretty much forget about it. The slow cooker performs unattended while you carry on with your workaday life. You can be away from the kitchen all day and return to a hot, delicious meal.

A Low-Tech Appliance

Slow cookers are amazingly low tech. The appliance usually consists of a metal casing and a stoneware insert with a tight-fitting lid. For convenience, this insert should be removable from the metal casing, making it easier to clean and increasing its versatility as a serving dish. The casing contains the heat source: electrical coils that usually surround the stoneware insert. These coils do their work using the energy it takes to power a 100-watt lightbulb. Because the slow cooker operates on such a small amount of energy, you can safely leave it turned on while you are away from home.

Slow Cooker Basics

Slow cookers are generally round or oval and range in size from 1 to 7 quarts. I feel there is a benefit to having two: a smaller (3 to 4 quart) one, which is ideal for making recipes with smaller yields, such as breakfast cereals and some desserts; and a larger (6 quart) oval one, which is necessary for cooking larger quantities, as well as for making recipes that call for setting a baking dish or pan inside the stoneware. Because the heating coils usually surround the stoneware, most slow cookers cook from the sides, rather than the bottom, which means you'll produce better results if the stoneware is at least half full. Some manufacturers sell a "slow cooker" that is actually a multi-cooker. It has a heating element at the bottom and, in my experience, it cooks faster than a traditional slow cooker. Also, since the heat source is at the bottom, it is possible that the food will scorch during the long cooking time unless it is stirred.

Your slow cooker should come with a booklet that explains how to use the appliance. I recommend that you read this carefully and/or visit the manufacturer's website for specific information on the model you purchased. I've cooked with a variety of slow cookers and have found that cooking times can vary substantially from one to another. Although it may not seem particularly helpful if you're just starting out, the only firm advice I can give is: Know your slow cooker. After trying a few of these recipes, you will get a sense of whether your slow cooker is faster or slower than the ones I use, and you will be able to adjust the cooking times accordingly.

Other variables that can affect cooking time are extreme humidity, power fluctuations and high altitudes. Be extra vigilant if any of these circumstances affects you.

Cooking Great-Tasting Food

The slow cooker's less-is-better approach is, in many ways, the secret of its success. The appliance does its work by cooking foods very slowly — from about 200°F (90°C) on the Low setting to 300°F (150°C) on High. This slow, moist cooking environment enables the appliance to produce mouth-watering braises, chilies and many other kinds of soups and stews, as well as delicious breakfast cereals and desserts.

Slow Cooker Tips

Understanding Your Slow Cooker
Like all appliances, the slow cooker has its unique way of doing things and, as a result, you need to understand how it works and adapt your cooking style accordingly. Success in the slow cooker, like success in the oven or on top of the stove, depends upon using proper cooking techniques. The slow cooker saves you time because it allows you to forget about the food once it is in the stoneware. But you still must pay attention to the advance preparation. Here are a few tips that will help to ensure slow cooker success.

Soften Vegetables
Although it requires using an extra pan, I am committed to softening most vegetables before adding them to the slow cooker. In my experience, this is not the most time-consuming part of preparing a slow cooker dish — it usually takes longer to peel and chop the vegetables, which you have to do anyway. But softening vegetables such as onions and carrots, dramatically improves the quality of the dish for two reasons: not only does it add color, it begins the process of caramelization, which breaks down their natural sugars and releases the flavor; it also extracts the fat-soluble components of foods, which further enriches the taste. Moreover, tossing herbs and spices with the softened vegetables emulsifies their flavor, helping to produce a sauce in which the flavors are better integrated into the dish than they would have been if this step had been skipped.

Reduce Liquid
As you use your slow cooker, one of the first things you will notice is that it generates a tremendous amount of liquid. Because slow cookers cook at a low heat, tightly covered, liquid doesn't evaporate as it does in the oven or on top of the stove. As a result, food made from traditional recipes will be watery. So the second rule of successful slow cooking is to reduce the amount of liquid. Naturally, you don't want to reduce the flavor, so I suggest using stock, rather than water, to cook most of the dishes. The other potential problem with liquid generation is that is can affect the results of starch dishes, such as cakes and some grains. One technique that works well with such dishes is to place folded tea towels over top of the stoneware before covering with the lid. This prevents accumulated moisture from dripping on the food.

Cut Root Vegetables into Thin Slices or Small Pieces
Perhaps surprisingly, root vegetables — carrots, parsnips, turnips and, particularly, potatoes — cook very slowly in the slow cooker. As a result, root vegetables should be thinly sliced or cut into small pieces no larger than 1-inch (2.5 cm) cubes.

Pay Attention to Cooking Temperature

Many desserts, such as those containing milk, cream or some leavening agents, need to be cooked on High. In these recipes, a Low setting is not suggested as an option. For recipes that aren't dependent upon cooking at a particular temperature, the rule of thumb is that 1 hour of cooking on High equals 2 to $2\frac{1}{2}$ hours on Low.

Don't Overcook

Although slow cooking reduces your chances of overcooking food, it is still not a "one size fits all" solution to meal preparation. Many vegetables, such as beans, lentils and root vegetables, need a good eight-hour cooking span and may even benefit from a longer cooking time. But others, such as green beans and cauliflower, are usually cooked within 6 hours on Low and will be overcooked and unappetizing if left for longer. One solution (which is not possible if you are cooking meat because of food safety concerns) is to extend the cooking time by assembling the dish ahead, then refrigerating it overnight in the stoneware. Because the mixture and the stoneware are chilled, the vegetables will take longer to cook. This is a useful technique if you are cooking more-tender vegetables and need to be away from the house all day.

Use Ingredients Appropriately

Some ingredients do not respond well to long, slow cooking at all, and should be added during the last 30 minutes of cooking, after the temperature has been increased to High. These include zucchini, peas, snow peas, fish, seafood, milk and cream (which will curdle if cooked too long.)

Although I love to cook with peppers, I've learned that most peppers become bitter if cooked for too long. The same holds true for cayenne pepper or hot pepper sauces such as Tabasco, and large quantities of spicy curry powder. (Small quantities of mild curry powder seem to fare well, possibly because natural sugars in the vegetables counter any bitterness.) The solution to this problem is to add fresh green or red bell peppers to recipes during the last 30 minutes of cooking, use cayenne pepper in small quantities, if at all, and add hot pepper sauce after the dish is cooked. All the recipes in this book address these concerns in the instructions.

Whole Leaf Herbs and Spices

For best results, use whole or coarsely ground, rather than finely ground, herbs and spices in the slow cooker. Spices, such as cumin seeds, which have been toasted and coarsely ground, and whole leaf herbs, such as dried thyme and oregano leaves, release their flavors slowly throughout the long cooking period, unlike ground spices and herbs, which tend to lose flavor during slow cooking. If you're using fresh herbs, add them finely chopped during the last hour of cooking unless you include the whole stem (this works best with thyme and rosemary).

I recommend the use of cracked black peppercorns rather than ground pepper in many of my recipes because they release flavor slowly during the long cooking process. "Cracked pepper" can be purchased in the spice sections of supermarkets, but I like to make my own in a mortar with a pestle. If you prefer to use ground black pepper, use one-quarter to half the amount of cracked black peppercorns called for in the recipe.

Using Dishes and Pans in the Slow Cooker

Some recipes, notably breads, need to be cooked in an extra dish placed in the slow cooker stoneware. Not only will you need a large oval slow cooker for this purpose, finding a dish or pan that fits into the stoneware can be a challenge. I've found that several kinds of dishes suit this purpose very well: Standard 7-inch (17.5 cm) square, 4-cup (1 L) and 6-cup (1.5 L) ovenproof baking dishes, a 6-cup (1.5 L) soufflé dish and 8-by 4-inch (20 by 10 cm) loaf pan. Before you decide to make a recipe requiring a baking dish, ensure that you have a container that will fit into your stoneware. I've noted the size and dimensions of the containers used in all relevant recipes. Be aware that varying the size and shape of the dish is likely to affect cooking times.

Maximize Slow Cooker Convenience

Although slow cookers can produce mouth-watering food, the appliance's other great strength is convenience. Where appropriate, all my recipes contain a Make Ahead tip to help you maximize this attribute. To get the most out of your slow cooker, consider the following:

- Prepare ingredients to the cooking stage the night before you intend to cook, to keep work to a minimum in the morning.
- Cook a recipe overnight and refrigerate until ready to serve.

Bread & Breakfast

Apple Cranberry Bread, see recipe overleaf

Apple Cranberry Bread

I love the combination of flavors in this delicious bread — a hint of orange combined with tart cranberries. It makes a great snack, a nutritious dessert and can even be eaten for breakfast.

MAKES 1 LOAF
FOR 8 SERVINGS

TIP

❖ **This bread, like the others in this book, can be made in almost any kind of baking dish that will fit into your slow cooker. I have a variety of baking pans that work well: a small loaf pan (about 8-by 4-inches/20 by 10 cm) makes a traditionally shaped bread; a round (6-cup/1.5 L) soufflé dish or a square (7-inch/17.5 cm) baking dish produces slices of different shapes. All taste equally good.**

- Large (minimum 5 quart) oval slow cooker
- Greased 8-by 4-inch (20 by 10 cm) approx. loaf pan or 6-cup (1.5 L) soufflé or baking dish (see Tip, left)

1 cup	all-purpose flour, unbleached if possible	250 mL
1 cup	whole wheat flour	250 mL
1/4 cup	milled flaxseeds	50 mL
2 tsp	baking powder	10 mL
1/2 tsp	salt	2 mL
1/2 tsp	ground cinnamon	2 mL
3/4 cup	Demerara or evaporated cane juice sugar (see Natural Wonders, page 259)	175 mL
1/4 cup	olive oil	50 mL
1	egg	1
2 tbsp	finely grated orange zest (2 oranges)	25 mL
3/4 cup	orange juice (1 large navel orange)	175 mL
1 tsp	vanilla	5 mL
1 cup	finely chopped peeled cored apple (about 1 apple)	250 mL
1 cup	fresh or frozen cranberries	250 mL

1. In a bowl or on a sheet of waxed paper, combine all-purpose and whole wheat flours, flaxseeds, baking powder, salt and cinnamon.

2. In a separate bowl, beat sugar, oil, egg, orange zest and juice and vanilla until thoroughly blended. Add dry ingredients, stirring just until blended. Fold in apple and cranberries.

3. Spoon batter into prepared pan. Cover tightly with foil and secure with a string. Place in slow cooker stoneware and pour in enough boiling water to come 1 inch (2.5 mL) up the sides of the dish. Cover and cook on High for 4 hours, until a tester inserted in the center comes out clean. Unmold and serve warm or let cool.

Mindful Morsels

Not only are oranges an excellent source of vitamin C, they are also a source of fiber, folacin, thiamin and potassium. They also contain calcium.

Natural Wonders

FLAXSEEDS

Sprinkled over your morning cereal or added to baked goods or smoothies, nutrient dense flaxseeds are an excellent supplement to your diet. In addition to being a source of iron, magnesium and potassium, flaxseeds are high in fiber so they help you to stay regular and keep your cholesterol levels under control. Moreover, flaxseeds are one of the best plant sources of heart-healthy omega-3 fats. They also contain lignans, a plant fiber that protects against cancer. In fact, the USDA lists 27 anticancer agents in flax. When using flaxseeds, buy the milled variety or grind them yourself, otherwise the seeds will pass through your system without providing nutritive value.

Nutrients Per Serving	
Calories	307
Protein	5.7 g
Carbohydrates	51.7 g
Fat (Total)	9.6 g
Saturated Fat	1.3 g
Monounsaturated Fat	5.6 g
Polyunsaturated Fat	2.0 g
Dietary Fiber	4.8 g
Sodium	227 mg
Cholesterol	23 mg

Good source of folacin, magnesium and iron.

Source of vitamin C and phosphorus.

Contains a high amount of dietary fiber.

Pumpkin Date Loaf

My husband always has a second helping of this scrumptious loaf, which is very moist and dense. If you feel like splurging, top the cake with a dollop of ice cream and serve it for dessert. Refrigerate any leftovers and serve them cold or, if you prefer, reheated in the microwave.

MAKES 1 LOAF
FOR 8 SERVINGS

TIPS

❖ **This bread, like the others in this book, can be made in almost any kind of baking dish that will fit into your slow cooker. I have a variety of baking pans that work well: a small loaf pan (about 8-by 4-inches/20 by 10 cm) makes a traditionally shaped bread; a round (6-cup/1.5 L) soufflé dish or a square (7-inch/17.5 cm) baking dish produces slices of different shapes. All taste equally good.**

❖ **If you prefer smaller round loaves, make this bread using three 19 oz (540 mL) vegetable tins, washed dried and sprayed with vegetable oil. Cover tops tightly with foil and reduce cooking time to 2 hours.**

- Large (minimum 5 quart) oval slow cooker
- Greased 8-by 4-inch (20 by 10 cm) approx. loaf pan or 6-cup (1.5 L) soufflé or baking dish (see Tips, left)

1 cup	all-purpose flour, unbleached if possible	250 mL
1 tsp	baking soda	5 mL
1/2 tsp	salt	2 mL
1/2 cup	finely chopped pitted soft dates, such as Medjool (5 to 6 dates)	125 mL
1/2 cup	finely chopped pecans	125 mL
2	eggs	2
1/2 cup	packed muscovado or evaporated cane juice sugar	125 mL
2 tbsp	olive oil	25 mL
1 cup	pumpkin purée (not pie filling)	250 mL
1 tsp	ground cinnamon	5 mL
1/2 tsp	freshly grated nutmeg	2 mL
1/4 tsp	ground ginger	1 mL

1. In a large bowl, mix together flour, baking soda and salt. Add dates and, using your fingers, separate any pieces of dates that are stuck together, ensuring that the bits are coated in flour. Add pecans and stir to blend. Make a well in the center.

2. In a separate bowl, beat eggs, sugar and olive oil until smooth and blended. Add pumpkin, cinnamon, nutmeg and ginger and mix well. Add to well in dry ingredients and mix just until blended.

3. Spoon batter into prepared pan. Cover tightly with foil and secure with a string. Place pan in slow cooker stoneware and pour in enough boiling water to come 1 inch (2.5 cm) up the sides. Cover and cook on High for 3 hours, until a tester inserted in the center of the loaf comes out clean. Unmold and serve warm or let cool.

Mindful Morsels

Like many spices, nutmeg has traditionally been used for medicinal purposes. Contemporary researchers are investigating the potential benefits of many spices to confirm whether traditional applications really work and the results look promising.

Natural Wonders

VITAMIN A

The pumpkin in this recipe is an excellent source of beta-carotene, the plant form of vitamin A. (For more on carotenoids, see Natural Wonders, page 47.) Although vitamin A is famous for keeping your eyes healthy, it has other important functions, such as contributing to your night-vision capabilities, supporting bone growth and keeping cells functioning well. Recent research suggests it may have anticarcinogenic properties, as well. It is a fat-soluble vitamin, which means your body may not effectively absorb and utilize the vitamin A in foods unless you have an adequate intake of dietary fat. However, your body stores fat soluble vitamins, so taking a high dose supplement isn't a good idea because any excess will remain in your body, where it has the potential to become toxic. Obtaining vitamin A from foods such as orange vegetables and fruits is the best strategy for good health.

Nutrients Per Serving	
Calories	250
Protein	4.4 g
Carbohydrates	37.5 g
Fat (Total)	10.2 g
Saturated Fat	1.4 g
Monounsaturated Fat	6.0 g
Polyunsaturated Fat	2.1 g
Dietary Fiber	2.9 g
Sodium	312 mg
Cholesterol	47 mg

Excellent source of vitamin A.

Good source of vitamin K.

Source of iron.

Contains a moderate amount of dietary fiber.

Banana Walnut Oat Bread

This moist and flavorful bread makes a delicious snack. You can also serve it as a dessert or for a breakfast on the run.

MAKES 1 LOAF
FOR 8 SERVINGS

TIPS

❖ This bread, like the others in this book, can be made in almost any kind of baking dish that will fit into your slow cooker. I have a variety of baking pans that work well: a small loaf pan (about 8-by 4-inches/20 by 10 cm) makes a traditionally shaped bread; a round (6-cup/1.5 L) soufflé dish or a square (7-inch/17.5 cm) baking dish produces slices of different shapes. All taste equally good.

❖ To ease cleanup, mix the dry ingredients on a sheet of waxed paper, instead of using a bowl.

- Large (minimum 5 quart) oval slow cooker
- Greased 8-by 4-inch (20 by 10 cm) approx. loaf pan or 6-cup (1.5 L) soufflé or baking dish (see Tips, left)

$1/3$ cup	butter, softened	75 mL
$2/3$ cup	Demerara or evaporated cane juice sugar	150 mL
2	eggs	2
3	ripe bananas, mashed (about $1\,1/4$ cups/300 mL)	3
$3/4$ cup	all-purpose flour, unbleached if possible	175 mL
$3/4$ cup	rolled oats (not quick-cooking)	175 mL
2 tbsp	milled flaxseeds	25 mL
2 tsp	baking powder	10 mL
$1/2$ tsp	salt	2 mL
$1/4$ tsp	baking soda	1 mL
$1/2$ cup	finely chopped walnuts	125 mL

1. In a bowl, beat butter and sugar until light and creamy. Add eggs, one at a time, beating until incorporated. Beat in bananas.

2. In a separate bowl (see Tips, left), combine flour, oats, flaxseeds, baking powder, salt and baking soda. Add to banana mixture, stirring just until combined. Fold in walnuts.

3. Spoon batter into prepared pan. Cover tightly with foil and secure with a string. Place pan in slow cooker stoneware and pour in enough boiling water to come 1 inch (2.5 cm) up the sides. Cover and cook on High for 3 hours, until a tester inserted in the center comes out clean. Unmold and serve warm or let cool.

Mindful Morsels

This bread is rich in heart healthy polyunsaturated fats. One slice contains 1.25 grams of omega-3 and 2.7 grams of omega-6 fatty acids.

Natural Wonders

BANANAS

Available year-round, bananas are one of our most healthful and versatile fruits. They make a great addition to breads, muffins and morning smoothies as well as a delicious snack on their own. A good source of vitamin B6, bananas also contain folacin and fiber and are one of the best food sources of potassium. Bananas do not contain any sodium, and eating a healthy diet that contains foods high in potassium and low in sodium appears to reduce the risk of high blood pressure. Bananas also contain a phytochemical called fructooligosaccharide, which has been shown to increase the ability to absorb calcium in laboratory situations. In addition, research suggests that bananas may be an especially potent force in battling kidney cancer. One study published in the *International Journal of Cancer* found that women who ate bananas four to six times a week reduced their chances of developing this disease by 50 percent.

Nutrients Per Serving	
Calories	327
Protein	6.0 g
Carbohydrates	44.1 g
Fat (Total)	15.3 g
Saturated Fat	5.9 g
Monounsaturated Fat	3.7 g
Polyunsaturated Fat	4.8 g
Dietary Fiber	3.0 g
Sodium	347 mg
Cholesterol	71 mg

Good source of vitamin B6, folacin, magnesium and potassium.

Source of phosphorus and iron.

Contains a moderate amount of dietary fiber.

Caraway Soda Bread

I love the caraway flavor in this classic Irish soda bread. It makes a great accompaniment to hearty soups and stews.

MAKES 1 LOAF OR 8 SERVINGS

TIPS

❖ **If you don't like the texture of whole caraway seeds, toast them in a dry skillet over medium heat, stirring, until fragrant, about 3 minutes, then grind them in a mortar or a spice grinder before adding to the dry ingredients.**

❖ **This bread, like the others in this book, can be made in almost any kind of baking dish that will fit into your slow cooker. I have a variety of baking pans that work well: a small loaf pan (about 8-by 4-inches/20 by 10 cm) makes a traditionally shaped bread; a round (6-cup/1.5 L) soufflé dish or a square (7-inch/17.5 cm) baking dish produces slices of different shapes. All taste equally good.**

- Large (minimum 5 quart) oval slow cooker
- Lightly greased 8-by 4-inch (20 by 10 cm) approx. loaf pan or 6-cup (1.5 L) soufflé or baking dish (see Tips, left)

1 cup	whole wheat flour	250 mL
1 cup	all-purpose flour, unbleached if possible	250 mL
2 tsp	caraway seeds (see Tips, left)	10 mL
2 tsp	granulated sugar	10 mL
1 tsp	baking soda	5 mL
1/2 tsp	salt	2 mL
3/4 cup	buttermilk	175 mL
2 tbsp	olive oil	25 mL

1. In a large bowl, mix together whole wheat and all-purpose flours, caraway seeds, sugar, baking soda and salt. Make a well in the center.

2. In measuring cup, stir together buttermilk and olive oil. Pour into well and mix just until blended. Knead several times to make dough fit the shape of your pan and place in prepared pan.

3. Cover pan tightly with aluminum foil. Place in slow cooker stoneware and pour in enough boiling water to come 1 inch (2.5 cm) up the sides of the dish. Cover and cook on High for 2 1/2 to 3 hours, until bread springs back when touched lightly in the center. Unmold and serve warm.

Mindful Morsels

Earthy and pungent, caraway is an ancient herb that has been used for medicinal and culinary purposes throughout history. Long recognized as a digestive aid, in recent years caraway seeds have been identified as a source of limonene, a powerful phytochemical that may help to protect against breast cancer.

Natural Wonders

WHOLE WHEAT FLOUR

Substituting whole wheat flour for some or all of the white flour in any recipe is a healthful strategy. Unlike all-purpose flour, whole wheat flour includes all three nutrient-rich parts of the wheat berry: the bran, the germ and the endosperm. (White flour uses only the endosperm.) Whole wheat flour has more protein, fiber, niacin, pantothenic acid and vitamins E and B6 than white flour. It is also much higher in magnesium and zinc. The fiber in whole wheat flour is one of its most valuable attributes. Another benefit to using whole wheat rather than white flour is its antioxidant strength. New research from Kansas State University is showing that the orthophenols in wheat contain powerful antioxidants.

Nutrients Per Serving	
Calories	153
Protein	4.5 g
Carbohydrates	25.2 g
Fat (Total)	4.1 g
Saturated Fat	0.7 g
Monounsaturated Fat	2.6 g
Polyunsaturated Fat	0.5 g
Dietary Fiber	2.4 g
Sodium	315 mg
Cholesterol	1 mg

Contains a moderate amount of dietary fiber.

See photo, page 22

Creamy Morning Millet with Apples

If you're tired of the same old breakfast, perk up your taste buds and expand your nutritional range by enjoying millet as a cereal. Don't worry about making more than you need. You can refrigerate leftovers for up to two days and reheat by portions in the microwave.

MAKES
4 TO 6 SERVINGS

TIPS

❖ If you prefer a non-creamy version, substitute water for the rice milk.

❖ Use plain or vanilla-flavored rice milk. Vary the quantity to suit your preference. Three 3 cups (750 mL) produces a firmer result. If you like your cereal to be creamy, use the larger quantity.

Nutrients Per Serving	
Calories	228
Protein	4.3 g
Carbohydrates	48.1 g
Fat (Total)	2.3 g
Saturated Fat	0.2 g
Monounsaturated Fat	1.0 g
Polyunsaturated Fat	0.8 g
Dietary Fiber	6.1 g
Sodium	138 mg
Cholesterol	0 mg

Good source of vitamin B12, phosphorus and magnesium

Source of calcium

Contains a very high amount of dietary fiber.

- Works best in a small (3½ quart) slow cooker (see Tips, page 29)
- Greased slow cooker stoneware

1 cup	millet (see Tips, page 26)	250 mL
3 to 4 cups	enriched rice milk or water (see Tips, left)	750 mL to 1 L
3	apples, peeled, cored and chopped	3
¼ tsp	salt	1 mL
	Chopped pitted dates, fresh berries and toasted nuts, optional	

1. In prepared slow cooker stoneware, combine millet, rice milk, apples and salt. Cover and cook on High for 4 hours or on Low for 8 hours or overnight. Stir well, spoon into bowls and sprinkle with fruit and/or nuts, if using.

VARIATION

Use half millet and half short-grain brown rice.

Mindful Morsels

For maximum health benefits, sprinkle this and other cereals with toasted nuts, which contain heart-healthy unsaturated fat.

Natural Wonders

MILLET

A nutritious whole grain, gluten-free millet is high in fiber and relatively high in protein. It contains the B-complex vitamins thiamin, niacin and riboflavin, as well as the minerals magnesium, iron and phosphorous. It also contains an assortment of beneficial phytochemicals. To boot, millet is particularly easy to digest.

See photo, page 23

Breakfast Rice

Simple yet delicious, this tasty combination couldn't be easier to make.

- **Works best in a small (3½ quart) slow cooker (see Tips, page 29)**
- **Greased slow cooker stoneware**

1 cup	brown rice	250 mL
4 cups	vanilla-flavored enriched rice milk	1 L
½ cup	dried cherries or cranberries	125 mL

1. In prepared slow cooker stoneware, combine rice, rice milk and cherries. Place a clean tea towel folded in half (so you will have two layers) over top of stoneware to absorb moisture. Cover and cook on High for 4 hours or on Low for up to 8 hours or overnight. Stir well and serve.

VARIATION

Use half rice and half wheat berries.

Mindful Morsels
Cherries (along with cranberries, blueberries and other red, purple and blue fruits) contain anthocyanins, a flavonoid with anti-inflammatory properties.

Natural Wonders
RICE
Few foods are more ubiquitous than rice, which is eaten around the world. Although many people consume white rice, brown rice is far more nutritious. A complex carbohydrate, it contains much more fiber than white rice, as well as B vitamins and minerals such as manganese, selenium and magnesium. Its bran layer contains the compound oryzanol, which may help keep cholesterol under control. It is rich in phytonutrients — when researchers measured the antioxidant activity of some whole grains, brown rice came in fourth behind corn, whole wheat and oats. Because it also contains essential oils, which become rancid at room temperature, brown rice should be stored in the refrigerator in an airtight container.

MAKES 4 SERVINGS

TIP
❖ Made with this quantity of liquid, the rice will be a bit crunchy around the edges, which suits my taste. If you prefer a softer version or will be cooking it longer than 8 hours, add ½ cup (125 mL) of water or rice milk to the recipe.

Nutrients Per Serving	
Calories	363
Protein	5.7 g
Carbohydrates	77.3 g
Fat (Total)	3.7 g
Saturated Fat	0.3 g
Monounsaturated Fat	2.2 g
Polyunsaturated Fat	1.1 g
Dietary Fiber	6.5 g
Sodium	93 mg
Cholesterol	0 mg

Excellent source of vitamin B12, calcium and phosphorus.

Good source of magnesium.

Source of vitamins A and B6.

Contains a very high amount of dietary fiber.

Multigrain Cereal with Fruit

A steaming bowl of this tasty cereal gets you off to a good start in the morning by providing a portion of the nutrients you'll need to remain energized and productive throughout the day.

MAKES 6 TO 8 SERVINGS

TIPS

❖ Like lentils, some millet may contain bits of dirt or discolored grains. If your millet looks grimy, rinse it thoroughly in a pot of water before using. Swish it around and remove any offending particles, then rinse under cold running water.

❖ The addition of salt adds a bit of depth to this cereal. If you're watching your sodium intake, feel free to omit it.

❖ If you're not using Medjool dates, which are naturally soft, place the chopped dates in a microwave-safe dish, cover with water and microwave on High for 30 seconds to soften before adding to cereal.

❖ This cereal has a tendency to get dry and brown around the edges if cooked for longer than 8 hours. If you need to cook it for longer, add an additional ½ cup (125 mL) of water.

- Works best in a small (3½ quart) slow cooker (see Tips, page 29)
- Greased slow cooker stoneware

½ cup	brown rice	125 mL
½ cup	millet (see Tips, left)	125 mL
½ cup	wheat berries	125 mL
2	medium all-purpose apples, peeled, cored and thinly sliced	2
4 cups	water (see Tips, left)	1 L
½ tsp	vanilla	2 mL
¼ tsp	salt, optional	1 mL
½ cup	chopped pitted soft dates, preferably Medjool (see Tips, left)	125 mL
	Chopped toasted nuts, optional	
	Wheat germ, optional	

1. In prepared slow cooker stoneware, combine rice, millet, wheat berries and apples. Add water, vanilla and salt, if using. Cover and cook on Low for up to 8 hours or overnight. Add dates and stir well. Serve sprinkled with toasted nuts and/or wheat germ, if using.

Mindful Morsels

Sprinkling your morning cereal with a tablespoon (15 mL) or two (25 mL) of wheat germ will significantly boost your nutrient intake because wheat germ is particularly nutrient dense. It contains fiber, folacin and vitamin E, along with a wide range of minerals. It also contains healthy omega-3 fats.

Natural Wonders

BREAKFAST

Breakfast is the most important meal of the day. Not only does a good breakfast help you feel energized and keep you productive throughout the day, it is also good for your heart and helps keep your weight under control. Research shows a link between eating breakfast, particularly whole-grain cereals, and lower levels of cholesterol. For instance, a study in the *American Journal of Clinical Nutrition* reported that healthy women who skipped breakfast paid the price with higher levels of blood cholesterol and lower levels of the hormone that helps to control blood sugar. They also snacked more during the day, consuming more calories than they would have if they enjoyed a morning meal.

Nutrients Per Serving	
Calories	232
Protein	5.0 g
Carbohydrates	52.2 g
Fat (Total)	1.4 g
Saturated Fat	0.2 g
Monounsaturated Fat	0.3 g
Polyunsaturated Fat	0.6 g
Dietary Fiber	6.1 g
Sodium	9 mg
Cholesterol	0 mg

Good source of magnesium and phosphorous.

Source of vitamin B6.

Contains a very high amount of dietary fiber.

Apple Oatmeal with Wheat Berries

This flavorful cereal is an adaptation of a recipe that appeared in Eat, Drink and Be Healthy: The Harvard Medical School Guide to Healthy Eating.

MAKES 6 SERVINGS

TIP

❖ The nutritional analysis on this recipe was done using sweetened cranberry cocktail, which adds 24 calories and 6 grams of carbohydrate to every serving of this cereal. If you prefer, use unsweetened cranberry juice from a natural foods store or well-stocked supermarket.

- Works best in a small (3½ quart) slow cooker (see Tips, page 29)
- Greased slow cooker stoneware

1½ cups	steel-cut oats	375 mL
½ cup	wheat berries	125 mL
2	apples, peeled, cored and chopped	2
½ tsp	ground cinnamon	2 mL
½ tsp	vanilla	2 mL
3½ cups	water	875 mL
1 cup	cranberry or apple juice (see Tip, left)	250 mL
	Evaporated cane juice sugar, toasted walnuts and wheat germ, optional	

1. In prepared slow cooker, combine steel-cut oats, wheat berries, apples, cinnamon and vanilla. Add water and cranberry juice. Cover and cook on High for 4 hours or on Low for 8 hours or overnight. Stir well. Top with sugar, walnuts and/or wheat germ, if using.

Nutrients Per Serving	
Calories	185
Protein	5.1 g
Carbohydrates	38.8 g
Fat (Total)	1.9 g
Saturated Fat	0.5 g
Monounsaturated Fat	0.5 g
Polyunsaturated Fat	0.8 g
Dietary Fiber	4.9 g
Sodium	6 mg
Cholesterol	0 mg

Good source of phosphorus and magnesium.

Source of vitamin C.

Contains a high amount of dietary fiber.

Mindful Morsels

Wheat berries and brown rice are sources of selenium, a mineral that may have cancer-protective properties.

Natural Wonders

STRESS-BUSTING BREAKFAST

Although breakfast has many benefits, most people aren't likely to identify it as a stress buster. But if you start the day off with a bowl of whole-grain cereal, that's exactly what it can be. Eating complex carbohydrates, such as the whole grains in this cereal, appears to replenish the brain chemical serotonin, which helps your body deal with stress. Magnesium, which is also found in whole grains, may help keep blood pressure under control.

Irish Oatmeal

Although rolled oats are very tasty, my favorite oat cereal is steel-cut oats, which are often sold under the name "Irish Oatmeal." They have more flavor than rolled oats and an appealing crunchy texture.

- **Works best in a small (3½ quart) slow cooker (see Tips, right)**
- **Greased slow cooker stoneware**

1 cup	steel-cut oats	250 mL
½ tsp	salt	2 mL
4 cups	water	1 L
	Raisins, chopped bananas or pitted dates, optional	
	Toasted nuts, seeds and milk, optional	

1. In prepared slow cooker, combine oats and salt. Add water. Cover and cook on High for 4 hours or on Low for 8 hours or overnight. Stir well. Stir in fruit to taste, or garnish with nuts, if using, or add milk, if desired.

MAKES 4 SERVINGS

TIPS

❖ **If you are cooking this cereal in a large oval slow cooker, reduce the cooking time by half.**

❖ **If you prefer a creamier version of this cereal make it using half skim or 2% evaporated milk and half water.**

Mindful Morsels

If you're concerned about osteoporosis, limit your intake of caffeine because drinking more than four cups of coffee a day may cause calcium to be excreted in the urine.

Natural Wonders

FRUIT, SEEDS AND NUTS

Although most whole-grain cereals are delicious served with milk or a dairy substitute, sprinkling your breakfast cereal with fruit, nuts and/or seeds expands your intake of nutrients and helps you get the servings you need from the various food groups. All these additions contain fiber. Berries add vitamin C and their own collection of phytochemicals. Nuts and seeds are high in essential fatty acids, among other benefits. Sunflower seeds are high in vitamin E and a good source of potassium. Pumpkin seeds are a source of vegetable protein and iron. They also contain magnesium and zinc.

Nutrients Per Serving	
Calories	90
Protein	3.6 g
Carbohydrates	15.8 g
Fat (Total)	1.5 g
Saturated Fat	0.4 g
Monounsaturated Fat	0.5 g
Polyunsaturated Fat	0.6 g
Dietary Fiber	2.1 g
Sodium	296 mg
Cholesterol	0 mg

Source of phosphorus.

Contains a moderate amount of dietary fiber.

Soups

Turkey and Corn Chowder with Barley, see recipe overleaf

Turkey and Corn Chowder with Barley

A steaming bowl of this zesty rib-sticking chowder will satisfy even the pickiest eater. It is equally good made with previously uncooked turkey or meat leftover from the holiday bird. Add whole grain rolls and a green or sliced tomato salad for a delicious light meal.

MAKES 10 SERVINGS

TIPS

❖ You can also make this soup using cooked leftover turkey. Use 3 cups (750 mL) shredded turkey and add it along with the green pepper after the soup has cooked.

❖ If you don't have pure ancho or New Mexico chili powder, use your favorite chili powder blend, instead.

❖ Add the jalapeño pepper if you like a bit of heat, or the chipotle pepper if you like a hint of smoke, as well.

MAKE AHEAD
This dish can be partially prepared before it is cooked. Complete Steps 1 and 2. Cover and refrigerate overnight or for up to 2 days. When you're ready to cook, continue with Step 3.

● **Large (minimum 6 quart) slow cooker**

1 tbsp	cumin seeds	15 mL
1 tbsp	olive oil	15 mL
2	onions, finely chopped	2
6	stalks celery, diced	6
4	cloves garlic, minced	4
2 tsp	dried oregano leaves, crumbled	10 mL
1/2 tsp	cracked black peppercorns	2 mL
8 cups	Homemade Chicken Stock (see recipe, page 35) or prepared chicken or turkey stock	2 L
3/4 cup	whole (hulled) or pot barley, rinsed (see Mindful Morsels, page 65)	175 mL
2 lbs	skinless boneless turkey, cut into 1/2-inch (1 cm) cubes (about 3 cups/750 mL)	1 kg
2 cups	frozen corn kernels	500 mL
1 tsp	ancho or New Mexico chili powder, dissolved in 2 tbsp (25 mL) freshly squeezed lemon juice (see Tips, left)	5 mL
1	green bell pepper, seeded and diced	1
1	jalapeño pepper or chipotle pepper in adobo sauce, diced, optional (see Tips, left)	1
	Finely chopped cilantro, optional	

1. In a dry skillet over medium heat, toast cumin seeds, stirring, until fragrant and they just begin to brown, about 3 minutes. Immediately transfer to a mortar or a spice grinder and grind. Set aside.

2. In the same skillet, heat oil over medium heat for 30 seconds. Add onions and celery and cook, stirring, until celery is softened, about 5 minutes. Add garlic, oregano, peppercorns and reserved cumin and cook, stirring, for 1 minute. Transfer to slow cooker stoneware. Add chicken stock and stir well.

3. Add barley, turkey and corn. Cover and cook on Low for 8 hours or on High for 4 hours, until turkey and barley are tender. Stir in chili powder solution. Add green pepper and jalapeño pepper, if using, and stir well. Cover and cook on High for 20 minutes, until pepper is tender. To serve, ladle into bowls and garnish with cilantro, if using.

Mindful Morsels
Ounce for ounce, nippy jalapeño peppers contain more nutrients than bell peppers, their sweet-tasting relatives.

Natural Wonders
VITAMIN B6
A serving of this tasty soup is an excellent source of vitamin B6. The peppers and the turkey are a source of this important nutrient, which will help to keep your body running in tip-top form. Vitamin B6 supports your nervous system, helping your body deal with stress. One study conducted at Tufts University's Human Nutrition Research Center on Aging found a link between lower levels of B6 and increased levels of irritability in the subjects studied. Vitamin B6 also helps your body create protein so it can make new cells. Due to its important role in cell formation, a B6 deficiency shows up promptly on the skin. Because skin is constantly renewing itself, it's likely to reveal problems with cell regeneration in advance of other organs. A skin disorder, such as eczema or seborrhea, may be one of the first symptoms of a deficiency of this vitamin. According to a recent study reported in the *Journal of the National Cancer Institute*, vitamin B6 may also lower the risk of colon cancer, one of the most common cancers in North America.

Nutrients Per Serving	
Calories	216
Protein	22.3 g
Carbohydrates	23.1 g
Fat (Total)	4.3 g
Saturated Fat	1.0 g
Monounsaturated Fat	2.1 g
Polyunsaturated Fat	0.9 g
Dietary Fiber	2.8 g
Sodium	97 mg
Cholesterol	56 mg

Excellent source of vitamin B6.

Good source of vitamin K, folacin, magnesium, potassium, phosphorus, iron and zinc.

Source of vitamin C.

Contains a moderate amount of dietary fiber.

Basic Vegetable Stock

These stock recipes, each of which make enough for two average soup recipes, can be made ahead and frozen. For convenience, cook them overnight in the slow cooker. If your slow cooker is not large enough to make a full batch, you can halve the recipes.

MAKES ABOUT 12 CUPS (3 L)

TIPS

❖ **To freeze stock, transfer to airtight containers in small, measured portions (2 cups/500 mL or 4 cups/1 L are handy), leaving at least 1 inch (2.5 cm) headspace for expansion. Refrigerate until chilled, cover and freeze for up to 3 months. Thaw in refrigerator or microwave before using.**

❖ **We have not included a nutrient analysis for Basic Vegetable Stock because it contains virtually no nutrients. The advantage to making your own vegetable stock is to reduce your consumption of sodium. One cup (250 mL) of this stock with no salt added, contains 0 mg of sodium. The same quantity of a typical prepared stock likely contains more than 500 mg of sodium.**

• **Large (minimum 6 quart) slow cooker**

8	carrots, scrubbed and coarsely chopped	8
6	stalks celery, coarsely chopped	6
3	onions, coarsely chopped	3
3	cloves garlic, coarsely chopped	3
6	sprigs parsley	6
3	bay leaves	3
10	black peppercorns	10
1 tsp	dried thyme leaves	5 mL
	Salt, optional	
12 cups	water	3 L

1. In slow cooker stoneware, combine carrots, celery, onions, garlic, parsley, bay leaves, peppercorns, salt to taste, if using, and water. Cover and cook on Low for 8 hours or on High for 4 hours. Strain and discard solids. Cover and refrigerate for up to 5 days or freeze in an airtight container.

VARIATION

Enhanced Vegetable Stock

To enhance 8 cups (2 L) Basic Vegetable or prepared stock, combine in a large saucepan over medium heat with 2 carrots, peeled and coarsely chopped, 1 tbsp (15 mL) tomato paste, 1 tsp (5 mL) celery seeds, 1 tsp (5 mL) cracked black peppercorns, ½ tsp (2 mL) dried thyme leaves, 4 parsley sprigs, 1 bay leaf and 1 cup (250 mL) white wine. Bring to a boil. Reduce heat to low and simmer, covered, for 30 minutes, then strain and discard solids.

Homemade Chicken Stock

There's nothing quite like the flavor of homemade chicken stock. It's very easy to make — you can cook it overnight, strain it in the morning and refrigerate it during the day. By the time you return home, the fat will have congealed on top of the stock and you can skim it off.

- **Large (minimum 6 quart) slow cooker**

4 lbs	bone-in skin-on chicken parts (see Tip, right)	2 kg
3	onions, coarsely chopped	3
4	carrots, scrubbed and coarsely chopped	4
4	stalks celery, coarsely chopped	4
6	sprigs parsley	6
3	bay leaves	3
10	black peppercorns	10
1 tsp	dried thyme leaves	5 mL
	Salt, optional	
12 cups	water	3 L

**MAKES ABOUT
12 CUPS (3 L)**

TIP

❖ **The more economical parts of the chicken, such as necks, backs, and wings, make the best stock.**

1. In slow cooker stoneware, combine chicken, onions, carrots, celery, parsley, bay leaves, peppercorns, thyme, salt, if using, and water. Cover and cook on High for 8 hours. Strain into a large bowl, discarding solids. Refrigerate liquid until fat forms on surface, about 6 hours. Skim off fat. Cover and refrigerate for up to 5 days.

Mindful Morsels

You can easily reduce your consumption of sodium by making your own stock and not adding salt. One cup (250 mL) of this stock, with no salt added, contains 21 mg of sodium. The same quantity of a typical prepared stock likely contains more than 500 mg of sodium. Healthy adults should consume no more than 2,400 mg of sodium a day.

Nutrients Per Serving	
Calories	21
Protein	2.7 g
Carbohydrates	0.1 g
Fat (Total)	1.1 g
Saturated Fat	0.3 g
Monounsaturated Fat	0.4 g
Polyunsaturated Fat	0.2 g
Dietary Fiber	0.1 g
Sodium	21 mg
Cholesterol	20 mg

Source of vitamin B6.

Mushroom Lentil Soup

Lentils and mushrooms are a classic combination for a reason — they blend deliciously because each brings out the best features of the other. This hearty soup with its deep earthy flavors makes a great main course in a bowl. Serve it on those evenings when everyone is coming and going at different times. Set out a loaf of whole grain bread and the fixin's for salad and let everyone help themselves.

MAKES 8 SERVINGS

TIPS

❖ If you're using a strongly flavored dried mushroom, such as porcini, to make this soup, 2 tbsp (25 mL) will be sufficient. But if you're using a mixture of mushrooms, some of which may be more mildly flavored, you may need an additional 1 tbsp (15 mL) or so.

❖ Lentils purchased in bulk may contain bits of dirt or discolored seeds. Before using, it is wise to rinse them thoroughly in a pot of water. Swish them around and remove any offending particles, then rinse thoroughly under cold running water.

MAKE AHEAD

This soup can be assembled before it is cooked. Complete Steps 1 and 2. Cover and refrigerate overnight or for up to 2 days. When you're ready to cook, continue with Step 3.

● **Large (minimum 5 quart) slow cooker**

2 cups	hot water	500 mL
2 tbsp	dried wild mushrooms (see Tips, left)	25 mL
1 tbsp	olive oil	15 mL
1	onion, finely chopped	1
4	stalks celery, diced	4
2	carrots, peeled and diced	2
1 tsp	chili powder	5 mL
1	can (28 oz/796) tomatoes, including juice, coarsely chopped	1
4 cups	Basic Vegetable Stock or Homemade Chicken Stock (see recipes, pages 34 and 35) or prepared stock	1 L
2 cups	brown or green lentils (see Tips, left)	500 mL
2 tbsp	freshly squeezed lemon juice	25 mL
	Freshly ground black pepper	
	Salt, optional	
	Plain yogurt, optional	
1/2 cup	finely chopped parsley leaves or chives	125 mL

1. In a heatproof bowl, combine hot water and dried mushrooms. Let stand for 30 minutes then strain through a fine sieve, reserving liquid. Pat mushrooms dry, chop finely and set aside.

2. In a large skillet, heat oil over medium heat for 30 seconds. Add onion, celery and carrots and cook, stirring, until carrots are softened, about 7 minutes. Add chili powder and reserved dried mushrooms and cook, stirring, for 1 minute. Add tomatoes with juice and bring to a boil. Transfer to slow cooker stoneware.

3. Add vegetable stock and lentils. Cover and cook on Low for 8 to 10 hours or on High for 4 to 5 hours, until vegetables are tender. Stir in lemon, ground pepper and salt to taste, if using. Ladle into bowls and drizzle with yogurt, if using. Garnish each serving with 1 tbsp (15 mL) parsley.

❖ **If you prefer a creamier soup, after the soup has finished cooking, scoop out about 2 cups (500 mL) of the solids, plus a little liquid and purée in a food processor. Return to the stoneware and continue as directed.**

Mindful Morsels
Not only are mushrooms very low in calories, they are also a source of potassium and zinc.

Nutrients Per Serving	
Calories	217
Protein	14.2 g
Carbohydrates	37.3 g
Fat (Total)	2.5 g
Saturated Fat	0.4 g
Monounsaturated Fat	1.4 g
Polyunsaturated Fat	0.5 g
Dietary Fiber	7.9 g
Sodium	188 mg
Cholesterol	0 mg

Natural Wonders
LENTILS
This recipe is high in complex carbohydrates, the healthy kind that nutritionists tell us we should be eating on a regular basis. The lentils, which account for 28.19 grams, are the major source of the carbohydrates in this recipe. Perhaps not surprisingly, as North Americans become increasingly health conscious, our consumption of legumes such as lentils has been rising. Once dismissed as "peasant food," legumes are now identified as "nutrient dense," and their consumption is linked with a wide range of health benefits. For instance, eating legumes, which are low on the glycemic index, helps to stabilize blood sugar, a great benefit for people with insulin resistance, hypoglycemia or diabetes.

While all legumes are highly nutritious, lentils have some advantages over other varieties. Firstly, unlike dried beans, they don't need to be soaked before cooking, which makes them more convenient. And secondly, since there's no time advantage to using canned versions in the slow cooker, you can use raw lentils, which contain almost no sodium. From a nutrient perspective, lentils are high in dietary fiber and an excellent source of iron.

Excellent source of vitamins A and K, folacin, phosphorus, potassium and iron.

Good source of vitamins C and B6, magnesium and zinc.

Contains a very high amount of dietary fiber.

VEGAN FRIENDLY

Mushroom Soup with Millet

Enhancing this soup with dried mushrooms and their soaking liquid produces a deeply flavored broth that lingers on the taste buds. A splash of soy sauce moves the flavor profile to the east. If you prefer a creamy finish, add a drizzle of plain yogurt or whipping cream. I like to serve this as a light main course with whole grain bread, followed by a platter of stir-fried bok choy.

MAKES 8 SERVINGS

TIPS

❖ **This quantity of dried mushrooms equates to half of a ¹/₂ oz (14 g) package.**

❖ **Millet is available in natural foods stores. Like lentils, some millet may contain bits of dirt or discolored grains. If your millet looks grimy, rinse it thoroughly in a pot of water before using. Swish it around and remove any offending particles, then rinse under cold running water. If you can't find millet, you can also make this soup with brown rice or a mixture of wild and brown rice (see Variation, page 39).**

MAKE AHEAD

This soup can be assembled before it is cooked. Complete Steps 1 through 3. Cover and refrigerate for up to 2 days. When you're ready to cook, continue with Step 4.

● **Large (minimum 5 quart) slow cooker**

3 cups	hot water	750 mL
2 tbsp	dried wild mushrooms (see Tips, left)	25 mL
¹/₂ cup	millet (see Tips, left)	125 mL
1 tbsp	olive oil	15 mL
2	onions, finely chopped	2
6	cloves garlic, minced	6
1 tbsp	minced gingerroot	15 mL
¹/₂ tsp	cracked black peppercorns	2 mL
2 lbs	button mushrooms, trimmed and thinly sliced	1 kg
6 cups	Basic Vegetable Stock (see recipe, page 34) or prepared vegetable stock (see Tips, right)	1.5
2	bay leaves	2
¹/₄ cup	reduced-sodium soy or tamari sauce	50 mL
	Salt, optional	
	Whipping (35%) cream or plain yogurt, optional	
¹/₂ cup	finely chopped green onions or parsley leaves	125 mL

1. In a heatproof bowl, combine hot water and dried mushrooms. Let stand for 30 minutes, then strain through a fine sieve, reserving liquid. Pat mushrooms dry, chop finely and set aside.

2. In a large skillet over medium heat, toast millet, stirring, until fragrant and beginning to turn golden, about 3 minutes. Transfer to slow cooker stoneware.

3. In same skillet, heat oil over medium heat for 30 seconds. Add onions and cook, stirring, until softened, about 3 minutes. Add reserved mushrooms, garlic, gingerroot and peppercorns and cook, stirring, for 1 minute. Add reserved mushroom liquid and bring to a boil. Transfer to slow cooker stoneware.

4. Add button mushrooms, vegetable stock, bay leaves and soy sauce. Cover and cook on Low for 6 to 8 hours or on High for 3 to 4 hours, until millet is tender. Discard bay leaves. Season to taste with salt, if using. Ladle into individual bowls, drizzle with cream, if using, and garnish each serving with 1 tbsp (15 mL) green onion.

VARIATION

Mushroom Soup with Rice
Substitute the millet with ¾ cup (175 mL) rinsed brown rice or a mixture of wild and brown rice.

❖ If you prefer, make this soup using 5 cups (1.25 L) reduced-sodium beef stock and 1 cup (250 mL) white wine or water, instead of the vegetable stock.

Mindful Morsels
Made with regular (not reduced-sodium) prepared vegetable stock and soy sauce, one serving of this soup would contain almost 1400 mg of sodium.

Natural Wonders

MILLET
I've included millet in this recipe because it's a nutritious whole grain that most people don't often eat. Adding this easily digested and gluten-free grain to your diet can help to expand the range of nutrients you consume. Millet contains magnesium, thiamin, riboflavin, niacin, folacin, iron, phosphorus and zinc, among other nutrients. And, like all whole grains, it is a source of dietary fiber. The Healthy Eating Pyramid developed by the Harvard School of Public Health places a strong emphasis on the consumption of whole grains and recommends eating some whole grain foods at most meals. If you don't have millet, you can make this soup using brown rice or a combination of brown and wild rice (see Variation, above) and still benefit from including whole grains in your diet.

Nutrients Per Serving	
Calories	108
Protein	4.2 g
Carbohydrates	18.8 g
Fat (Total)	2.6 g
Saturated Fat	0.4 g
Monounsaturated Fat	1.3 g
Polyunsaturated Fat	0.5 g
Dietary Fiber	3.7 g
Sodium	307 mg
Cholesterol	0 mg

Good source of vitamin K and potassium.

Source of vitamins C and B6, phosphorus and iron.

Contains a moderate amount of dietary fiber.

See photo, page 40

Leafy Greens Soup

This delicious country-style soup is French in origin and based on the classic combination of leeks and potatoes, with the addition of healthful leafy greens. Sorrel, which has an intriguing but bitter taste, adds delightful depth to the flavor. Sorrel is available from specialty greengrocers or at farmers' markets during the summer, but if you're unsuccessful in locating it, arugula or parsley also work well in this recipe.

MAKES 8 SERVINGS

TIP

❖ **To clean leeks: Fill a sink full of lukewarm water. Split the leeks in half lengthwise and submerge them in the water, swishing them around to remove all traces of dirt. Transfer to a colander and rinse thoroughly under cold water.**

MAKE AHEAD

This soup can be partially prepared before it is cooked. Complete Step 1, cover and refrigerate overnight or for up to 2 days. When you're ready to cook, continue with Steps 2 and 3.

• **Large (minimum 5 quart) slow cooker**

1 tbsp	butter or olive oil	15 mL
1 tbsp	olive oil	15 mL
6	small leeks, white and light green parts only, cleaned and thinly sliced (see Tip, left)	6
4	cloves garlic, minced	4
1 tsp	salt	5 mL
1 tsp	dried tarragon	5 mL
1/2 tsp	cracked black peppercorns	2 mL
6 cups	Basic Vegetable Stock or Homemade Chicken Stock (see recipes, pages 34 and 35) or prepared stock	1.5 L
3	medium potatoes, peeled and cut into 1/2 inch (1 cm) cubes	3
4 cups	packed torn Swiss chard leaves (about 1 bunch)	1 L
1 cup	packed torn sorrel, arugula or parsley leaves	250 mL
	Whipping (35%) cream, optional	
	Garlic croutons, optional	

1. In a large skillet over medium heat, melt butter and olive oil. Add leeks and cook, stirring, until softened, about 5 minutes. Add garlic, salt, tarragon and peppercorns and cook, stirring, for 1 minute. Add stock and bring to a boil. Transfer to slow cooker stoneware.

See photo, page 41

2. Stir in potatoes. Cover and cook on Low for 8 hours or on High for 4 hours, until potatoes are tender. Add Swiss chard and sorrel, in batches, stirring after each to submerge the leaves in the liquid. Cover and cook on High for 20 minutes, until greens are tender.

3. Working in batches, purée soup in a food processor or blender. (You can also do this in the stoneware using an immersion blender.) Spoon into individual serving bowls and drizzle with cream and/or top with croutons, if using.

Mindful Morsels

A diet rich in folacin and vitamin B6, nutrients plentiful in Swiss chard and sorrel, plays a role in maintaining homocysteine levels. Elevated homocysteine levels have been associated with heart disease.

Natural Wonders

SWISS CHARD

I've added Swiss chard to this traditional leek and potato soup because along with kale, collards and other dark leafy greens, it is a nutritional superstar. A relative of the beet family, Swiss chard is a good source of numerous vitamins and minerals, including vitamins K, A and C, as well as magnesium and potassium. A half cup (125 mL) serving of Swiss chard contains more than 150 percent of the recommended daily value of vitamin K. Like all leafy greens Swiss chard is loaded with antioxidants. It contains vitamin E, a free radical fighter, and beta-carotene, which helps to keep your eyes healthy. In the realm of breaking news, some researchers think the anthocyanins in Swiss chard may prevent cancers of the digestive tract. Other research indicates that consumption of chard may be linked with reduced rates of colon cancer. And, with just 35 calories a cup (250 mL) adding chard to your meal plan makes great sense as part of any weight control program.

Nutrients Per Serving	
Calories	122
Protein	3.6 g
Carbohydrates	21.8 g
Fat (Total)	3.5 g
Saturated Fat	1.2 g
Monounsaturated Fat	1.7 g
Polyunsaturated Fat	0.4 g
Dietary Fiber	5.1 g
Sodium	475 mg
Cholesterol	5 mg

Excellent source of vitamins A, C and K, magnesium, potassium and iron.

Good source of vitamin B6 and folacin.

Source of calcium.

Contains a high amount of dietary fiber.

Beet Soup with Lemongrass and Lime

This Thai-inspired soup, which is served cold, is elegant and refreshing. Its jewel-like appearance and intriguing flavors make it a perfect prelude to any meal. I especially like to serve it at summer dinners in the garden.

MAKES 8 SERVINGS

TIP

❖ **I often use coconut oil when making this soup because its pleasantly nutty taste complements the Thai flavors in this soup.**

MAKE AHEAD

Ideally, make this soup the day before you intend to serve it so it can chill overnight in the refrigerator.

● **Works in slow cookers from 3½ to 6 quarts**

1 tbsp	olive oil or extra virgin coconut oil (see Tip, left)	15 mL
1	onion, chopped	1
4	cloves garlic, minced	4
2 tbsp	minced gingerroot	25 mL
2	stalks lemongrass, trimmed, smashed and cut in half crosswise	2
2 tsp	cracked black peppercorns	10 mL
6	medium beets, peeled and chopped (about 2½ lbs/1.25 kg)	6
6 cups	Basic Vegetable Stock (see recipe, page 34) or prepared vegetable stock	1.5 L
1	red bell pepper, seeded and diced	1
1	long red chile pepper, seeded and diced, optional	1
	Zest and juice of 1 lime	
	Salt, optional	
	Coconut cream, optional	
	Finely chopped cilantro	

1. In a skillet, heat oil over medium heat for 30 seconds. Add onion and cook, stirring, until softened, about 3 minutes. Add garlic, gingerroot, lemongrass and peppercorns and cook, stirring, for 1 minute. Transfer to slow cooker stoneware.

2. Add beets and stock. Cover and cook on Low for 8 hours or on High for 4 hours, until beets are tender. Add red pepper and chile pepper, if using. Cover and cook on High for 30 minutes, until peppers are tender. Remove lemongrass and discard.

3. Working in batches, purée soup in a food processor or blender. (You can also do this in the stoneware using an immersion blender.) Transfer to a large bowl. Stir in lime zest and juice. Season to taste with salt, if using. Chill thoroughly, preferably overnight.

4. When ready to serve, spoon into individual bowls, drizzle with coconut cream, if using, and garnish with cilantro.

Mindful Morsels

The peppers in this recipe are a source of capsaicin, which researchers are studying for its anti-inflammatory properties.

Natural Wonders

BEETS

Over half of the carbohydrates in one serving of this soup (10.7 grams) come from the beets, which are extremely nutritious. The consumption of beets, especially in the form of freshly squeezed beet juice, has long been a folk medicine tonic. Some have even linked beets with cancer-curing power. While these claims have likely been overstated, recent evidence indicates that eating beets may, indeed, help your body defend itself against cancer and other diseases. Beets contain anthocyanins, a group of phytochemicals that researchers are studying for their ability to fight cancer and their anti-inflammatory powers, among other benefits.

High in natural sugar yet low in calories, beets are also an excellent source of folacin, an important B vitamin that can be challenging to obtain through dietary sources. Beets are also a source of potassium, which helps your muscles and metabolism function. They also contain certain phytochemicals that appear to bind cholesterol in the digestive tract, protecting the body against heart disease. One word of caution: Because beets — especially the greens — contain oxalic acid people with kidney or gallbladder problems may want to be cautious about eating them. And don't panic if you see red in your urine or stool after eating beets. It's not blood, but beeturia, a harmless condition.

Nutrients Per Serving	
Calories	85
Protein	2.4 g
Carbohydrates	16.3 g
Fat (Total)	2.0 g
Saturated Fat	0.3 g
Monounsaturated Fat	1.3 g
Polyunsaturated Fat	0.3 g
Dietary Fiber	2.9 g
Sodium	85 mg
Cholesterol	0 mg

Excellent source of vitamin C and folacin.

Good source of potassium.

Source of vitamin A.

Contains a moderate amount of dietary fiber.

Gingery Carrot Soup with Orange and Parsley

In my books, carrots and ginger always make a superlative combination. Here, they are enhanced with zesty orange and a hit of earthy parsley to produce a delicious and versatile soup. Serve this with whole grain bread and a tossed green salad for a light but nourishing supper or as a first course to a more substantial meal. If you prefer a creamy soup and a hint of exotic coconut flavor, add a drizzle of coconut milk and use coconut oil to soften the onions.

MAKES 8 SERVINGS

TIPS

❖ **I provide a range of quantities for the ginger to suit individual tastes. If you find ginger a bit assertive, use the smaller amount. If you like its flavor go for the larger quantity.**

❖ **Because you are using the skin of the fruit to add flavor to this soup, I recommend buying organically grown oranges for use in this recipe.**

❖ **Use flat-leaf rather than curly parsley because it has more flavor.**

MAKE AHEAD

This soup can be partially prepared before cooking. Complete Step 1, cover and refrigerate overnight or for up to 2 days. When you're ready to cook, continue with Steps 2 and 3.

• **Works in slow cookers from 3½ to 6 quarts**

1 tbsp	olive oil or extra virgin coconut oil	15 mL
2	onions, chopped	2
2 to 3 tbsp	minced gingerroot (see Tips, left)	25 to 45 mL
1 tbsp	finely grated orange zest (see Tips, left)	15 mL
1 tsp	cracked black peppercorns	5 mL
2	bay leaves	2
6 cups	thinly sliced peeled carrots (about 6 large carrots)	1.5 L
4 cups	Basic Vegetable Stock or Homemade Chicken Stock (see recipes, pages 34 and 35) or prepared stock	1 L
1½ cups	freshly squeezed orange juice	375 mL
1 cup	packed parsley leaves (see Tips, left)	250 mL
	Salt, optional	
	Coconut milk, optional	

1. In a skillet, heat oil over medium heat for 30 seconds. Add onions and cook, stirring, until softened, about 3 minutes. Add gingerroot, orange zest, peppercorns and bay leaves and cook, stirring, for 1 minute. Transfer to slow cooker stoneware. Add carrots and vegetable stock and stir well.

2. Cover and cook on Low for 8 hours or on High for 4 hours, until carrots are tender. Add orange juice and parsley. Cover and cook on High for 20 minutes, until heated through. Discard bay leaves.

3. Working in batches, purée soup in a food processor or blender. (You can also do this in the stoneware using an immersion blender.) Season to taste with salt, if using. Ladle into serving bowls and drizzle with coconut milk, if using. Serve hot.

Mindful Morsels

Ginger adds more than flavor to this soup. It is a great digestive and recent studies show that it contains beta-ionone, a phytochemical with promising cancer-fighting properties.

Natural Wonders
CAROTENOIDS

Although it contains a range of nutrients, this soup is particularly rich in carotenoids, powerful antioxidants that protect the body from numerous diseases, such as age-related macular degeneration, heart disease and certain cancers. Beta-carotene, which is found in carrots, among other sources, is, perhaps, the best-known of these phytonutrients. Among its potential benefits, beta-carotene is thought to boost the immune system. A 2003 study published in the *Asia Pacific Journal of Clinical Nutrition* found a link between dietary intake of beta-carotene and increased bone density in older women. Research indicates that food is the best source of this valuable nutrient, since recent studies testing the benefits of supplements have produced inconsistent results.

Another carotenoid, beta-cryptoxanthin, which is found in oranges, helps to keep your respiratory track healthy and may lower your risk of developing rheumatoid arthritis. It may also protect against esophageal, lung and colon cancers. One study indicated that a diet high in beta-cryptoxanthin might reduce the risk of lung cancer by as much as 30 percent.

Nutrients Per Serving	
Calories	88
Protein	1.8 g
Carbohydrates	16.8 g
Fat (Total)	2.1 g
Saturated Fat	0.3 g
Monounsaturated Fat	1.3 g
Polyunsaturated Fat	0.3 g
Dietary Fiber	3.0 g
Sodium	58 mg
Cholesterol	0 mg

Excellent source of vitamins A, C and K.

Good source of potassium.

Source of vitamin B6.

Contains a moderate amount of dietary fiber.

Turkey and Black Bean Soup

This hearty soup is a meal in a bowl. I like to serve it with a simple green or shredded carrot salad and crusty whole grain bread for a great weeknight meal. The quantity of chili powder, combined with a chipotle pepper, produces a zesty result. If you're heat-averse, reduce the quantity of chili powder and use a jalapeño instead of a chipotle pepper.

MAKES 8 SERVINGS

TIPS

❖ If you prefer a thicker, more integrated soup, purée the drained beans in a food processor or mash with a potato masher before adding to the stoneware.

❖ You can also make this soup using cooked leftover turkey. Use 2¹⁄₂ cups (625 mL) of shredded turkey and add it along with the bell peppers.

❖ If you don't have ancho chili powder, you can substitute an equal quantity of New Mexico chili powder, your favorite chili powder blend or ¹⁄₄ tsp (1 mL) cayenne pepper.

MAKE AHEAD

This dish can be partially prepared before it is cooked. Complete Step 1. Cover and refrigerate overnight or for up to 2 days. When you're ready to cook, continue with Steps 2 and 3.

• **Large (minimum 6 quart) slow cooker**

1 tbsp	olive oil	15 mL
2	onions, finely chopped	2
2	carrots, peeled and diced	2
2	stalks celery, diced	2
4	cloves garlic, minced	4
1 tbsp	dried oregano leaves, crumbled	15 mL
1 tsp	cracked black peppercorns	5 mL
1 tsp	finely grated lime zest	5 mL
2 tbsp	cumin seeds, toasted (see Tips, right)	25 mL
¹⁄₄ cup	tomato paste	50 mL
6 cups	Homemade Chicken Stock (see recipe, page 35) or prepared chicken or turkey stock	1.5 L
2	cans (14 to 19 oz/398 to 540 mL) black beans, drained and rinsed, or 2 cups (500 mL) dried black beans, soaked, cooked and drained (see Basic Beans, page 250)	2
	Salt, optional	
2¹⁄₂ cups	cubed (¹⁄₂ inch/1 cm) skinless boneless turkey breast (one 1¹⁄₂ lb/750 g bone-in turkey breast) (see Tips, left)	625 mL
2 tsp	ancho chili powder, dissolved in 2 tbsp (25 mL) freshly squeezed lime juice (see Tips, left)	10 mL
1	jalapeño pepper or chipotle pepper in adobo sauce, minced	1
1	green bell pepper, diced	1
1	red bell pepper, diced	1

1. In a skillet, heat oil over medium heat for 30 seconds. Add onions, carrots and celery and cook, stirring, until softened, about 7 minutes. Add garlic, oregano, peppercorns, lime zest and toasted cumin and cook, stirring, for 1 minute. Add tomato paste and stir well. Transfer to slow cooker stoneware. Stir in chicken stock and beans. Season to taste with salt, if using.

2. Add turkey and stir well. Cover and cook on Low for 6 hours or on High for 3 hours, until turkey is cooked and mixture is bubbly.

3. Add ancho solution and stir well. Add jalapeño and green and red bell peppers and stir well. Cover and cook on High for 20 minutes, until peppers are tender.

❖ **To toast cumin seeds:** Place seeds in a dry skillet over medium heat and cook, stirring, until fragrant and seeds just begin to brown, about 3 minutes. Immediately transfer to a mortar or a spice grinder and grind.

Mindful Morsels

Isoflavones are healthful compounds found in some vegetables, such as soy and legumes. Research suggests that it is best to get isoflavones from food sources, such as the black beans in this soup, since they do not seem to be beneficial when isolated from whole foods.

Natural Wonders

COMPLEX CARBOHYDRATES

A steaming bowl of this flavorful soup will fill you up but not out because it is low in saturated fat and high in complex carbohydrates. There are two kinds of carbs: simple (bad) and complex (good). Simple carbs, such as white bread and heavily sugared drinks, are low in nutrients and quickly digested, causing blood sugar to spike. They have been linked with a higher incidence of degenerative diseases such as diabetes. The complex kind, such as whole grains and legumes, contain more nutrients, including fiber and are digested more slowly, which helps to stabilize blood sugar. Researchers have found that meals containing significant quantities of high-fiber plant foods make people feel full before they consume a substantial number of calories, which may help you to keep your weight under control.

Nutrients Per Serving	
Calories	231
Protein	24.7 g
Carbohydrates	23.6 g
Fat (Total)	4.8. g
Saturated Fat	1.0 g
Monounsaturated Fat	2.4 g
Polyunsaturated Fat	1.0 g
Dietary Fiber	7.8 g
Sodium	364 mg
Cholesterol	52 mg

Excellent source of vitamins A, C and B6, potassium and iron.

Good source of vitamin K, folacin, magnesium, phosphorus and zinc.

Contains a very high amount of dietary fiber.

See photo, page 50

Two-Bean Soup with Pistou

I love the flavors in this classic French country soup: the hint of licorice in the fennel and the nip of paprika is nicely balanced by the pleasing blandness of the potatoes and beans.

MAKES 8 SERVINGS

TIPS

❖ **If your market is out of fennel, use 6 stalks of diced celery instead.**

❖ **Adding the green beans while they are still frozen ensures that they will not be mushy when the soup has finished cooking. If you prefer to use fresh green beans, cut them into 2-inch (5 cm) lengths and cook them in a pot of boiling salted water for 4 minutes, until tender crisp. Add them to the slow cooker after stirring in the paprika.**

MAKE AHEAD

You can partially prepare this soup ahead of time. Complete Step 1. Cover and refrigerate overnight or for up to 2 days. When you're ready to cook, continue with Steps 2 and 3.

• **Large (minimum 6 quart) slow cooker**

1 tbsp	olive oil	15 mL
3	onions, finely chopped	3
2	carrots, peeled and diced	2
1	bulb fennel, base and leafy stems discarded, bulb thinly sliced on the vertical and cut into 1/2-inch (1 cm) lengths (see Tips, left)	1
1 tsp	fennel seeds, toasted (see Tips, right)	5 mL
1	can (28 oz/796) diced tomatoes, including juice	1
6 cups	Basic Vegetable Stock or Homemade Chicken Stock (see recipes, pages 34 and 35) or prepared stock	1.5 L
2	potatoes, peeled and shredded	2
2	cans (each 14 to 19 oz/398 to 540 mL) white beans, drained and rinsed, or 2 cups (500 mL) dried white beans, soaked, cooked and drained (see Basic Beans, page 250)	2
2 cups	frozen sliced green beans (see Tips, left)	500 mL
2 tsp	paprika dissolved in 1 tbsp (15 mL) water	10 mL
	Salt, optional	
	Freshly ground black pepper	

PISTOU

1 cup	packed fresh basil leaves	250 mL
4	cloves garlic, minced	4
1/2 cup	finely grated Parmesan cheese	125 mL
1/4 cup	extra virgin olive oil	50 mL

1. In a skillet, heat oil over medium heat for 30 seconds. Add onions, carrots and fennel bulb and cook, stirring, until vegetables are softened, about 7 minutes. Add toasted fennel

See photo, page 51

seeds and cook, stirring, for 1 minute. Add tomatoes with juice and bring to a boil. Transfer to slow cooker stoneware.

2. Add stock, potatoes, white beans and green beans. Cover and cook on Low for 8 hours or on High for 4 hours, until vegetables are tender. Stir in paprika solution and season to taste with salt, if using, and pepper. Cover and cook on High for 20 minutes.

3. *Pistou:* In a food processor fitted with a metal blade, combine basil, garlic and Parmesan. Process until smooth. Slowly add olive oil down the feeder tube until integrated. Ladle soup into bowls and top each serving with a dollop of pistou.

VARIATION

For a more substantial soup add 2 cups (500 mL) cooked small pasta, such as elbow macaroni along with the paprika.

❖ **To toast fennel seeds: Place in a dry skillet over medium heat and cook, stirring, until seeds are fragrant, about 3 minutes. Immediately transfer to a mortar or a spice grinder and grind.**

Mindful Morsels

We've tested this recipe using canned beans, which are high in sodium. The beans in this recipe contribute 251 mg of sodium per serving. You may want to look for reduced-sodium varieties or cook your own with no added salt.

Natural Wonders
SODIUM AND POTASSIUM

If you're concerned about your blood pressure, then you're likely watching your intake of sodium because high salt intake has been linked with hypertension. To keep your sodium intake under control, avoid prepared and processed foods. To control hypertension, keep an eye on the amount of potassium you consume. Researchers have found that a diet high in potassium can actually reduce the effects of consuming too much sodium. Most fruit, vegetables, meat and fish are high in this important mineral. The potassium in this recipe is distributed across the vegetables. Each serving of this soup contains just over 1,000 milligrams of this important mineral, or 25 percent of the daily value.

Nutrients Per Serving	
Calories	270
Protein	10.4 g
Carbohydrates	35.2 g
Fat (Total)	11.1 g
Saturated Fat	2.4 g
Monounsaturated Fat	6.8 g
Polyunsaturated Fat	1.1 g
Fiber	10.0 g
Sodium	549 mg
Cholesterol	5 mg

Excellent source of vitamins A and K and potassium.

Good source of vitamins C and B6, folacin, magnesium, calcium, phosphorus and iron.

Contains a high amount of dietary fiber.

Thai-Style Pumpkin Soup

This soup is both versatile and delicious. It has an exotic combination of flavors and works well as a prelude to a meal. If you prefer a more substantial soup, top each serving with cooked shrimp or scallops, or add some brown rice (see Variation, page 55).

MAKES 8 SERVINGS

TIP

❖ **Coconut cream is the thick part of the liquid that accumulates on the top of canned coconut milk. Scoop out the required quantity, then stir the remainder well for use in the soup.**

MAKE AHEAD

This soup can be partially prepared before it is cooked. Complete Step 1. Cover and refrigerate overnight or for up to 2 days. When you're ready to cook, continue with Steps 2 and 3.

• **Large (minimum 6 quart) slow cooker**

1 tbsp	olive oil or extra virgin coconut oil	15 mL
2	onions, finely chopped	2
4	cloves garlic, minced	4
2 tbsp	minced gingerroot	25 mL
1 tsp	cracked black peppercorns	5 mL
2	stalks lemongrass, trimmed, smashed and cut in half crosswise	2
1 tbsp	cumin seeds, toasted (see Tips, page 49)	15 mL
8 cups	cubed, peeled pumpkin or other orange squash (2-inch/5 cm cubes)	2 L
6 cups	Basic Vegetable Stock or Homemade Chicken Stock (see recipes, pages 34 and 35) or prepared stock	1.5 L
1 cup	coconut milk	250 mL
1 tsp	Thai red curry paste	5 mL
	Finely grated zest and juice of 1 lime	
¼ cup	toasted pumpkin seeds, optional	50 mL
	Cherry tomatoes, halved, optional	
	Finely chopped cilantro	

1. In a skillet, heat oil over medium heat for 30 seconds. Add onions and cook, stirring, until softened, about 3 minutes. Add garlic, gingerroot, peppercorns, lemongrass and toasted cumin and cook, stirring, for 1 minute. Transfer to slow cooker stoneware. Add pumpkin and stock.

2. Cover and cook on Low for 8 hours or on High for 4 hours, until pumpkin is tender. Skim off 1 tbsp (15 mL) of the coconut cream (see Tip, left). In a small bowl, combine with curry paste and blend well. Add to slow cooker along with remaining coconut milk and lime zest and juice. Cover and

cook on High until heated through, about 20 minutes. Discard lemongrass.

3. Working in batches, purée soup in a food processor or blender. (You can also do this in the stoneware using an immersion blender.) Ladle into bowls, and garnish with pumpkin seeds and/or tomatoes, if using, and cilantro.

VARIATION

For a more substantial soup, add 1 cup (250 mL) brown rice, rinsed, along with the pumpkin. You can also finish the soup with a topping of cooked salad shrimp or scallops (about 1 pound (500 g). If using scallops, pat them dry, cut into quarters and dust with 1 tsp (5 mL) of your favorite chili powder. Sauté in 1 tbsp (15 mL) olive or coconut oil, in 2 batches, for about 1½ minutes per side.

Mindful Morsels
Pumpkin seeds are a source of linoleic fatty acids, vitamin E, vegetable protein and iron.

Natural Wonders
COCONUT OIL
Almost all of the saturated fat in this recipe comes from the coconut milk. For decades, coconut oil, the fat in coconut milk, has been derided as a health hazard because it contains a significant amount of saturated fat. Now, researchers are beginning to piece together a case urging its inclusion in our diets. Coconut oil is very high in antioxidants and lauric acid, which some researchers believe make it an excellent immune-system booster. It is a "low-fat" fat (1 gram contains only 6.8 calories compared with 9 calories per gram of fat, which is the norm) and a "medium chain" fat, which means it is quickly burned by the body. Consequently, researchers are studying its potential in weight-loss programs, and the preliminary results are encouraging.

Nutrients Per Serving	
Calories	130
Protein	2.5 g
Carbohydrates	14.3 g
Fat (Total)	8.4 g
Saturated Fat	5.7 g
Monounsaturated Fat	1.8 g
Polyunsaturated Fat	0.4 g
Fiber	2.4 g
Sodium	9 mg
Cholesterol	0 mg

Good source of vitamin A, magnesium, potassium and iron.

Source of vitamin C and phosphorus.

Contains a moderate amount of dietary fiber.

Vichyssoise with Celery Root and Watercress

This refreshing soup is delicious, easy to make and can be a prelude to the most sophisticated meal. More nutritious than traditional vichyssoise, it has a pleasing nutty flavor that may be enhanced with a garnish of chopped toasted walnuts. In the summer, I aim to have leftovers in the refrigerator and treat myself to a small bowl for a yummy afternoon snack.

MAKES
8 TO 10 SERVINGS

TIPS

❖ Since celery root oxidizes quickly on contact with air, be sure to use as soon as you have peeled and chopped it, or toss with 1 tbsp (15 mL) lemon juice to prevent discoloration.

❖ To cool the soup more quickly, transfer it to a large bowl before refrigerating.

MAKE AHEAD

This dish can be partially prepared before it is cooked. Complete Step 1. Cover and refrigerate overnight or for up to 2 days. When you're ready to cook, continue with Steps 2 and 3.

• Large (minimum 5 quart) slow cooker

1 tbsp	olive oil	15 mL
3	leeks, white and light green parts only, cleaned and coarsely chopped (see Tip, page 42)	3
2	cloves garlic, minced	2
1/2 tsp	cracked black peppercorns	2 mL
6 cups	Homemade Chicken Stock or Basic Vegetable Stock (see recipes, pages 34 and 35) or prepared stock	1.5 L
1	large celery root, peeled and sliced	1
2	bunches (each about 4 oz/125 g) watercress, tough parts of the stems removed	2
	Salt, optional	
1/2 cup	whipping (35%) cream or soy milk	125 mL
	Toasted chopped walnuts, optional	
	Watercress sprigs, optional	

1. In a skillet, heat oil over medium heat for 30 seconds. Add leeks and cook, stirring, until softened, about 5 minutes. Add garlic and peppercorns and cook, stirring, for 1 minute. Transfer to slow cooker stoneware. Add stock and stir well.

2. Stir in celery root. Cover and cook on Low for 6 hours or on High for 3 hours, until celery root is tender. Stir in watercress until wilted.

3. Working in batches, purée mixture in a food processor or blender. (You can also do this in the stoneware using an immersion blender. Season to taste with salt, if using. Stir in cream and refrigerate until thoroughly chilled, about 4 hours (see Tips, left). To serve, ladle into bowls and garnish with toasted walnuts and/or watercress sprigs, if using.

Mindful Morsels

Virtually all of the saturated fat in a serving of this soup (2.6 grams) comes from the whipping cream. If you are concerned about your intake of saturated fat, use soy milk instead.

Natural Wonders

WATERCRESS

Enhancing a dish with peppery watercress brings more than zip to the table. It also adds a wide range of nutrients to your diet. A dark leafy green, watercress contains important nutrients such as vitamins A, C and K, as well as the minerals calcium and potassium. Like all leafy greens, watercress is loaded with antioxidants, such as beta-carotene, which help to slow down the aging process and protect you from disease. It also contains bioflavonoids, which appear to work in synergy with vitamin C, enhancing its antioxidant ability, among other benefits. A member of the Cruciferous family, watercress also contains a compound known as phenylethyl isothiocyanate, which is thought to protect against lung cancer.

Nutrients Per Serving	
Calories	103
Protein	3.6 g
Carbohydrates	9.2 g
Fat (Total)	6.4 g
Saturated Fat	3.0 g
Monounsaturated Fat	2.5 g
Polyunsaturated Fat	0.4 g
Dietary Fiber	2.4 g
Sodium	85 mg
Cholesterol	27 mg

Excellent source of vitamin K.

Good source of vitamin B6 and potassium.

Source of vitamins A and C.

Contains a moderate amount of dietary fiber.

Caldo Verde

This soup, which is Portuguese in origin, is usually made with white beans and kale. This version, which uses chickpeas and collard greens, is equally delicious and also lends itself to many adaptations. If you can't find collards, use kale, and feel free to substitute white beans for the chickpeas. Serve this as the centerpiece of a soup-and-salad meal. Add crusty whole grain bread or ciabatta and a salad of grated carrots with a lemon juice and extra virgin olive oil vinaigrette.

MAKES 8 SERVINGS

TIP

❖ Shred collard greens as if you were making a chiffonade of basil leaves. Remove the stems, including the thick vein that runs up the bottom of the leaf and thoroughly wash the leaves by swishing them around in a sink full of warm water. On a cutting board, stack the leaves, 2 or 3 at a time. Roll them into a cigar shape and slice as thinly as you can.

MAKE AHEAD

This dish can be assembled before it is cooked. Complete Steps 1 and 2. Cover and refrigerate overnight or for up to 2 days. When you're ready to cook, continue with Step 3.

- Large (minimum 5 quart) slow cooker

1 tsp	cumin seeds	5 mL
1 tbsp	olive oil	15 mL
2	onions, finely chopped	2
2	carrots, peeled and diced	2
2	cloves garlic, minced	2
1/2 tsp	cracked black peppercorns	2 mL
6 cups	Homemade Chicken Stock (see recipe, page 35) or prepared chicken or turkey stock	1.5 L
2	cans (each 14 to 19 oz/398 to 540 mL) chickpeas, drained and rinsed, or 2 cups (500 mL) dried chickpeas, soaked, cooked and drained (see Basic Beans, page 250)	2
2	potatoes, peeled and diced	2
	Salt, optional	
2 tsp	paprika, dissolved in 2 tbsp (25 mL) lemon juice	10 mL
4 cups	shredded collard greens (about one 12 oz/375 g bunch) (see Tip, left)	1 L
4 oz	cooked smoked sausage, such as cured chorizo or kielbasa, sliced and chopped into bite-size pieces, optional	125 g
	Red wine vinegar, optional	

1. In a large dry skillet over medium heat, toast cumin seeds, stirring, until fragrant and they just begin to brown, about 3 minutes. Immediately transfer to a mortar or a spice grinder and grind. Set aside.

2. In same skillet, heat oil over medium heat for 30 seconds. Add onions and carrots and cook, stirring, until carrots are softened, about 7 minutes. Add garlic, peppercorns and reserved cumin and cook, stirring, for 1 minute. Transfer to slow cooker stoneware. Add chicken stock and chickpeas and stir well.

3. Add potatoes and stir well. Cover and cook on Low for 8 hours or on High for 4 hours, until potatoes are tender. Season to taste with salt, if using. If you prefer a smooth soup, working in batches, purée soup in a food processor or blender and return to slow cooker. (You can also do this in the stoneware using an immersion blender.) Stir in paprika mixture. Add collards, in batches, stirring each to submerge before adding the next batch. Add sausage, if using. Cover and cook on High until collards are tender, about 30 minutes. Season to taste with vinegar, if using.

Mindful Morsels

If you are trying to reduce your consumption of sodium, cook dried chickpeas with no added salt. This recipe was tested using canned chickpeas, which contribute almost all of the sodium, 204 mg per serving.

Natural Wonders
STRESS BUSTERS

Think of this soup as a steaming bowl of comfort. Many of the nutrients it contains, such as complex carbohydrates, vitamin B6, folacin and magnesium, help your body manage stress. Complex carbohydrates, such as chickpeas, are a source of B vitamins, which help your body produce the brain chemical serotonin, known to moderate symptoms of depression and anxiety. Some research links folacin with antidepressant effects, and among its benefits, magnesium may help your muscles to relax. It is also important to get an adequate amount of vitamin C if you're feeling stressed.

Nutrients Per Serving	
Calories	190
Protein	7.9 g
Carbohydrates	33.0 g
Fat (Total)	3.7 g
Saturated Fat	0.6 g
Monounsaturated Fat	1.8 g
Polyunsaturated Fat	0.9 g
Dietary Fiber	6.1 g
Sodium	243 mg
Cholesterol	5 mg

Excellent source of vitamins A, B6 and K.

Good source of folacin, potassium and magnesium.

Source of vitamin C, calcium and phosphorus.

Contains a very high amount of dietary fiber.

See photo, page 60

New World Leek and Potato Soup

I call this soup "new world" because it's a variation on the classic French leek and potato soup, using sweet potatoes and peppers, two ingredients that Christopher Columbus introduced to Europe during his explorations of the Americas. Serve small quantities as a prelude to a celebratory meal, or add whole grain bread and a tossed green salad for a light supper.

MAKES 8 SERVINGS

TIPS

❖ **If you prefer, use one red and one green bell pepper.**

❖ **To clean leeks: Fill a sink full of lukewarm water. Split the leeks in half lengthwise and submerge them in the water, swishing them around to remove all traces of dirt. Transfer to a colander and rinse thoroughly under cold water.**

MAKE AHEAD
This dish can be partially prepared before it is cooked. Complete Steps 1 and 2. Cover and refrigerate overnight or for up to 2 days. When you're ready to cook, continue with Steps 3 and 4.

● Large (minimum 5 quart) slow cooker

1 tbsp	cumin seeds	15 mL
1 tbsp	olive oil	15 mL
4	large leeks, white part with just a bit of green, cleaned and thinly sliced (see Tips, left)	4
4	cloves garlic, minced	4
1/2 tsp	cracked black peppercorns	2 mL
6 cups	Basic Vegetable Stock or Homemade Chicken Stock (see recipes, pages 34 and 35) or prepared stock	1.5 L
2 lbs	sweet potatoes, peeled and cut into 1-inch (2.5 cm) cubes (about 3 potatoes)	1 kg
2	green bell peppers, diced (see Tips, left)	2
1	long red chile pepper, minced, optional	1
	Salt, optional	
1/2 cup	whipping (35%) cream or soy milk	125 mL
	Roasted red pepper strips, optional	
	Finely snipped chives	

1. In a large dry skillet over medium heat, toast cumin seeds, stirring, until fragrant and they just begin to brown, about 3 minutes. Immediately transfer to a mortar or a spice grinder and grind. Set aside.

2. In same skillet, heat oil over medium heat for 30 seconds. Add leeks and cook, stirring, until softened, about 5 minutes. Add garlic, peppercorns and reserved cumin and cook, stirring, for 1 minute. Transfer to slow cooker stoneware. Add vegetable stock.

See photo, page 61

3. Add sweet potatoes. Cover and cook on Low for 7 to 8 hours or on High for 3 to 4 hours, until potatoes are tender. Add green peppers and chile pepper, if using. Cover and cook on High for 20 to 30 minutes, until peppers are tender. Season to taste with salt, if using.

4. Working in batches, purée soup in a food processor or blender. (You can also do this in the stoneware using an immersion blender.) To serve, ladle soup into bowls, drizzle with cream and garnish with roasted red pepper strips, if using, and chives.

Mindful Morsels

With the addition of peppers, and the substitution of sweet for regular potatoes, this delicious soup is even more nutritious than the traditional version.

Natural Wonders
COLORFUL FOOD

This colorful soup is more than a pretty to look at. The pigments that provide plant foods with their vibrant hues also signal the nutrients they contain and their disease-fighting properties. Sweet potatoes are one of the best sources of beta-carotene, which our bodies convert to vitamin A, and a source of vitamin B6, among other nutrients. Peppers are a great source of vitamin C and are high in bioflavonoids, which are thought to protect against cancer. Leeks contain folacin and iron along with kaempferol, an antioxidant that shows promise in protecting against cancer. To maximize the disease-fighting properties of plant foods, nutritionists tell us to eat at least three different-color vegetables and two different-color fruits every day. A bowl of this tasty soup goes a long way toward helping you achieve that goal.

Nutrients Per Serving	
Calories	222
Protein	5.1 g
Carbohydrates	33.5 g
Fat (Total)	8.4 g
Saturated Fat	3.8 g
Monounsaturated Fat	3.2 g
Polyunsaturated Fat	0.8 g
Dietary Fiber	4.2 g
Sodium	44 mg
Cholesterol	34 mg

Excellent source of vitamins A, B6 and C.

Good source of folacin, potassium and iron.

Contains a high amount of dietary fiber.

Scotch Broth

This hearty meal-in-a bowl is known as Scotland's pot-au-feu, a traditional boiled dinner. It is usually made with lamb, but I have an old Scottish recipe that suggests beef or a "good marrow bone" may be substituted. I like to serve this as a light dinner, accompanied by a simple green salad and warm crusty rolls.

MAKES 10 SERVINGS

TIP

❖ **To clean leeks: Fill a sink full of lukewarm water. Split the leeks in half lengthwise and submerge them in the water, swishing them around to remove all traces of dirt. Transfer to a colander and rinse thoroughly under cold water.**

MAKE AHEAD

This dish can be partially prepared before it is cooked. Heat 1 tbsp (15 mL) oil and complete Step 2. Cover and refrigerate overnight or for up to 2 days. When you're ready to cook, either brown the lamb as outlined in Step 1 or add it to the stoneware without browning. Stir well and continue with Step 3.

• **Large (minimum 6 quart) slow cooker**

1 to 2 tbsp	olive oil (approx.)	15 to 25 mL
1 lb	lamb shoulder or stewing beef, trimmed of fat and diced	500 g
3	leeks, white and light green parts only, cleaned and thinly sliced (see Tip, left)	3
4	stalks celery, diced	4
4	carrots, peeled and diced	4
2	parsnips, peeled and diced	2
2 tsp	dried thyme leaves, crumbled	10 mL
1/2 tsp	cracked black peppercorns	2 mL
1	bay leaf	1
8 cups	beef stock	2 L
	Salt	
1 cup	whole (hulled) or pot barley, rinsed (see Mindful Morsels, right)	250 mL
1 cup	green peas, thawed if frozen	250 mL
1/2 cup	finely chopped parsley leaves	125 mL

1. In a skillet, heat 1 tbsp (15 mL) oil over medium-high heat for 30 seconds. Add lamb, in batches, and cook, stirring, until browned, about 1 minute per batch. Transfer to slow cooker stoneware

2. Reduce heat to medium. Add more oil to pan, if necessary. Add leeks, celery, carrots and parsnips and cook, stirring, until vegetables are softened, about 7 minutes. Add thyme and peppercorns and cook, stirring, for 1 minute. Transfer to slow cooker stoneware. Stir in bay leaf, beef stock and salt to taste. Stir in barley.

3. Cover and cook on Low for 7 hours or on High for 3½ hours, until vegetables are tender. Stir in green peas and cook on High for 20 minutes, until tender. Discard bay leaf. Serve hot, liberally garnished with parsley.

Mindful Morsels

Although pearl barley is more readily available, make an effort to find whole (also known as hulled) barley when making the recipes in this book. It contains more nutrients, including fiber, than its refined relative. Pot barley, which is more refined than whole barley, is also a preferable alternative to pearl barley as it maintains some of the bran.

Natural Wonders

B VITAMINS

This recipe is a good source of vitamins B6, B12 and folacin, which, taken together, may help to prevent heart disease. This triumvirate works in concert to recycle artery-clogging homocysteine into methionine, an essential amino acid that helps your body to perform many important functions. Moreover, although researchers don't understand why it works, a recent study reported that a combination of B12 and folacin taken after a stroke reduces the incidence of subsequent hip fractures. As a group, the B vitamins (there are eight in all) work together to support brain function and ensure that your body has an adequate supply of energy. They also help you to cope with stress by increasing serotonin production and counteracting fatigue. If you're feeling chronically tired, irritable and anxious, you may be suffering from a deficiency of B vitamins.

Nutrients Per Serving	
Calories	210
Protein	13.0 g
Carbohydrates	30.4 g
Fat (Total)	4.7 g
Saturated Fat	1.2 g
Monounsaturated Fat	2.2 g
Polyunsaturated Fat	0.6 g
Dietary Fiber	4.9 g
Sodium	811 mg
Cholesterol	26 mg

Excellent source of vitamins A and K.

Good source of vitamins B6 and B12, folacin, magnesium and potassium and zinc.

Source of vitamin C and phosphorus.

Contains a high amount of dietary fiber.

Curried Parsnip Soup with Green Peas

Flavorful and elegant, this soup makes a great introduction to a more substantial meal. Served with whole grain bread, it is also a satisfying lunch. I like to complete this soup with a drizzle of whipping cream, which gives a smooth and sophisticated finish, but if you're averse to that much dairy fat, substitute coconut milk, plain yogurt or a bit of soy creamer.

MAKES 8 SERVINGS

TIPS

❖ **If you are using large parsnips in this recipe, cut away the woody core and discard.**

❖ **To enhance the Asian flavors and expand the range of nutrients you consume, substitute extra virgin coconut oil for the olive oil. Its flavors blend very well with the others in this recipe.**

MAKE AHEAD

This dish can be partially prepared before it is cooked. Complete Steps 1 and 2. Cover and refrigerate overnight or for up to 2 days. When you're ready to cook, continue with Steps 3 and 4.

• **Large (minimum 5 quart) slow cooker**

2 tsp	cumin seeds	10 mL
1 tsp	coriander seeds	5 mL
1 tbsp	olive oil or extra virgin coconut oil	15 mL
2	onions, finely chopped	2
4	cloves garlic, minced	4
1/2 tsp	cracked black peppercorns	2 mL
1	piece (1 inch/2.5 cm) cinnamon stick	1
1	bay leaf	1
6 cups	Basic Vegetable Stock or Homemade Chicken Stock (see recipes, pages 34 and 35) or prepared stock	1.5 L
4 cups	sliced peeled parsnips (about 1 lb/500 g) (see Tips, left)	1 L
2 tsp	curry powder, dissolved in 4 tsp (20 mL) freshly squeezed lemon juice	10 mL
2 cups	sweet green peas, thawed if frozen	500 mL
1/3 cup	whipping (35%) cream or coconut milk	75 mL

1. In a large dry skillet over medium heat, toast cumin and coriander seeds, stirring, until fragrant and cumin seeds just begin to brown, about 3 minutes. Immediately transfer to a mortar or a spice grinder and grind. Set aside.

2. In same skillet, heat oil over medium heat for 30 seconds. Add onions and cook, stirring, until softened, about 3 minutes. Add garlic, peppercorns, cinnamon stick, bay leaf and reserved cumin and coriander and cook, stirring, for 1 minute. Transfer to slow cooker stoneware. Add vegetable stock and parsnips and stir well.

3. Cover and cook on Low for 6 hours or on High for 3 hours, until parsnips are tender. Discard cinnamon stick and bay leaf.

4. Working in batches, purée soup in a food processor or blender. (You can also do this in the stoneware using an immersion blender.) Return to slow cooker stoneware. Add curry powder solution, green peas and whipping cream. Cover and cook on High for 20 minutes, until peas are tender and cream is heated through.

Mindful Morsels

Although coconut milk is high in saturated fat, it is a delicious and vegan-friendly alternative to whipping cream in this soup.

Natural Wonders

PARSNIPS

When thinking about vegetables, parsnips are usually a bit of an afterthought, which is unfortunate. I love their sweet, nutty flavor, and they make a refreshing change from more common root vegetables, such as turnips and carrots, particularly during the winter. In fact, the best parsnips are harvested after the first frost, just when the supply of other fresh local vegetables begins to taper off.

Their positive nutritional profile is another reason for consuming this vegetable, which belongs to the family (Umbelliferous) that includes carrots, celery, coriander and parsley. These vegetables contain phenolic acids, which scientists are studying for their anticarcinogenic properties. A source of fiber, parsnips also contain folacin, potassium and vitamins C and K. Recent studies link consumption of vitamin K with increased bone density in women and fewer hip fractures in members of both sexes (for more about vitamin K, see Natural Wonders, page 143).

Nutrients Per Serving	
Calories	146
Protein	3.4 g
Carbohydrates	22.2 g
Fat (Total)	5.7 g
Saturated Fat	2.5 g
Monounsaturated Fat	2.5 g
Polyunsaturated Fat	0.4 g
Dietary Fiber	4.3 g
Sodium	40 mg
Cholesterol	13 mg

Good source of folacin and potassium.

Source of vitamins C and K and phosphorus.

Contains a high amount of dietary fiber.

Cabbage Borscht

Served with dark rye bread this hearty soup makes a soul-satisfying meal. I prefer the flavor when it's made with a combination of beef and vegetable stock, but if you're a vegetarian, the vegetable stock works well, too.

MAKES 8 SERVINGS

TIP

❖ **If you prefer a smoother soup, do not purée the vegetables in Step 2. Instead, wait until they have finished cooking, and purée the soup in the stoneware using an immersion blender before adding the vinegar and cabbage. Allow the soup time to reheat (cook on High for 10 or 15 minutes) before adding the cabbage to ensure that it cooks.**

MAKE AHEAD

This dish can be partially prepared before it is cooked. Complete Steps 1 and 2. Cover and refrigerate overnight or for up to 2 days. When you're ready to cook, continue with Step 3.

● **Large (minimum 6 quart) slow cooker**

1 tbsp	olive oil	15 mL
2	onions, finely chopped	2
4	stalks celery, diced	4
2	carrots, peeled and diced	2
4	cloves garlic, minced	4
1 tsp	caraway seeds	5 mL
1 tsp	salt	5 mL
1/2 tsp	cracked black peppercorns	2 mL
1	can (28 oz/796 mL) tomatoes, including juice, coarsely chopped	1
1 tbsp	brown sugar	15 mL
3	medium beets, peeled and diced	3
1	potato, peeled and diced	1
4 cups	Basic Vegetable Stock (see recipe, page 34) or 2 cups (500 mL) each prepared vegetable and beef stock	1 L
1 tbsp	red wine vinegar	15 mL
4 cups	finely shredded cabbage	1 L
	Sour cream, optional	
	Finely chopped dill	

1. In a skillet, heat oil over medium heat for 30 seconds. Add onions, celery and carrots and cook, stirring, until carrots are softened, about 7 minutes. Add garlic, caraway seeds, salt and peppercorns and cook, stirring, for 1 minute.

2. Transfer to a food processor fitted with a metal blade (see Tip, left). Add half the tomatoes with juice and process until smooth. Transfer to slow cooker stoneware. Add remaining tomatoes, brown sugar, beets and potato to food processor and process until smooth. Transfer to slow cooker stoneware. Add vegetable stock.

3. Cover and cook on Low for 6 hours or on High for 3 hours, until vegetables are tender. Add vinegar and cabbage and stir well. Cover and cook on High for 20 to 30 minutes, until cabbage is tender. To serve, ladle into bowls, add a dollop of sour cream, if using, and garnish with dill.

VARIATION

If you're not a vegetarian, and prefer a more substantial soup, add thinly sliced kielbasa to the soup bowls before adding the garnish(es).

Mindful Morsels

Most North Americans do not consume enough fruits and vegetables. A person who needs 2,000 calories a day should be eating at least $4\frac{1}{2}$ cups (1.125 L) of fruits and vegetables every day. One serving of this soup will provide almost a quarter of that amount.

Nutrients Per Serving	
Calories	98
Protein	2.8 g
Carbohydrates	19.2 g
Fat (Total)	2.2 g
Saturated Fat	0.3 g
Monounsaturated Fat	1.3 g
Polyunsaturated Fat	0.3 g
Dietary Fiber	3.3 g
Sodium	487 mg
Cholesterol	0 mg

Natural Wonders

CABBAGE

Cabbage is such a healthful vegetable that it is known as a "functional food," which means it has been designated by the National Cancer Institute as a food with high cancer-fighting power. Cabbage contains two particularly potent cancer-fighting phytochemicals: indoles, which protect against breast cancer by helping to metabolize estrogen; and isothiocyanates, which help the body to detoxify carcinogens. Research shows that people who consume significant quantities of cabbage have particularly low rates of colon cancer. Low in calories, cabbage is a source of vitamin C, folacin, potassium and dietary fiber. One caveat: if you have thyroid problems you might want to limit your consumption of this vegetable because cabbage contains substances that may interfere with thyroid functioning.

Excellent source of vitamin A.

Good source of vitamins C, B6 and K, potassium and folacin.

Contains a moderate amount of dietary fiber.

See photo, page 70

Harira

This traditional Moroccan soup, often made with lamb, is usually served during Ramadan at the end of a day of fasting. This vegetarian version is finished with a dollop of harissa, a spicy North African sauce, which adds flavor and punch. Served with whole grain bread, harira makes a great light meal. A salad of shredded carrots topped with a sprinkling of currants adds color to the meal and complements the Middle Eastern flavors.

MAKES 8 SERVINGS

TIPS

❖ **To prepare chiles for Harissa:** Remove the stems and combine with 1 cup (250 mL) boiling water in a small bowl. Ensure they are submerged and set aside for 30 minutes until soft. Drain and coarsely chop.

❖ **To toast seeds for Harissa:** Combine caraway, coriander and cumin seeds in a dry skillet over medium heat. Cook, stirring, until fragrant, about 3 minutes. Immediately transfer to a mortar or a spice grinder and grind.

MAKE AHEAD

Harira can be partially prepared before it is cooked. Complete Step 1. Cover and refrigerate overnight or for up to 2 days. When you're ready to cook, continue with Step 2.

• **Large (minimum 5 quart) slow cooker**

1 tbsp	olive oil	15 mL
2	onions, coarsely chopped	2
4	stalks celery, diced	4
2	cloves garlic, minced	2
1 tbsp	turmeric	15 mL
1 tbsp	grated lemon zest	15 mL
1/2 tsp	cracked black peppercorns	2 mL
1	can (28 oz/796 mL) diced tomatoes, including juice	1
4 cups	Basic Vegetable Stock or Homemade Chicken Stock (see recipes, pages 34 and 35) or prepared stock	1 L
1 cup	dried red lentils, rinsed	250 mL
1	can (14 to 19 oz/398 to 540 mL) chickpeas, drained and rinsed, or 1 cup (250 mL) dried chickpeas, soaked, cooked and drained (see Basic Beans, page 250)	1
1/2 cup	finely chopped parsley	125 mL
	Harissa (see recipe, page 73)	

1. In a skillet, heat oil over medium heat for 30 seconds. Add onions and celery and cook, stirring, until celery is softened, about 5 minutes. Add garlic, turmeric, lemon zest and peppercorns and cook, stirring, for 1 minute. Add tomatoes with juice and bring to a boil. Transfer to slow cooker stoneware.

2. Add stock, lentils and chickpeas and stir well. Cover and cook on Low for 6 to 8 hours or on High for 3 to 4 hours, until mixture is hot and bubbly and lentils are tender. Stir in parsley. Ladle into bowls and pass the harissa at the table.

See photo, page 71

Harissa

In a mini-chopper, combine 3 reconstituted red chile peppers (see Tips, left), 2 tsp (10 mL) each toasted caraway and coriander seeds, 1 tsp (5 mL) toasted cumin seeds (see Tips, left), 2 reconstituted sun-dried tomatoes, 4 cloves garlic, 1½ tbsp (22 mL) lemon juice, 1 tbsp (15 mL) sweet paprika and ½ tsp (2 mL) salt and process until combined. Add 3 tbsp (45 mL) extra virgin olive oil and process until smooth and blended. Store, covered, in the refrigerator for up to 1 month, covering the paste with a bit of olive oil every time you use it. Makes ⅓ cup (75 mL).

Mindful Morsels

Enjoy the vegetables in this soup as a diet high in fruit and vegetables lowers risk of heart disease and stroke.

Natural Wonders

VEGETARIANS

If you have a vegetarian or two in your household, here's a soup you can serve knowing that many of their nutritional needs will be met. As more and more people, especially adolescents, adopt a vegetarian lifestyle, ensuring that they consume all the nutrients they need becomes increasingly challenging. For instance, growing bodies need more protein, iron, zinc and calcium than those that have matured. The legumes in this soup provide a smattering of these nutrients in varying quantities. While vegetarians may have to work harder than non-vegetarians to get a full range of nutrients from dietary sources, the good news is that being vegetarian may reduce the risk of high blood pressure, type-2 diabetes, certain kinds of cancer, and heart disease.

Nutrients Per Serving	
Calories	201
Protein	10.2 g
Carbohydrates	33.3 g
Fat (Total)	4.2 g
Saturated Fat	0.6 g
Monounsaturated Fat	2.4 g
Polyunsaturated Fat	0.8 g
Dietary Fiber	7.0 g
Sodium	314 mg
Cholesterol	0 mg

Excellent source of vitamins B6 and K, folacin, potassium and iron.

Good source of vitamin C, phosphorus, magnesium and zinc.

Source of vitamin A.

Contains a very high amount of dietary fiber.

Vegetable Gumbo

This tasty vegetable soup reminds me of a delicious version of one of my favorite canned soups when I was a kid. Served with whole grain bread, it makes an excellent lunch. If you're feeling indulgent and longing for comfort food that dredges up childhood memories, add a grilled cheese sandwich made with Cheddar cheese and whole wheat bread. Yum.

MAKES 6 SERVINGS

TIPS

❖ **This quantity of rice, combined with the okra, produces a dense soup, which condenses even more when refrigerated overnight. If you prefer a more soup-like consistency, add an additional cup (250 mL) of stock.**

❖ **Okra is a great thickener for broths but be sure not to overcook it because it will become unpleasantly sticky. Choose young okra pods 2 to 4 inches (5 to 10 cm) long, that don't feel sticky to the touch, in which case they are too ripe. Gently scrub the pods, cut off the top and tail and slice.**

MAKE AHEAD
This dish can be partially prepared before it is cooked. Complete Step 1. Cover and refrigerate overnight or for up to 2 days. When you're ready to cook, continue with Step 2.

• **Large (minimum 5 quart) slow cooker**

1 tbsp	olive oil	15 mL
2	onions, finely chopped	2
6	stalks celery, diced	6
4	cloves garlic, minced	4
2 tsp	dried thyme leaves, crumbled	10 mL
1/2 tsp	cracked black peppercorns	2 mL
1	bay leaf	1
1	can (28 oz/796 mL) diced tomatoes, including juice	1
1/2 cup	brown rice (see Tips, left)	125 mL
4 cups	Basic Vegetable Stock or Homemade Chicken Stock (see recipes, pages 34 and 35) or prepared stock	1 L
2 tsp	paprika, dissolved in 4 tsp (20 mL) lemon juice	10 mL
	Salt, optional	
2 cups	sliced okra (1/4-inch/0.5 cm slices) (see Tips, left)	500 mL
1	green bell pepper, diced	1

1. In a skillet, heat oil over medium heat for 30 seconds. Add onions and celery and cook, stirring, until celery is softened, about 5 minutes. Add garlic, thyme, peppercorns and bay leaf and cook, stirring, for 1 minute. Add tomatoes with juice and bring to a boil. Transfer to slow cooker stoneware.

2. Add brown rice and stock. Cover and cook on Low for 6 hours or on High for 3 hours, until rice is tender. Discard bay leaf. Add paprika solution and stir well. Season to taste with salt, if using. Stir in okra and green pepper. Cover and cook on High for 20 minutes, until pepper is tender.

Mindful Morsels

The brown rice in this recipe replaces the roux (flour cooked in oil) traditionally used to thicken gumbo. This reduces the quantity of fat and replaces refined flour with a healthy whole grain, adding fiber and other nutrients to the soup.

Natural Wonders

OKRA

Okra is a traditional ingredient in gumbo, where it is often used as a thickener in place of filé powder. But okra adds much more to this soup than a thick consistency. This low-cal vegetable is also a source of many nutrients, including vitamins C and B6, folacin, thiamin and magnesium. The pectin in okra, which enables it to thicken this soup, is a source of soluble fiber and helps keep blood cholesterol levels under control. Okra also contains glutathione a cancer-fighting antioxidant. One study found that people who consumed high amounts of glutathione, were half as likely to develop cancers of the throat and mouth than those with low levels of this compound.

Nutrients Per Serving	
Calories	148
Protein	4.5 g
Carbohydrates	28.0 g
Fat (Total)	3.2 g
Saturated Fat	0.5 g
Monounsaturated Fat	1.9 g
Polyunsaturated Fat	0.6 g
Dietary Fiber	4.7 g
Sodium	238 mg
Cholesterol	0 mg

Excellent source of vitamins C and K and potassium.

Good source of vitamins A and B6, magnesium, folacin and iron.

Source of calcium and phosphorus.

Contains a high amount of dietary fiber.

Cockaleekie

This chicken and leek soup has been around for hundreds of years and qualifies as Scottish comfort food. Although the prunes seem unconventional, having tried the soup with and without this ingredient I prefer the addition of prunes, which add a pleasing sweetness and depth to the broth and complement the other flavors. However, if you have negative feelings about prunes, they may be omitted, and the recipe produces something approaching a classic chicken soup with barley. To complete the meal, add a green salad or sliced tomatoes, in season, and whole grain bread.

MAKES 8 SERVINGS

TIP

❖ **If you're not using the prunes, add 1 cup (250 mL) additional chicken stock along with the barley.**

MAKE AHEAD

This dish can be partially prepared before it is cooked. Complete Steps 1 through 3. Cover and refrigerate overnight or for up to 2 days. When you're ready to cook, continue with Step 4.

• **Large (minimum 6 quart) slow cooker**

20	pitted prunes, finely chopped (about 1 cup/250 mL) whole pitted prunes), optional (see Tip, left)	20
1¹/₂ cups	water	375 mL
2 lbs	skinless boneless chicken thighs	1 kg
1 tbsp	olive oil	15 mL
4	large leeks, white part with just a bit of green, cleaned and thinly sliced (see Tip, page 42)	4
4	stalks celery, diced	4
4	carrots, peeled and diced	4
1 tsp	dried thyme leaves, crumbled	5 mL
¹/₂ tsp	cracked black peppercorns	2 mL
4	whole cloves	4
1	piece (1 inch/2.5 cm) cinnamon stick	1
6 cups	Homemade Chicken Stock (see recipe, page 35) or prepared chicken stock	1.5 L
1 cup	whole (hulled) or pot barley, rinsed (see Mindful Morsels, page 65)	250 mL
¹/₂ cup	finely chopped parsley	125 mL

1. In a small bowl, combine prunes and water. Stir well. Cover and set aside.

2. Arrange chicken over bottom of slow cooker stoneware.

3. In a large skillet, heat oil over medium heat for 30 seconds. Add leeks, celery and carrots and cook, stirring, until softened, about 7 minutes. Add thyme, peppercorns, cloves and cinnamon stick and cook, stirring for 1 minute. Transfer to slow cooker stoneware.

4. Add chicken stock and barley. Cover and cook on Low for 6 hours or on High for 3 hours, until chicken is falling apart and barley is tender. Discard cloves and cinnamon stick. Add prunes and soaking water, if using. Stir well. Cover and cook on High for 30 minutes, until flavors have melded. Ladle into bowls and garnish with parsley.

Mindful Morsels

Prunes do more than relieve constipation. They are rich in malic acid, which helps to keep you energized.

Natural Wonders
KEEPING BLOOD PRESSURE UNDER CONTROL

Among other benefits, eating nutrient-rich vegetables, fruits and whole grains, particularly those high in potassium and magnesium, will help to keep your blood pressure under control. Studies show that people who have low intakes of these important minerals are more likely to have high blood pressure.

If do you have high blood pressure, try tweaking your lifestyle before taking medication. Experts tell us that making two or more dietary-lifestyle changes may control blood pressure as well as drug therapy, which is usually effective but may initiate negative side effects. Maintaining a healthy weight and being active are an excellent start, as is limiting your sodium intake. Experts now recommend 1,500 mg of sodium a day for those who have been diagnosed with high blood pressure. Don't focus on the salt shaker — most of the salt we consume is invisible, lurking in processed foods such as canned soups and snacks, as well as fast foods. Eliminating these foods from your diet and replacing them with healthy whole foods will go a long way toward keeping your blood pressure under control. Use homemade rather than prepared stocks when making soups and stews (see recipes, pages 34 and 35) and look for canned legumes with no salt added in natural foods stores, or cook your own, which is very easy to do using a slow cooker (see recipe for Basic Beans, page 250).

Nutrients Per Serving	
Calories	299
Protein	27.2 g
Carbohydrates	31.2 g
Fat (Total)	7.5 g
Saturated Fat	1.7 g
Monounsaturated Fat	3.0 g
Polyunsaturated Fat	1.7 g
Dietary Fiber	5.1 g
Sodium	166 mg
Cholesterol	109 mg

Excellent source of vitamins A, B6 and K, iron and zinc.

Good source of folacin, magnesium, potassium and phosphorus.

Source of vitamin C.

Contains a high amount of dietary fiber.

Chestnut Soup

Impress your guests with this deliciously different soup. French in origin, it makes an elegant starter to any meal. In France it is often accentuated with a licorice-flavored herb such as chervil or tarragon. Here I have added the Chinese spice, star anise, which adds a particularly delectable depth to the stock. Feel free to double the recipe if you are feeding more people.

MAKES
4 TO 6 SERVINGS

TIPS

❖ **If you are using prepared chestnut purée in this recipe, check the label to make sure it doesn't contain sugar. Some versions of this product are destined for dessert rather than main course use. Canned purée is very congealed and you'll need to soften it up a bit before adding to the broth. I suggest breaking it into little pieces and beating it in a bowl with a bit of the hot broth, or puréeing it in a food processor.**

MAKE AHEAD
This dish can be partially prepared before it is cooked. Complete Steps 1 and 2. Cover and refrigerate overnight or for up to 2 days. When you're ready to cook, continue with Step 3.

• **Works in slow cookers from 3½ to 6 quarts**

GARLIC CROUTONS

1 tbsp	olive oil or duck fat (see Mindful Morsels, right)	15 mL
2	cloves garlic, minced	2
1	slice country-style bread, cut into ¼-inch (0.5 cm) cubes	1
	Sea salt, optional	
1 tbsp	olive oil or duck fat	15 mL
⅓ cup	minced onion	75 mL
2	carrots, peeled and diced	2
2	stalks celery, diced	2
1	whole star anise	1
¼ tsp	freshly ground black pepper	1 mL
4 cups	Homemade Chicken Stock or Basic Vegetable Stock (see recipes, pages 34 and 35) or prepared stock	1 L
1 cup	unsweetened chestnut purée (see Tips, left)	250 mL
1 tbsp	chopped fresh tarragon, chervil or parsley	15 mL
1 tbsp	port wine, optional	15 mL
	Whipping (35 %) cream, optional	

1. *Garlic Croutons:* In a skillet, heat oil over medium heat for 30 seconds. Add garlic and cook, stirring, for 1 minute. Add bread and cook, stirring, until golden, about 2 minutes. Drain on paper towel-lined plate and sprinkle with sea salt to taste, if using. If not using immediately, transfer to an airtight container. Set aside until ready to use.

2. In a skillet, heat oil over medium heat for 30 seconds. Add onion, carrots and celery and cook, stirring, until softened, about 7 minutes. Add star anise and black pepper and cook, stirring, for 1 minute. Transfer to slow cooker stoneware. Stir in stock.

3. Cover and cook on Low for 6 to 8 hours or on High for 3 to 4 hours, until vegetables are very tender. Stir in chestnut purée and tarragon. Cover and cook for 30 minutes, until flavors meld. Working in batches, purée soup in a food processor or blender. (You can also do this in the stoneware using an immersion blender.) Stir in port wine, if using. Ladle into bowls and drizzle with cream, if using. Garnish with croutons.

❖ **If you have leftover chestnut purée, use it to enhance mashed potatoes. Blend it with some warm milk, season with salt and pepper and beat into the potatoes.**

Mindful Morsels

When softening vegetables you can substitute rendered duck fat for olive oil. Many gourmands love the flavor it adds to any recipe. Since virtually half its fat (49 percent) is monounsaturated, occasionally using duck fat, which can be purchased from specialty food stores, can be part of a healthy eating strategy.

Natural Wonders

CHESTNUTS

Like all nuts, chestnuts are nutritious. Although they contain a number of important nutrients, such as vitamins C and B6, folacin and fiber, chestnuts differ from other nuts in significant ways. For one thing, they contain a greater proportion of carbohydrate, which is why they taste so sweet and are relatively high in many B vitamins. Unlike other nuts, they are low in fat, which means they have fewer calories. One ounce of roasted chestnuts contains 69 calories, compared with 166 calories in a comparable quantity of peanuts and 210 calories in the same quantity of macadamia nuts. Moreover, almost all of the fat in chestnuts is unsaturated, equally divided between monounsaturates and polyunsaturates, which make them a very healthy food choice.

Nutrients Per Serving	
Calories	156
Protein	4.0 g
Carbohydrates	21.8 g
Fat (Total)	6.2 g
Saturated Fat	1.0 g
Monounsaturated Fat	3.9 g
Polyunsaturated Fat	0.9 g
Dietary Fiber	4.8 g
Sodium	83 mg
Cholesterol	13 mg

Excellent source of vitamins A and B6.

Good source of vitamin K, folacin and potassium.

Source of vitamin C.

Contains a high amount of dietary fiber.

Greek-Style Split Pea Soup

This is a soup version of the Greek appetizer fava, a purée of yellow split peas often topped with capers or stewed tomatoes. Here I've suggested the addition of a persillade made with red wine vinegar as a flavor enhancer, but you can also finish the soup with a dollop of warm tomato sauce. For a smoother result, purée the soup after it has finished cooking.

MAKES 8 SERVINGS

TIP

❖ Traditional wisdom suggests that yellow split peas do not need to be soaked before cooking. However, I have found that without a good pre-soaking they are a bit tough.

MAKE AHEAD

This soup can be partially prepared before it is cooked. Complete Steps 1 and 2. Cover and refrigerate overnight or for up to 2 days. When you're ready to cook, continue with Steps 3 and 4.

• Large (minimum 5 quart) slow cooker

2 cups	yellow split peas (see Tip, left)	500 mL
1 tbsp	olive oil	15 mL
2	onions, finely chopped	2
4	stalks celery, diced	4
4	carrots, peeled and diced	4
4	cloves garlic, minced	4
1 tsp	dried oregano leaves, crumbled	5 mL
1/2 tsp	cracked black peppercorns	2 mL
6 cups	Enhanced Vegetable Stock (see Variation, page 34)	1.5 L
	Salt, optional	
	Extra virgin olive oil, optional	

PERSILLADE (optional)

1 cup	packed parsley leaves, finely chopped	250 mL
4	cloves garlic, minced	4
4 tsp	red wine vinegar	20 mL

1. In a large pot, combine split peas and 8 cups (2 L) cold water. Bring to a boil over medium-high heat and boil rapidly for 3 minutes. Turn off element and set aside for 1 hour. Drain and rinse thoroughly. Set aside.

2. In a skillet, heat oil over medium heat for 30 seconds. Add onions, celery and carrots and cook, stirring, until carrots are softened, about 7 minutes. Add garlic, oregano and peppercorns and cook, stirring, for 1 minute. Transfer to slow cooker stoneware. Add reserved split peas and stock and stir well.

3. Cover and cook on Low for 8 to 10 hours or on High for 4 to 5 hours, until peas are tender. Add salt to taste, if using.

4. *Persillade (optional):* In a bowl, combine parsley, garlic and vinegar. (You can also make this in a mini-chopper.) Set aside at room temperature for 30 minutes to allow flavors to develop. To serve, ladle soup into individual bowls, drizzle with extra virgin olive oil, if using, and garnish with persillade, if using.

VARIATIONS

Instead of the persillade, top each serving of soup with a dollop of warm tomato sauce.

Quebec-Style Split Pea Soup

Add a leftover ham bone and any extra meat, chopped, to the slow cooker along with the split peas. Substitute 1 tsp (5 mL) dried thyme leaves for oregano and regular vegetable stock for the enhanced version. Top with garlic croutons instead of persillade.

Mindful Morsels

Most of the fiber (4.3 grams) in a serving of this soup comes from the split peas. The carrots contribute 1 gram.

Natural Wonders

DRIED PEAS

All legumes are an excellent source of fiber, but yellow split peas contain more than most. Dried peas, like all legumes, contain both types of fiber: soluble fiber, which may help to keep cholesterol low; and insoluble fiber, which helps to keep you regular and wards off intestinal problems, such as irritable bowel syndrome and diverticular disease, an inflammation of the intestine. Dried peas are also a source of isoflavones, the phytochemicals that are touted for their apparent ability to act as phytoestrogens, thereby relieving many of the symptoms associated with menopause, among other benefits. Dried peas also contain folacin, potassium and iron.

Nutrients Per Serving	
Calories	230
Protein	13.4 g
Carbohydrates	39.5 g
Fat (Total)	2.4 g
Saturated Fat	0.3 g
Monounsaturated Fat	1.4 g
Polyunsaturated Fat	0.5 g
Fiber	6.2 g
Sodium	47 mg
Cholesterol	0 mg

Excellent source of vitamins A and K, folacin and potassium.

Good source of magnesium, phosphorus, iron and zinc.

Source of vitamin B6.

Contains a very high amount of dietary fiber.

Poultry, Seafood & Fish

Caribbean Fish Stew, see recipe overleaf

Caribbean Fish Stew

I love the combination of flavors in this tasty stew. The allspice and the Scotch bonnet peppers add a distinctly island tang. For a distinctive and delicious finish, be sure to include the dill. Serve this with crusty rolls to soak up the sauce, a fresh green salad and some crisp white wine.

MAKES 8 SERVINGS

TIP

❖ **One Scotch bonnet pepper is probably enough for most people, but if you're a heat seeker, use two. You can also use habanero peppers instead.**

MAKE AHEAD

This dish can be partially prepared before it is cooked. Complete Steps 1 and 2. Cover and refrigerate overnight or for up to 2 days. When you're ready to cook, continue with Step 3.

• **Works in slow cookers from 3½ to 6 quarts**

2 tsp	cumin seeds	10 mL
6	whole allspice	6
1 tbsp	olive oil	15 mL
2	onions, finely chopped	2
4	cloves garlic, minced	4
2 tsp	dried thyme leaves, crumbled	10 mL
1 tsp	turmeric	5 mL
1 tbsp	grated orange or lime zest	15 mL
½ tsp	cracked black peppercorns	2 mL
1	can (28 oz/796 mL) tomatoes, including juice, coarsely chopped	1
2 cups	fish stock	500 mL
	Salt	
1 to 2	Scotch bonnet peppers, minced	1 to 2
2 cups	sliced okra (¼ inch/0.5 cm)	500 mL
1½ lbs	skinless grouper fillets, cut into bite-size pieces	750 g
8 oz	shrimp, cooked, peeled and deveined	250 g
½ cup	finely chopped dill, optional	125 mL

1. In a large dry skillet over medium heat, toast cumin seeds and allspice, stirring, until fragrant and cumin seeds just begin to brown, about 3 minutes. Immediately transfer to a mortar or a spice grinder and grind. Set aside.

2. In same skillet, heat oil over medium heat for 30 seconds. Add onions and cook, stirring, until softened, about 3 minutes. Add garlic, thyme, turmeric, orange zest, peppercorns and reserved cumin and allspice and cook, stirring, for 1 minute. Add tomatoes with juice and fish stock and bring to a boil. Season with salt to taste. Transfer to slow cooker stoneware.

3. Cover and cook on Low for 6 hours or on High for 3 hours. Add chili peppers, okra, fish fillets and shrimp. Cover and cook on High for 20 minutes, until fish flakes easily with a fork and okra is tender. Stir in dill, if using.

Mindful Morsels

Finishing this stew with a liberal serving of dill adds flavor and nutrients, such as vitamin C and a smattering of vitamin A and folacin. Dill also contains phytochemicals, some of which may help protect against cancer.

Natural Wonders

FISH

In terms of cancer prevention, it makes sense to pass on the red meat and eat fish instead. A study conducted by French researchers who tracked the diets of half a million people aged 35 to 70, who were cancer-free for an average of five years when the study began, found that as fish consumption rose, rates of colon cancer appeared to drop. Those who ate the most fish (an average of 3 ounces/90 g per day), including canned and smoked fish, lowered their risk of this form of cancer by almost one-third.

Other studies confirm that eating fish regularly can help to protect against certain types of cancer. A Canadian study of more than 7,000 participants found that those who got most of their fat calories from fish were 28 percent less likely to have leukemia, 36 percent less likely to have multiple myeloma and 29 percent less likely to have non-Hodgkins' lymphoma. A Spanish study found that people who ate fish had fewer incidences of three other types of cancer: ovarian, pancreatic and cancers of all parts of the digestive tract.

Nutrients Per Serving	
Calories	172
Protein	24.2 g
Carbohydrates	10.5 g
Fat (Total)	3.8 g
Saturated Fat	0.7 g
Monounsaturated Fat	1.7 g
Polyunsaturated Fat	0.8 g
Dietary Fiber	2.4 g
Sodium	320 mg
Cholesterol	64 mg

Excellent source of vitamin B6 and potassium.

Good source of vitamins C, B12 and K, folacin, magnesium, phosphorus and iron.

Source of vitamin A and calcium.

Contains a moderate amount of dietary fiber.

Chicken Cassoulet

This hearty one-dish meal is always a hit — I particularly like the dill finish, which adds an intriguing hint of flavor. I like to serve this with an abundance of whole grain bread to soak up the luscious sauce. A salad of shredded carrots makes a nice accompaniment.

MAKES 8 SERVINGS

TIP

❖ If you're using small cremini mushrooms (my preference in this recipe), just remove the stems and use them whole. Cut larger ones in half or quarters, depending on the size. If using portobello mushrooms, remove the stems and gills and cut each into 6 equal wedges.

MAKE AHEAD

This dish can be partially prepared before it is cooked. Complete Step 1. Cover and refrigerate bean mixture for up to 2 days. When you're ready to cook, continue with Steps 2 and 3.

• **Large (minimum 6 quart) slow cooker**

1 tbsp	olive oil	15 mL
2	onions, finely chopped	2
8	carrots, peeled and sliced	8
4	stalks celery, sliced	4
4	cloves garlic, minced	4
2 tsp	herbes de Provence	10 mL
1 tsp	salt	5 mL
1 tsp	cracked black peppercorns	5 mL
1	can (28 oz/796 mL) tomatoes, including juice, coarsely chopped	1
1 cup	chicken or vegetable stock	250 mL
2	cans (each 14 to 19 oz/398 to 540 mL) white beans or 2 cups (500 mL) dried white beans, soaked, cooked and drained (see Basic Beans, page 250)	2
2	bay leaves	2
2 lbs	skinless bone-in chicken thighs (about 8 thighs)	1 kg
1 lb	cremini or portobello mushrooms (see Tip, left)	500 g
1/2 cup	finely chopped dill	125 mL

1. In a large skillet, heat oil over medium heat for 30 seconds. Add onions, carrots and celery and cook, stirring, until carrots are softened, about 7 minutes. Add garlic, herbes de Provence, salt and peppercorns and cook, stirring for 1 minute. Add tomatoes with juice, chicken stock, beans and bay leaves and bring to a boil. Remove from heat.

2. Spoon half of the bean mixture into slow cooker stoneware. Lay chicken evenly over top. Arrange mushrooms evenly over chicken. Spoon remainder of sauce over mushrooms.

3. Cover and cook on Low for 6 hours or on High for 3 hours, until juices run clear when chicken is pierced with a fork. Stir in dill. Cover and cook on High for 15 minutes, until flavors meld.

Mindful Morsels

The nutritional analysis for this recipe was done using regular prepared chicken stock and canned beans. If the quantity of sodium concerns you, use Homemade Chicken Stock (see recipe, page 35) and cook dried white beans with no salt added.

Natural Wonders

FIBER

This recipe is an excellent source of fiber, more than half of which (5.4 grams) comes from the beans. You can nurture your heart and help to keep your weight under control by regularly adding fiber-rich legumes, such as beans, to your diet. One long-term study, which followed approximately 10,000 subjects for a 19-year period, found that participants who consumed 21 grams of fiber a day had a 12 percent reduction in coronary heart disease and an 11 percent reduction in cardiovascular disease, compared with those who consumed only 5 grams a day. Studies also show that a high intake of fiber-rich foods protects against obesity. Because legumes are nutrient dense, they combine the ability to quickly satiate with nutritional wallop. In other words, you don't need to consume a lot of calories to feel satisfied, while meeting nutritional objectives.

Nutrients Per Serving	
Calories	281
Protein	24.4 g
Carbohydrates	32.7 g
Fat (Total)	6.8 g
Saturated Fat	1.4 g
Monounsaturated Fat	2.6 g
Polyunsaturated Fat	1.5 g
Dietary Fiber	10.3 g
Sodium	948 mg
Cholesterol	69 mg

Excellent source of vitamins A, B6 and K, magnesium, potassium, iron and zinc.

Good source of vitamin C, folacin, calcium and phosphorus.

Contains a very high amount of dietary fiber.

Indian-Style Chicken with Puréed Spinach

This mouth-watering dish is an adaptation of one of my favorite recipes from Suneeta Vaswani's terrific book Easy Indian Cooking. *I usually serve it as the centerpiece of a meal, accompanied by rice and/or whole wheat chapati.*

MAKES 8 SERVINGS

TIPS

❖ If you don't have a 14 oz (398 mL) can of diced tomatoes, use 2 cups (500 mL) canned tomatoes with juice, coarsely chopped.

❖ If using fresh spinach, be sure to remove the stems, and if it has not been pre-washed, rinse it thoroughly in a basin of lukewarm water. You will need to push it well down in the blender or food processor before puréeing in batches. If using frozen spinach, thaw it first and squeeze the water out.

MAKE AHEAD

This dish can be partially prepared before it is cooked. Complete Step 1. Cover and refrigerate chicken. Complete Steps 2 and 3. Cover and refrigerate separately from chicken. The next day, continue with Steps 4 and 5.

• **Large (minimum 5 quart) oval slow cooker**

4 lbs	skinless bone-in chicken thighs (about 16 thighs)	2 kg
¼ cup	freshly squeezed lemon juice	50 mL
1 tbsp	cumin seeds	15 mL
2 tsp	coriander seeds	10 mL
2 tbsp	olive oil	25 mL
2	onions, thinly sliced on the vertical	2
1 tbsp	minced peeled gingerroot	15 mL
1 tbsp	minced garlic	15 mL
1 tsp	turmeric	5 mL
1 tsp	cracked black peppercorns	5 mL
1 tsp	salt, or to taste (see Tips, right)	5 mL
1	can (14 oz/398 mL) diced tomatoes, including juice (see Tips, left)	1
2	packages (each 10 oz/300 g) fresh or frozen spinach (see Tips, left)	2
1 to 2	long red or green chiles, chopped	1 to 2
1 cup	chicken stock	250 mL
	Juice of 1 lime or lemon	

1. Rinse chicken under cold running water and pat dry. In a bowl, combine chicken and lemon juice. Toss well and set aside for 20 to 30 minutes.

2. In a dry skillet over medium heat, toast cumin and coriander seeds, stirring, until fragrant and cumin seeds just begin to brown, about 3 minutes. Immediately transfer to a mortar or a spice grinder and grind. Set aside.

3. In same skillet, heat oil over medium-high heat for 30 seconds. Add onions and cook, stirring, until they begin to color, about 5 minutes. Reduce heat to medium and cook, stirring, until

golden, about 12 minutes. Add reserved cumin and coriander, gingerroot, garlic, turmeric, peppercorns and salt and cook, stirring, for 1 minute. Stir in tomatoes with juice and bring to a boil. Remove from heat.

4. Arrange marinated chicken evenly over the bottom of the slow cooker stoneware. Pour tomato mixture over top. Cover and cook on Low for 6 hours or on High for 3 hours, until juices run clear when chicken is pierced with a fork.

5. In a blender or food processor, combine spinach, chile(s) and chicken stock. Pulse until spinach is puréed. Add to chicken and stir well. Cover and cook on High for 20 minutes, until mixture is bubbly. Just before serving, stir in lime juice.

❖ **One chile produces a medium-hot result. Add a second chile only if you're a true heat seeker.**

❖ **The nutrient analysis on this recipe was done using 1 tsp (5 mL) of salt. If you're concerned about your sodium intake, use less.**

Mindful Morsels
One serving of this dish provides almost 400 percent of the daily value of vitamin K, virtually all of which comes from the spinach.

Natural Wonders
CUMIN
Cumin, a spice with a unique peppery yet earthy flavor, is used liberally in many cuisines. But there's more to this versatile spice than aromatics: Like most spices, cumin, which contains the essential minerals calcium, iron, potassium and manganese, has nutrient value. Traditional wisdom is that cumin improves digestion, and new research explains why it has this effect. Cumin stimulates the pancreas, producing enzymes that help the body digest food and assimilate nutrients. Researchers are also exploring the possibility that the spice may also have cancer-preventing properties.

When using cumin, I like to use the whole seeds, which I toast and grind. Not only does toasting bring out the spice's pleasant nuttiness, it makes the kitchen deliciously fragrant. Also, whole seeds maintain their freshness much longer than ground powder. Stored in an airtight container in a cool dry place, away from light, cumin seeds will keep for as long as three years, whereas ground cumin keeps only for a year.

Nutrients Per Serving	
Calories	290
Protein	34.9 g
Carbohydrates	9.7 g
Fat (Total)	12.4 g
Saturated Fat	2.7 g
Monounsaturated Fat	5.3 g
Polyunsaturated Fat	2.5 g
Dietary Fiber	2.9 g
Sodium	665 mg
Cholesterol	138 mg

Excellent source of vitamins A, B6 and K, folacin, magnesium, potassium, iron and zinc.

Good source of vitamin C.

Source of calcium.

Contains a moderate amount of dietary fiber.

Chicken Cacciatore with Broccoli

This dish is a classic because it's so tasty. The addition of broccoli to the traditional ingredients adds flavor as well as nutrients. Serve this over hot polenta or pasta for a delicious meal.

MAKES 6 SERVINGS

TIP

❖ I like to use Italian San Marzano tomatoes when making this recipe because they have more flavor than domestic varieties. If you can't find them, add 1 tbsp (15 mL) tomato paste, along with the tomatoes.

MAKE AHEAD

This dish can be partially prepared before it is cooked. Complete Step 1. Cover and refrigerate overnight or for up to 2 days. When you're ready to cook, continue with Steps 2 and 3.

• Large (minimum 5 quart) slow cooker

2 tbsp	olive oil, divided	25 mL
2	onions, finely chopped	2
4	cloves garlic, minced	4
1 tsp	dried oregano leaves, crumbled	5 mL
1/2 tsp	salt	2 mL
1/2 tsp	cracked black peppercorns	2 mL
8 oz	cremini mushrooms	250 g
1 cup	dry white wine or chicken stock	250 mL
1	can (28 oz/796 mL) tomatoes, including juice, coarsely chopped (see Tip, left)	1
12	skinless bone-in chicken thighs (about 3 lbs/1.5 kg)	12
2	dried red chile peppers, optional	2
1	green bell pepper, diced	1
4 cups	broccoli florets, blanched	1 L

1. In a skillet, heat 1 tbsp (15 mL) of the olive oil over medium heat for 30 seconds. Add onions and cook, stirring, until softened, about 3 minutes. Add garlic, oregano, salt and peppercorns and cook, stirring, for 1 minute. Add mushrooms and toss to coat. Add white wine and tomatoes with juice and bring to a boil.

2. Arrange chicken over bottom of slow cooker stoneware. Cover with sauce. Cover and cook on Low for 6 hours or on High for 3 hours, until juices run clear when chicken is pierced with a fork. Using a slotted spoon, transfer chicken to a heatproof serving dish and keep warm in oven.

3. In a skillet, heat remaining 1 tbsp (15 mL) of the oil over medium heat for 30 seconds. Add chile peppers, if using, and cook, stirring, for 1 minute. Add bell pepper and cook, stirring, until softened, about 3 minutes. Add tomato sauce from slow cooker stoneware and bring to a boil. Reduce heat and simmer until slightly reduced and thickened, about 10 minutes. Add broccoli and cook until heated through. Combine with chicken and serve.

Mindful Morsels

Not only are the mushrooms in this recipe very low in calories, they are also a good source of potassium, which helps control blood pressure, and zinc, which helps the immune system to function.

Natural Wonders
COMBINING FOODS

Eating a variety of foods with a view toward maximizing the range of nutrients we consume has long been recognized as a healthy eating strategy. Now scientists are telling us there is even more reason to enjoy a varied diet. The more we learn about the phytochemicals in food, the more we understand that the relationships among the various components of foods also play a role in their healthful properties. Different phytochemicals interact with different organs, tissues and cells, and studies are now showing that foods interact synergistically. For instance, while tomatoes and broccoli have both been identified as cancer fighters, tomatoes rely on lycopene to do this job and broccoli uses glucosinolates. A study published in the *Journal of Nutrition* shows that rats fed broccoli and tomatoes together had less tumor growth than those eating a diet containing either food alone. Another study done by Britain's Institute of Food Research combined broccoli and chicken. Chicken is high in the mineral selenium, and broccoli contains sulforaphone, both of which have cancer-fighting properties. Researchers found the combination of broccoli and chicken was up to 13 times more powerful than when either food was consumed alone.

Nutrients Per Serving	
Calories	318
Protein	35.5 g
Carbohydrates	14.6 g
Fat (Total)	13.4 g
Saturated Fat	2.8 g
Monounsaturated Fat	6.0 g
Polyunsaturated Fat	2.7 g
Dietary Fiber	3.6 g
Sodium	546 mg
Cholesterol	138 mg

Excellent source of vitamins C, B6 and K, potassium and zinc.

Good source of vitamin A, magnesium, folacin and iron.

Source of calcium and phosphorus.

Contains a moderate amount of dietary fiber.

See photo, page 92

French Basil Chicken

I call this French Basil Chicken to distinguish it from the well-known dish Thai basil chicken, which is also a staple at our house. This version combines chicken with the complementary flavors of tomato, artichoke and sweet red pepper. A healthy quantity of finely chopped fresh basil leaves is stirred in at the end. I like to serve this with fluffy rice garnished with plenty of toasted pine nuts.

MAKES
6 TO 8 SERVINGS

TIPS

❖ If you prefer, substitute an equal amount of chicken stock for the wine, but be aware that you may need to reduce the amount of salt. Prepared stock varies in saltiness. Taste the stock you are using and if it seems salty, reduce the quantity of added salt. If you are concerned about sodium in your diet, use a reduced-sodium stock or make your own with no salt added (see Homemade Chicken Stock, page 35).

❖ If your supermarket carries 19 oz (540 mL) cans of diced tomatoes, by all means substitute for the 14 oz (398 mL) called for in the recipe.

MAKE AHEAD
This recipe can be partially prepared before it is cooked. Complete Step 1. Cover and refrigerate overnight or for up to 2 days. When you're ready to cook, continue with Step 2.

• **Works in slow cookers from 3½ to 6 quarts**

1 tbsp	olive oil	15 mL
2	onions, finely chopped	2
4	cloves garlic, minced	4
1 tsp	herbes de Provence	5 mL
½ tsp	salt, or to taste	2 mL
½ tsp	cracked black peppercorns	2 mL
1 tbsp	all-purpose flour	15 mL
½ cup	dry white wine (see Tips, left)	125 mL
1 cup	chicken stock (see Tips, left)	250 mL
1	can (14 oz/398 mL) diced tomatoes, including juice (see Tips, left)	1
1	can (14 oz/398 mL) artichoke hearts, drained, rinsed and quartered	1
3 lbs	skinless bone-in chicken thighs (about 12 thighs)	1.5 kg
2 cups	diced red bell pepper	500 mL
½ cup	finely chopped fresh basil leaves	125 mL

1. In a skillet, heat oil over medium heat for 30 seconds. Add onions and cook, stirring, until softened, about 3 minutes. Add garlic, herbes de Provence, salt and peppercorns and cook, stirring, for 1 minute. Add flour and cook, stirring, for 1 minute. Add wine and cook, stirring, for 1 minute. Add chicken stock and tomatoes with juice and bring to a boil. Stir in artichoke hearts and remove from heat.

2. Arrange chicken pieces evenly over the bottom of slow cooker stoneware and cover with tomato mixture. Cover and cook on Low for 6 hours or on High for 3 hours, until juices run clear when chicken is pierced with a fork. Stir in red pepper and basil. Cover and cook on High for 30 minutes, or until pepper is tender.

See photo, page 93

Mindful Morsels

Onions are the base for so many soups, stews and sauces that we take them for granted. But onions contain many nutrients, including quercetin, a flavonoid that may stop the growth of colon cancer.

Natural Wonders

HERBS

Culinary herbs do more than add color and flavor to a dish: they also have significant health benefits. For instance, USDA researchers have found that many culinary herbs such as sage, dill, thyme, rosemary and oregano are loaded with antioxidants. It's also worth knowing that more than half of the vitamin K in this recipe comes from the basil. Fragrant and pungent, basil also contains flavonoids, a group of phytochemcials that may protect cells and chromosomes from free radical damage. Along with isoflavones and ellagic acid, flavonoids belong to the polyphenol family of phytochemcials, which appear to have the ability to fight viruses and cancer. Moreover, a study published in the *American Journal of Clinical Nutrition* in 2002 linked a high intake of flavonoids with a lower incidence of heart disease and stroke. Research focused on basil's volatile oils has shown promising results in another area. Because these compounds restrict bacterial growth, researchers are exploring their potential value in treating antibiotic-resistant bacteria. Basil also contains eugenol, which inhibits activity of an enzyme causing inflammatory conditions such as arthritis.

Nutrients Per Serving	
Calories	230
Protein	26.5 g
Carbohydrates	12.4 g
Fat (Total)	8.3 g
Saturated Fat	1.9 g
Monounsaturated Fat	3.2 g
Polyunsaturated Fat	1.8 g
Dietary Fiber	3.4 g
Sodium	549 mg
Cholesterol	103 mg

Excellent source of vitamins C, B6 and K.

Good source of vitamin A, magnesium, potassium, zinc, folacin and iron.

Contains a moderate amount of dietary fiber.

Chicken with Leeks in Walnut Sauce

This French country dish is one way of increasing your consumption of walnuts, which although relatively high in calories are extremely good for you (see Natural Wonders, right). I like to serve this tasty stew with parsleyed potatoes and a sliced tomato salad to add color to the meal. If you're worried about your waistline, go for an after-dinner walk.

MAKES
6 TO 8 SERVINGS

TIP

❖ To clean leeks: Fill a sink full of lukewarm water. Split the leeks in half lengthwise and submerge them in the water, swishing them around to remove all traces of dirt. Transfer to a colander and rinse thoroughly under cold water.

MAKE AHEAD

This dish can be partially prepared before it is cooked. Complete Step 1. Cover and refrigerate overnight or for up to 2 days. When you're ready to cook, continue with Steps 2 and 3.

• Works in slow cookers from 3½ to 6 quarts

1 tbsp	olive oil	15 mL
4	leeks, white part with a bit of green, cleaned and thinly sliced (see Tip, left)	4
4	stalks celery, diced	4
2	cloves garlic, minced	2
1 tsp	dried tarragon leaves, crumbled	5 mL
½ tsp	cracked black peppercorns	2 mL
1 tbsp	all-purpose flour	15 mL
2 cups	chicken stock	500 mL
	Salt, optional	
3 lbs	skinless bone-in chicken thighs (about 12 thighs)	1.5 kg

WALNUT SAUCE

1 cup	walnuts halves	250 mL
1 cup	loosely packed parsley leaves	250 mL
1	clove garlic, minced	1
1 tbsp	extra virgin olive oil	15 mL
1 tbsp	red wine vinegar	15 mL
	Salt, optional	

1. In a skillet, heat oil over medium heat for 30 seconds. Add leeks and celery and cook, stirring, until softened, about 5 minutes. Add garlic, tarragon and peppercorns and cook, stirring, for 1 minute. Add flour and cook, stirring, for 1 minute. Add chicken stock and bring to a boil. Cook, stirring, until slightly thickened, about 2 minutes. Season to taste with salt, if using.

2. Arrange chicken evenly over bottom of slow cooker stoneware and cover with leek mixture. Cover and cook on Low for 6 hours or on High for 3 hours, until juices run clear when chicken is pierced with a fork.

3. *Walnut Sauce:* Meanwhile, in a food processor fitted with a metal blade, combine walnuts, parsley and garlic. Process until finely ground. With motor running, gradually add olive oil, then vinegar through the feed tube, processing until smooth. Season to taste with salt, if using. Add to stoneware and stir well. Cover and cook on High for 15 minutes, until walnuts are heated through.

Mindful Morsels
A serving of this recipe provides 1.44 grams of healthy omega-3 fatty acids.

Natural Wonders
WALNUTS AND OMEGA-3 FATTY ACIDS

Although a serving of this tasty stew contains 19.5 grams of fat, most of that fat is polyunsaturated, which contains healthful omega-3 fatty acids. Contemporary farming and food processing techniques have reduced the quantity of these essential fats in the North American diet. However, consumption of omega-3 fatty acids has been linked with various health benefits, including lower rates of heart disease and stroke. Although there are no recommended daily values for this nutrient in the U.S., the World Health Organization suggests getting 3 grams of omega 3's daily. Walnuts are one of the few plant foods that are rich in this valuable nutrient.

In addition to omega-3 fatty acids, walnuts are a source of vitamin B6, magnesium and potassium and contain arginine, an essential amino acid. Walnuts are also bursting with plant sterols, which help lower cholesterol, and, like all nuts and seeds, are high in fiber. Numerous studies show a strong link between the consumption of nuts and reduced rates of coronary artery disease. So enjoy a small handful of nuts every day — they will help keep the doctor away.

Nutrients Per Serving	
Calories	320
Protein	27.4 g
Carbohydrates	9.4 g
Fat (Total)	19.5 g
Saturated Fat	3.0 g
Monounsaturated Fat	5.8 g
Polyunsaturated Fat	8.9 g
Dietary Fiber	3.0 g
Sodium	364 mg
Cholesterol	103 mg

Excellent source of vitamins B6 and K and zinc.

Good source of folacin, magnesium, potassium and iron.

Source of vitamin C.

Contains a moderate amount of dietary fiber.

Spicy Peanut Chicken

This is a lively dish, chock-full of many flavors, all of which work together to create the "yum" factor. I like to serve this over brown basmati rice to add fiber and complete the meal.

**MAKES
6 TO 8 SERVINGS**

MAKE AHEAD

This dish can be partially prepared before it is cooked. Complete Step 1. Cover and refrigerate overnight or for up to 2 days. When you're ready to cook, continue with Steps 2 and 3.

• **Works in slow cookers from 3½ to 6 quarts**

Amount	Ingredient	Metric
1 tbsp	olive or extra virgin coconut oil	15 mL
2	onions, finely chopped	2
2	carrots, peeled and diced	2
4	stalks celery, diced	4
4	cloves garlic, minced	4
1 tbsp	minced gingerroot	15 mL
½ tsp	cracked black peppercorns	2 mL
1 cup	chicken stock	250 mL
3 lbs	skinless bone-in chicken thighs (about 12 thighs)	1.5 kg
3 tbsp	smooth natural peanut butter	45 mL
2 tbsp	freshly squeezed lemon juice	25 mL
2 tbsp	reduced-sodium soy sauce	25 mL
2 tsp	Thai red curry paste	10 mL
½ cup	coconut milk	125 mL
2 cups	sweet green peas, thawed if frozen	500 mL
1	red bell pepper, diced	1
¼ cup	chopped roasted peanuts	50 mL
½ cup	finely chopped cilantro	125 mL

1. In a skillet, heat oil over medium heat for 30 seconds. Add onions, carrots and celery and cook, stirring, until carrots are softened, about 7 minutes. Add garlic, gingerroot and peppercorns and cook, stirring, for 1 minute. Add chicken stock and bring to a boil.

2. Arrange chicken over bottom of slow cooker stoneware and add vegetable mixture. Cover and cook on Low for 5 hours or on High for 2½ hours, until juices run clear when chicken is pierced with a fork.

3. In a bowl, combine peanut butter, lemon juice, soy sauce and red curry paste. Mix well. Add to slow cooker stoneware and stir well. Add coconut milk, peas and red pepper and stir well. Cover and cook on High for 20 minutes, until pepper is tender and mixture is hot. Garnish with peanuts and cilantro and serve.

Mindful Morsels

When making this dish, using extra virgin coconut oil to soften the onions adds a depth of coconut flavor to the sauce and nutrients to your diet.

Natural Wonders

PEANUTS

Although they have many of the healthful features of nuts, despite their name, peanuts are not really a nut but a legume. They are rich in monounsaturated fats, the same kind found in olive oil. A source of vitamin E, niacin, folacin and magnesium, peanuts also contain an array of healthful antioxidants. These include resveratrol, which is found in red wine and thought to be linked to lower rates of cardiovascular disease, and polyphenols, which appear to have antiviral and anticarcinogenic properties. Peanuts also contain arginine, an amino acid, which boosts nitric oxide thereby fostering healthy blood vessels. Eating peanuts can also help to prevent gallstones. The Nurses' Health Study found that women who ate at least 1 ounce (30 g) of nuts, peanuts or peanut butter a week, lowered their risk of developing gallstones by 25 percent. The one problem with peanuts is that many people are highly allergic to them, so make sure you are not serving a dish containing peanuts to anyone who might have a peanut allergy.

Nutrients Per Serving	
Calories	334
Protein	33.0 g
Carbohydrates	14.7 g
Fat (Total)	16.2 g
Saturated Fat	5.3 g
Monounsaturated Fat	6.0 g
Polyunsaturated Fat	3.3 g
Dietary Fiber	3.6 g
Sodium	471 mg
Cholesterol	114 mg

Excellent source of vitamins A, C, B6 and K, phosphorus, magnesium and zinc.

Good source of folacin, potassium and iron.

Contains a moderate amount of dietary fiber.

Chicken Chili and Barley Casserole

This flavorful dish, which bridges the gap between chicken chili and a baked casserole, is a hit with all family members. It's a great dish for those evenings when everyone is coming and going at different times. Just leave the slow cooker setting on warm and the fixings for salad.

MAKES 8 SERVINGS

TIPS

❖ Although they tend to be high in fat, used in moderation, sausages are an easy way to add flavor to any dish. The problem is, many contain unwanted additives. It's worth seeking out a source that sells additive-free sausages made from naturally raised meat or, failing that, to explore making your own.

❖ Just about any chili powder works well in this recipe: ancho, New Mexico or a prepared blend.

❖ Chorizo is usually quite spicy so add the jalapeño only if you're a heat seeker.

MAKE AHEAD

This dish can be partially prepared before it is cooked. Complete Step 1. Cover and refrigerate overnight or for up to 2 days. When you're ready to cook, continue with Steps 2 and 3.

• Large (minimum 5 quart) slow cooker

1 tbsp	cumin seeds, toasted (see Tips, page 49)	15 mL
1 tbsp	olive oil	15 mL
2	fresh chorizo sausages, casings removed and crumbled (about 4 oz/125 g total)	2
2	onions, finely chopped	2
4	cloves garlic, minced	4
1 tsp	dried oregano leaves, crumbled	5 mL
1 tsp	cracked black peppercorns	5 mL
1	can (28 oz/796 mL) tomatoes, including juice, coarsely chopped	1
2 cups	chicken stock	500 mL
1 cup	whole (hulled) or pot barley, rinsed	250 mL
1	can (14 to 19 oz/398 to 540 mL) white beans, drained and rinsed (see Mindful Morsels, right)	1
1 lb	boneless skinless chicken thighs, cut into bite-size pieces	500 g
2	red bell peppers, diced	2
2 tsp	chili powder, dissolved in 1 tbsp (15 mL) lime juice (see Tips, left)	10 mL
1	jalapeño pepper, seeded and minced, optional (see Tips, left)	1
1 to 2	avocados, diced (see Tips, right)	1 to 2
2 tbsp	freshly squeezed lime juice	25 mL
	Salt, optional	
	Finely chopped red onion and cilantro	

1. In a large skillet, heat oil over medium heat for 30 seconds. Add sausage and onions and cook, stirring, until onions are softened and no hint of pink remains in sausage, about 4 minutes. Add garlic, oregano, peppercorns and toasted

cumin and cook, stirring, for 1 minute. Add tomatoes with juice and bring to a boil. Transfer to slow cooker stoneware.

2. Add chicken stock, barley, beans and chicken and stir well. Cover and cook on Low for 6 hours or on High for 3 hours, until juices run clear when chicken is pierced with a fork and barley is tender. Stir in bell peppers, chili powder solution and jalapeño pepper, if using. Cover and cook for 20 minutes, until peppers are tender.

3. Meanwhile, in a bowl, combine avocados, lime juice and salt to taste, if using. To serve, ladle casserole onto plates, top with avocado mixture and garnish with onion and cilantro.

❖ I've included a range in the quantity of avocados because they vary so much in size. Use two if yours are extremely small. One if it's large.

Mindful Morsels

If you're watching your intake of sodium make your own chicken stock with no added salt and use 1 cup (250 mL) cooked dried white beans (see Basic Beans, page 250) instead of the canned.

Natural Wonders

AVOCADOS

At first glance this recipe might seem a bit high in fat but most is the healthy unsaturated kind. The avocado in one serving of this recipe provides 2.4 grams of monounsaturated fat and 0.5 grams of polyunsaturated fat. Although they are high in calories, ounce for ounce, avocados are extremely nutritious. They are a great source of folacin and are high in potassium and fiber. They also contain carotenoids and vitamin E, which appear to work together to battle prostate cancer cells. Recent studies also show that avocados help your body make better use of antioxidants. Adding avocado to a salad containing baby spinach, lettuce and carrots dramatically enhanced absorption of alpha-carotene, beta-carotene and lutein. Similarly, when avocado was added to tomato salsa, lycopene absorption was increased by 4.4 times and beta-carotene absorption was 2.6 times higher than without the avocado.

Nutrients Per Serving	
Calories	404
Protein	23.1 g
Carbohydrates	46.2 g
Fat (Total)	15.0 g
Saturated Fat	3.8 g
Monounsaturated Fat	7.4 g
Polyunsaturated Fat	2.3 g
Dietary Fiber	10.4 g
Sodium	867 mg
Cholesterol	60 mg

Excellent source of vitamins C and B6, folacin, magnesium, potassium, iron and zinc.

Good source of vitamins A and K and phosphorus.

Contains a very high amount of dietary fiber.

See photo, page 102

Turkey in Cranberry Leek Sauce

Here's a simple, yet delicious treatment for a whole turkey breast. Serve this with mashed potatoes and steamed green beans for a traditional comfort food meal, or substitute a whole grain, such as brown rice or quinoa, for the potatoes to increase the nutrient density.

MAKES 6 SERVINGS

TIP

❖ I've left the skin on the turkey breast and browned it before cooking to more closely approximate the result of a traditional roast turkey. If you're concerned about your consumption of fat, remove the skin and skip Step 1. Place the skinless breast in the stoneware and continue with Step 2.

MAKE AHEAD

This dish can be partially prepared before it is cooked. Heat oil and complete Step 2. Cover and refrigerate overnight or for up to 2 days. When you're ready to cook, complete Steps 1 and 3.

- Large (minimum 5 quart) slow cooker
- Instant-read thermometer

1 tbsp	olive oil	15 mL
1	skin on bone-in turkey breast (about 1 1/2 lbs/750 g) (see Tip, left)	1
2	medium leeks, white part only with just a bit of green, cleaned and thinly sliced (see Tip, page 96)	2
2	cloves garlic, minced	2
2 tsp	dried thyme leaves	10 mL
1/2 tsp	cracked black peppercorns	2 mL
1 tbsp	all-purpose flour	15 mL
1 cup	chicken or turkey stock	250 mL
	Salt, optional	
1/2 cup	dried cranberries	125 mL
2 tbsp	finely chopped parsley	25 mL

1. In a skillet, heat oil over medium-high heat for 30 seconds. Add turkey breast, skin side down, and cook until nicely browned, about 4 minutes. Transfer, skin side up, to slow cooker stoneware.

2. Reduce heat to medium. Add leeks and cook, stirring, until softened, about 5 minutes. Add garlic, thyme and peppercorns and cook, stirring, for 1 minute. Add flour and cook, stirring, for 1 minute. Add chicken stock and cook, stirring, until mixture begins to thicken, about 2 minutes. Season to taste with salt, if using. Stir in cranberries.

3. Transfer sauce to slow cooker stoneware, covering turkey with sauce. Cover and cook on Low for 5 1/2 to 6 hours or on High for 2 1/2 to 3 hours, until an instant-read thermometer inserted into center of breast registers 175°F (80°C). To serve, transfer to a platter and garnish with parsley.

See photo, page 103

Mindful Morsels

There is enough protein in one serving of this dish to provide almost half the daily requirement for an average adult woman (46 grams). Adult men need about 56 grams of protein a day.

Nutrients Per Serving	
Calories	218
Protein	21.7 g
Carbohydrates	13.2 g
Fat (Total)	8.5 g
Saturated Fat	1.9 g
Monounsaturated Fat	4.2 g
Polyunsaturated Fat	1.5 g
Dietary Fiber	1.8 g
Sodium	221 mg
Cholesterol	54 mg

Natural Wonders

TURKEY

Turkey is one of the best sources of complete protein because once the skin is removed, it is a very lean meat. While the jury is still out on the risks and benefits of a high-protein diet, the Nurses' Health Study found that women who consumed about 110 grams of protein a day were 25 percent less likely to have suffered a heart attack or to have died from heart disease than those who consumed less protein, about 68 grams a day.

In addition to being rich in protein, turkey is also a good source of important B vitamins — niacin, B6 and B12 — as well as zinc, an immune system protector that can be challenging to obtain from dietary sources. The body can utilize the zinc in turkey and other meats more readily than that from non-meat sources. Turkey is also a good source of the trace mineral selenium, which supports a number of bodily functions. Recent research indicates that selenium may reduce the risk of coronary artery disease and protect the body from prostate, colorectal and lung cancers. Some researchers suggest taking selenium before spending time in the sun because it may reduce the occurrence of skin cancer.

Good source of vitamins B6 and K, phosphorus, potassium, iron and zinc.

Moroccan-Style Chicken with Prunes and Quinoa

A variation on a traditional Moroccan tagine, this delicious dish makes the most of the bittersweet combination of prunes, honey and lemon. The addition of garlic, oregano and a smattering of black pepper completes the flavor profile. Traditionally, this dish is served with couscous, but I've used quinoa, which is every bit as tasty and more nutritious (see Natural Wonders, page 209).

MAKES 8 SERVINGS

TIPS

❖ If you are marinating the chicken overnight, refrigerate the prune mixture.

❖ Some quinoa has a resinous coating called saponin, which needs to be rinsed off. To ensure your quinoa is saponin-free, before cooking fill a bowl with warm water and swish the kernels around, then transfer to a sieve and rinse thoroughly under cold running water.

MAKE AHEAD

This dish can be partially prepared before it is cooked. Complete Steps 1 and 2. Cover and refrigerate overnight or for up to 2 days. When you're ready to cook, continue with Steps 3 through 5.

• **Works in slow cookers from 3½ to 6 quarts**

1½ cups	chopped pitted prunes	375 mL
1½ cups	water	375 mL
1 tbsp	liquid honey	15 mL
1 tsp	grated lemon zest	5 mL
4	cloves garlic, minced	4
1 tbsp	dried oregano leaves, crumbled	15 mL
1 tbsp	grated lemon zest	15 mL
½ tsp	salt	2 mL
½ tsp	cracked black peppercorns	2 mL
2 lbs	skinless bone-in chicken thighs (about 8 thighs)	1 kg
2 cups	chicken stock	500 mL
¼ cup	freshly squeezed lemon juice	50 mL
3 cups	water	750 mL
1½ cups	quinoa, rinsed (see Tips, left)	375 mL

1. In a bowl, combine prunes, 1½ cups (375 mL) of the water, honey and lemon zest. Cover and set aside (see Tips, left).

2. In slow cooker stoneware, combine garlic, oregano, lemon zest, salt and peppercorns. Add chicken and toss until evenly coated with mixture. Cover and refrigerate for at least 1 hour or overnight.

3. Add chicken stock and lemon juice to stoneware and stir well. Cover and cook on Low for 5 hours or on High for 2½ hours, until juices run clear when chicken is pierced with a fork. Add prunes with liquid. Cover and cook on High for 30 minutes to meld flavors.

4. Meanwhile, in a pot over high heat, bring 3 cups (750 mL) of the water to a boil. Reduce heat to medium. Add quinoa in a steady stream, stirring to prevent lumps from forming and return to a boil. Cover, reduce heat to low and simmer until tender and liquid is absorbed, about 15 minutes. Set aside.

5. To serve, spoon quinoa onto a plate and top with chicken mixture.

Mindful Morsels

I've used nutrient-dense quinoa in this recipe, even though couscous is a more conventional accompaniment. Although whole wheat varieties are available, most of the couscous sold in North America is "instant" and made from refined durum wheat from which the bran and germ have been removed.

Natural Wonders

PRUNES

When the new U.S. dietary guidelines were rolled out in 2005, the recommended number of daily servings of fruits and vegetables increased from 5 to 9. People consuming 2,000 calories a day are advised to eat 2 cups (500 mL) of fruit a day. Adding prunes to your diet as an enhancement to the main course can help you to achieve that goal.

Simply stated, prunes are highly nutritious. They contain antioxidant phenols and beta-carotene. They are also a source of potassium, which helps to keep blood pressure under control and may promote healthy bones by decreasing calcium excretion. But prunes are best known as an excellent source of fiber. Just ¼ cup (50 mL) of prunes contains 3 grams of dietary fiber, which is associated with a wide range of healthful benefits, in addition to keeping you regular. Prunes are also low on the glycemic index, which is good news for people with diabetes.

Nutrients Per Serving	
Calories	283
Protein	17.7 g
Carbohydrates	42.5 g
Fat (Total)	5.3 g
Saturated Fat	1.0 g
Monounsaturated Fat	1.6 g
Polyunsaturated Fat	1.6 g
Dietary Fiber	5.5 g
Sodium	440 mg
Cholesterol	53 mg

Excellent source of magnesium and iron.

Good source of vitamins B6 and K, potassium and zinc.

Source of vitamin C and phosphorus.

Contains a high amount of dietary fiber.

Turkey, Mushroom and Chickpea Sauce

Kids always want seconds of this lip-smacking sauce, which is delicious over chunky pasta, brown rice or polenta. For a change, try it over hot quinoa, whose new world origins resonate with turkey. Add a tossed green salad for a great weekday meal.

MAKES 6 SERVINGS

TIPS

❖ If you don't have a mortar or a spice grinder, place the toasted fennel seeds on a cutting board and use the bottom of a wine bottle or measuring cup to grind them.

❖ If you don't have hot paprika, use regular paprika instead with a pinch of cayenne.

MAKE AHEAD

This dish can be partially prepared before it is cooked. Complete Steps 1 and 2. Cover and refrigerate overnight or for up to 2 days. When you're ready to cook, continue with Step 3.

• **Works in slow cookers from 3½ to 6 quarts**

½ tsp	fennel seeds (see Tips, left)	2 mL
1 tbsp	olive oil	15 mL
1 lb	ground turkey	500 g
2	onions, minced	2
4	stalks celery, diced	4
2	cloves garlic, minced	2
1 tsp	dried oregano leaves, crumbled	5 mL
1 tsp	salt	5 mL
½ tsp	cracked black peppercorns	2 mL
8 oz	cremini mushrooms, trimmed and quartered	250 g
1	can (28 oz/796 mL) tomatoes, including juice, coarsely chopped	1
1 cup	vegetable, chicken or turkey stock	250 mL
1	can (14 to 19 oz/398 to 540 mL) chickpeas, drained and rinsed, or 1 cup (250 mL) dried chickpeas, soaked, cooked and drained (see Basic Beans, page 250)	1
2 tsp	hot paprika (see Tips, left) dissolved in 1 tbsp (15 mL) lemon juice	10 mL
1	red bell pepper, diced	1

1. In a dry skillet over medium heat, toast fennel seeds, stirring, until fragrant, about 3 minutes. Immediately transfer to a mortar or a spice grinder and grind (see Tips, left). Set aside.

2. In same skillet, heat oil over medium heat for 30 seconds. Add turkey, onions and celery and cook, stirring, until celery is softened and no hint of pink remains in the turkey, about 6 minutes. Add garlic, oregano, salt and peppercorns and cook, stirring, for 1 minute. Add mushrooms and toss to coat.

Add tomatoes with juice and stock and bring to a boil. Transfer to slow cooker stoneware. Add chickpeas and stir well.

3. Cover and cook on Low for 6 hours or on High for 3 hours, until mixture is hot and bubbly. Add paprika solution and stir well. Add bell pepper and stir well. Cover and cook on High for 20 minutes, until pepper is tender.

Mindful Morsels

If you're concerned about your intake of sodium, use homemade stock with no added salt (see Homemade Chicken Stock, page 35, or Basic Vegetable Stock, page 34) and cooked dried chickpeas.

Natural Wonders

PROTEIN SOURCES

About one-third of the calories in this recipe come from protein. While our bodies need protein, unless you're a vegetarian it's not difficult to obtain an adequate supply of this macronutrient eating an average North American diet. However, it is wise to pay attention to the source of the protein you consume, because many high-protein foods are also high in saturated fat.

Take red meat, for example. Three ounces (90 g) of beef top sirloin provides about 28 grams of protein and 3.1 grams of saturated fat. Compare that to the same quantity of skinless turkey breast, which delivers about 27 grams of protein and only 1 gram of saturated fat, a comparable amount of protein and a third of the saturated fat. The ground turkey in one serving of this recipe, which combines white and dark meat, which is higher in fat, contains 13.2 grams of protein and 1.7 grams of saturated fat. The chickpeas are another source of protein, although legumes don't contain the full range of amino acids. (Combine a legume such as chickpeas with a whole grain, such as brown rice or polenta, to create a complete protein.) The chickpeas in one serving of this recipe provide 2.6 grams of vegetable protein and 0.1 gram of saturated fat.

Nutrients Per Serving	
Calories	260
Protein	19.0 g
Carbohydrates	26.5 g
Fat (Total)	9.6 g
Saturated Fat	2.2 g
Monounsaturated Fat	4.2 g
Polyunsaturated Fat	2.2 g
Dietary Fiber	5.7 g
Sodium	977 mg
Cholesterol	60 mg

Excellent source of vitamins C and B6 and potassium.

Good source of vitamins A and K, folacin, magnesium, phosphorus, iron and zinc.

Source of calcium.

Contains a high amount of dietary fiber.

Peppery Turkey Casserole

With five different kinds of peppers this dish is a testament to the depth and variety of this useful ingredient. I've added quinoa because it's so nutritious and isn't commonly included in the North American diet. Here, I've stirred it in after the dish has finished cooking to make a casserole, but if you prefer, serve it on the side.

MAKES 8 SERVINGS

TIPS

❖ **For convenience use bottled roasted red peppers or if you prefer, roast your own.**

❖ **Some quinoa has a resinous coating called saponin, which needs to be rinsed off. To ensure your quinoa is saponin-free, before cooking fill a bowl with warm water and swish the kernels around, then transfer to a sieve and rinse thoroughly under cold running water.**

MAKE AHEAD

This dish can be partially prepared before it is cooked. Complete Step 1. Cover and refrigerate overnight or for up to 2 days. When you're ready to cook, continue with Steps 2 through 5.

• **Works in slow cookers from 3½ to 6 quarts**

1 tbsp	olive oil	15 mL
2	onions, finely chopped	2
4	cloves garlic, minced	4
2 tsp	dried oregano leaves, crumbled	10 mL
½ tsp	cracked black peppercorns	2 mL
1 cup	dry white wine	250 mL
1	can (14 oz/398 mL) diced tomatoes, including juice (see Tips, page 134)	1
2 cups	chicken or turkey stock	500 mL
	Salt, optional	
1½ lbs	bone-in turkey breast, skin removed, cut into ½-inch (1 cm) cubes (about 2½ cups/625 mL)	750 g
2 tsp	sweet paprika, dissolved in 2 tbsp (25 mL) water	10 mL
1	jalapeño pepper, finely chopped	1
2	green bell peppers, diced	2
1	roasted red bell pepper, diced	1
3 cups	water	750 mL
1½ cups	quinoa, rinsed (see Tips, left)	375 mL

1. In a skillet, heat oil over medium heat for 30 seconds. Add onions and cook, stirring, until softened, about 3 minutes. Add garlic, oregano and peppercorns and cook, stirring, for 1 minute. Add white wine and tomatoes with juice and bring to a boil. Transfer to slow cooker stoneware. Add chicken stock and stir well. Season to taste with salt, if using.

2. Add turkey and stir well. Cover and cook on Low for 6 hours or on High for 3 hours, until turkey is tender.

3. Add paprika solution, jalapeño pepper, bell peppers and roasted red pepper to slow cooker stoneware and stir well. Cover and cook on High for 30 minutes, until peppers are tender.

4. Meanwhile, in a pot, bring water to a boil. Add quinoa in a steady stream, stirring to prevent lumps from forming, and return to a boil. Cover, reduce heat to low and simmer until tender and liquid is absorbed, about 15 minutes. Set aside.

5. When peppers are tender, add cooked quinoa to slow cooker stoneware and stir well. Serve immediately.

VARIATION

Peppery Turkey Stew

Omit the quinoa. Serve the stew over hot rice or mashed potatoes.

Mindful Morsels

Although many culinary herbs act as antioxidants, of those they have studied, USDA researchers have found oregano to have the most powerful antioxidant activity.

Natural Wonders

VITAMIN B6

A serving of this dish provides about 30 percent of the daily value of vitamin B6. The bell peppers and the turkey are a source of this vitamin, which is best known for keeping skin healthy. But B6 plays a role in keeping your mind sharp and it boosts serotonin, which helps to keep depression at bay. It also helps your body make new cells to produce infection-fighting antibodies and it appears to alleviate morning sickness in pregnant women. According to a recent study reported in the *Journal of the National Cancer Institute*, vitamin B6 may also lower the risk of colon cancer, one of the most common cancers in North America. A deficiency of this vitamin can lead to depression and certain skin conditions.

Nutrients Per Serving	
Calories	256
Protein	22.2 g
Carbohydrates	30.5 g
Fat (Total)	5.2 g
Saturated Fat	0.9 g
Monounsaturated Fat	2.3 g
Polyunsaturated Fat	1.3 g
Dietary Fiber	3.5 g
Sodium	385 mg
Cholesterol	37 mg

Excellent source of vitamins C and B6, phosphorus, magnesium, potassium and iron.

Good source of zinc.

Source of vitamin A.

Contains a moderate amount of dietary fiber.

See photo, page 112

Two-Bean Turkey Chili

This delicious chili, which has just a hint of heat, is perfect for family get-togethers. Add a tossed green salad, sprinkled with shredded carrots, and whole grain rolls.

MAKES 8 SERVINGS

TIPS

❖ You can also make this chili using leftover turkey. Use 3 cups (750 mL) of shredded cooked turkey and add along with the bell peppers.

❖ Add the jalapeño pepper if you're a heat seeker, or the chipotle in adobo sauce, if you like a hint of smoke, as well.

MAKE AHEAD

This dish can be partially prepared before it is cooked. Complete Step 1. Cover and refrigerate overnight or for up to 2 days. When you're ready to cook continue with Steps 2 and 3.

• **Works in slow cookers from 3½ to 6 quarts**

1 tbsp	olive oil	15 mL
2	onions, finely chopped	2
4	stalks celery, diced	4
6	cloves garlic, minced	6
2 tsp	dried oregano leaves, crumbled	10 mL
½ tsp	cracked black peppercorns	2 mL
	Zest of 1 lime	
1 tbsp	cumin seeds, toasted (see Tips, page 49)	15 mL
2 tbsp	fine cornmeal	25 mL
1 cup	chicken or turkey stock	250 mL
1	can (28 oz/796 mL) tomatoes, including juice, coarsely chopped	1
2 lbs	bone-in turkey breast, skin removed, cut into ½-inch (1 cm) cubes (about 3 cups/750 mL)	1 kg
2	cans (each 14 to 19 oz/398 to 540 mL) pinto beans, drained and rinsed (see Mindful Morsels, right)	2
2 cups	frozen sliced green beans	500 mL
1 tbsp	New Mexico or ancho chili powder, dissolved in 2 tbsp (25 mL) lime juice	15 mL
1	each green and red bell pepper, diced	1
1	can (4.5 oz/127 mL) diced mild green chiles	1
1	jalapeño pepper or chipotle pepper in adobo sauce, diced, optional (see Tips, left)	1

1. In a skillet, heat oil over medium heat for 30 seconds. Add onions and celery and cook, stirring, until celery is softened, about 5 minutes. Add garlic and cook, stirring, for 1 minute. Add oregano, peppercorns, lime zest and toasted cumin and cook, stirring, for 1 minute. Add cornmeal and toss to

See photo, page 113

coat. Add chicken stock and cook, stirring, until mixture boils, about 1 minute. Add tomatoes with juice and return to a boil. Transfer to slow cooker stoneware.

2. Add turkey, pinto beans and green beans and stir well. Cover and cook on Low for 8 hours or on High for 4 hours, until turkey is tender and mixture is bubbly.

3. Add chili powder solution, green and red bell peppers, mild green chiles, and jalapeno, if using. Cover and cook on High for 30 minutes, until bell peppers are tender.

Mindful Morsels

To reduce sodium, use dried beans (see Basic Beans, page 250) or canned organic pinto beans with no salt added. The brand I use, which is very tasty, is seasoned with kombu seaweed and contains only 17 mg of sodium per ½ cup (125 mL) serving.

Natural Wonders

CHILE PEPPERS

From mild and fruity to smoky and just plain fiery, chiles add depth as well as heat to any dish. They also add nutrition and medicinal value. In general terms, red chiles are more nutritious than green ones, and the hotter the chile, the more capsaicin it contains. Capsaicin is the substance that gives chiles their burn and provides many of their health benefits. With their identifiable ability to clear congestion, chile peppers have long been used as a natural remedy for the common cold. Today, scientists are exploring their ability to fight heart attacks and strokes, among other benefits. As a good source of the antioxidants vitamin C and beta-carotene, chiles also provide good immune-system support. They also contain bioflavonoids, which researchers believe may have cancer-preventing properties.

Nutrients Per Serving	
Calories	277
Protein	29.6 g
Carbohydrates	30.7 g
Fat (Total)	4.5 g
Saturated Fat	1.0 g
Monounsaturated Fat	2.3 g
Polyunsaturated Fat	0.9 g
Dietary Fiber	7.7 g
Sodium	764 mg
Cholesterol	51 mg

Excellent source of vitamins C, B6 and K, phosphorus, magnesium, potassium and iron.

Good source of vitamin A, folacin and zinc.

Source of calcium.

Contains a very high amount of dietary fiber.

Creamy Tuna Casserole

In this family-friendly dish tuna is combined with pasta, mushrooms and other vegetables in a delectable creamy base. If you have time, make the Crispy Crumb Topping, which adds crunch and a bit of punch in the form of Parmesan cheese. Serve this with a tossed green salad for a tasty and nutritious weekday meal.

MAKES 6 SERVINGS

TIPS

❖ **For added fiber use whole wheat pasta.**

❖ **Crumbs made from white bread will make a tasty topping, but those made from whole wheat bread will be higher in nutrients, including fiber.**

MAKE AHEAD

This recipe can be assembled before it is cooked. Complete Steps 1 and 2. Cover and refrigerate overnight. When you're ready to cook, continue with Steps 3 and 4.

- Works in slow cookers from 3½ to 6 quarts
- Greased slow cooker stoneware

8 oz	small tubular pasta, such as penne	250 g
1 tbsp	olive oil	15 mL
1	onion, minced	1
4	stalks celery, diced	4
8 oz	mushrooms, sliced	250 g
½ tsp	dried tarragon or thyme leaves, crumbled	2 mL
½ tsp	cracked black peppercorns	2 mL
1	can (10 oz/284 mL) reduced-sodium condensed cream of celery soup, undiluted	1
2 tbsp	cream cheese, softened	25 mL
2	cans (each 6½ oz/184 g) solid white tuna, drained and flaked	2

CRISPY CRUMB TOPPING (optional)

1 tbsp	butter	15 mL
½ tsp	salt	2 mL
2 cups	fresh bread crumbs (see Tips, left)	500 mL
2 tbsp	freshly grated Parmesan cheese	25 mL

1. In a pot of boiling salted water, cook pasta until tender to the bite, about 8 minutes. Drain and transfer to prepared slow cooker stoneware.

2. Meanwhile, in a large skillet, heat oil over medium heat for 30 seconds. Add onion, celery and mushrooms and cook, stirring, until celery is softened, about 6 minutes. Add tarragon and peppercorns and stir well. Gradually add soup, stirring to dissolve any lumps. Add cream cheese and cook, stirring, until melted and incorporated into sauce. Stir in tuna. Transfer to slow cooker stoneware. Stir well.

3. Cover and cook on Low for 4 to 5 hours or on High for 2 to 2½ hours, until hot and bubbly.

4. *Crispy Crumb Topping (optional):* In a skillet over medium heat, melt butter and salt. Add bread crumbs and cook, stirring, until they start to brown, about 5 minutes. Remove from heat and stir in Parmesan. Spread evenly over top of the cooked casserole and serve.

Mindful Morsels

Look for solid white albacore tuna, which is higher in healthy omega-3 fatty acids than most other varieties of canned tuna. Avoid flaked tuna, which is bound together with food additives.

Natural Wonders

MAGNESIUM

This recipe is a good source of magnesium, a mineral that supports every major system in our bodies. Among its most important functions, magnesium helps to keep bones strong, and an insufficient intake of this mineral may increase the risk of osteoporosis in older women. It also supports the nervous system, working with calcium to help keep nerves relaxed and healthy. Without an adequate supply of magnesium, muscles may react, triggering cramps and spasms. Muscle tension, anxiety and heart disease are among the ailments linked with a magnesium deficiency. Magnesium helps to regulate a brain receptor, and recent research indicates that it may keep memory functioning as we age. A magnesium deficiency may be triggered by over-consumption of alcohol, which increases its secretion in the urine, so watch your intake of this mineral if you're inclined to over-imbibe.

Nutrients Per Serving	
Calories	297
Protein	17.4 g
Carbohydrates	36.1 g
Fat (Total)	9.1 g
Saturated Fat	2.3 g
Monounsaturated Fat	3.6 g
Polyunsaturated Fat	2.5 g
Dietary Fiber	3.5 g
Sodium	603 mg
Cholesterol	25 mg

Good source of folacin, phosphorus, magnesium, potassium and iron.

Source of vitamins B6 and K.

Contains a moderate amount of dietary fiber.

Cioppino

This zesty stew originated on the San Francisco pier, where it was prepared using whatever was bountiful in the catch that day. The rouille adds flavor and richness, and you don't need to worry about adding a small dollop per serving if your mayonnaise is made with an extra virgin olive oil. Serve this with a crusty country-style bread, such as ciabatta, and a green salad.

MAKES 8 SERVINGS

TIPS

❖ When making cioppino, I like to use Italian San Marzano tomatoes, which are thick and flavorful. If you have access to this excellent product, you can omit the tomato paste.

❖ If you don't have fish stock, use 2 cups (500 mL) water combined with 2 cups (500 mL) bottled clam juice.

MAKE AHEAD

This dish can be partially prepared before it is cooked. Complete Step 1. Cover and refrigerate overnight or for up to 2 days. When you're ready to cook, continue with Steps 2 through 4.

• Large (minimum 5 quart) slow cooker

1 tbsp	olive oil	15 mL
2	onions, finely chopped	2
1	bulb fennel, cored and chopped	1
6	cloves garlic, minced	6
4	anchovy fillets, finely chopped	4
1 tsp	cracked black peppercorns	5 mL
1/2 tsp	fennel seeds, toasted (see Tip, page 53)	2 mL
1 tbsp	tomato paste (see Tips, left)	15
1	can (28 oz/796 mL) tomatoes, including juice, coarsely chopped	1
1 cup	dry white wine	250 mL
4 cups	fish stock	1 L
1 lb	skinless firm white fish, such as snapper, cut into bite-size pieces	500 g
8 oz	cooked peeled shrimp, thawed if frozen	250 g
8 oz	cooked crabmeat	250 g
1	red bell pepper, diced	1
1	long red chile pepper, diced, optional	1
	Salt, optional	

EASY ROUILLE (optional)

1/3 cup	mayonnaise	75 mL
2	cloves garlic, puréed	2
1 tbsp	extra virgin olive oil	15 mL
1 tsp	freshly squeezed lemon juice	5 mL
1/4 tsp	hot or regular paprika	1 mL
	Croutons, optional	

1. In a skillet, heat oil over medium heat for 30 seconds. Add onions and fennel and cook, stirring, until softened, about 3 minutes. Add garlic, anchovies, peppercorns and toasted fennel and cook, stirring, for 1 minute. Stir in tomato paste. Add tomatoes with juice and white wine and bring to a boil. Transfer to slow cooker stoneware.

2. Add fish stock and stir well. Cover and cook on Low for 6 to 8 hours or on High for 3 to 4 hours. Add fish, shrimp, crabmeat, red pepper and chile pepper, if using and stir well. Cover and cook on High for 20 minutes, until fish flakes easily when pierced with a fork and seafood is heated through. Season to taste with salt.

3. *Easy Rouille (optional):* In a small bowl, combine mayonnaise, garlic, olive oil, lemon juice and paprika. Mix until thoroughly blended.

4. To serve, ladle cioppino into warm bowls, garnish each serving with croutons, if using, and a dollop of rouille, if using.

Mindful Morsels

Eating fish may reduce your risk of stroke. One study found that women who ate fish two to four times a week were 27 percent less likely to have a stroke than women who ate fish once a month.

Natural Wonders

FENNEL

Including fennel in your diet is a good way to expand your nutrient range and increase your intake of beneficial antioxidants. Like celery, fennel, a member of the parsley family, is low in calories, but it is more nutritious than celery. Fennel contains an unusual combination of disease-fighting phytonutrients, including anethole, which scientists are currently studying for its anti-inflammatory and cancer-preventing properties. Fennel also contains dietary fiber, folacin and potassium, among other nutrients. Fennel seeds have long been used by herbalists to treat digestive problems.

Nutrients Per Serving	
Calories	199
Protein	28.8 g
Carbohydrates	11.0 g
Fat (Total)	4.4 g
Saturated Fat	0.8 g
Monounsaturated Fat	1.8 g
Polyunsaturated Fat	0.9 g
Dietary Fiber	2.3 g
Sodium	558 mg
Cholesterol	100 mg

Excellent source of vitamin B12, phosphorus, magnesium and potassium.

Good source of vitamins C and B6, folacin and zinc.

Source of vitamin A and calcium.

Contains a moderate amount of dietary fiber.

Salmon Loaf

This tasty loaf, accompanied by a tossed green salad is a favorite weekday meal at our house. If you don't have tomato sauce, homemade chili sauce or another tomato-based relish also makes a nice finish. Or try a yogurt-based sauce such as tzatziki.

MAKES 6 SERVINGS

TIP

❖ If you prefer and you have a large oval slow cooker, you can make this in a 8-by 4-inch (20 by 10 cm) loaf pan, lightly greased. You won't need the foil strip, but you will need to cover the pan tightly with foil after filling it with the salmon mixture. Then the foil should be secured with a string or elastic band. Place the pan in the slow cooker stoneware and pour in enough boiling water to come 1 inch (2.5 cm) up the sides. Cover and cook on Low for 6 hours or on High for 3 hours, or until loaf is set.

MAKE AHEAD

This dish can be prepared before it is cooked. Complete Steps 1 through 3. Cover and refrigerate overnight. When you're ready to cook, continue with Step 4.

- **Works in slow cookers from 3½ to 6 quarts**

1 tbsp	olive oil	15 mL
1	large onion, finely chopped (about 1½ cups/375 mL)	1
4	stalks celery, finely chopped (about 1½ cups/375 mL)	4
8 oz	mushrooms, thinly sliced	250 g
½ tsp	dried tarragon, crumbled	2 mL
½ tsp	freshly ground black pepper	2 mL
3	eggs	3
2 tbsp	freshly squeezed lemon juice	25 mL
2	cans (each 7½ oz/213 g) wild salmon, including bones and juice, skin removed, if desired	2
½ cup	finely chopped parsley	125 mL
¾ cup	dry bread crumbs (approx.)	175 mL
	Warm tomato sauce, optional	

1. In a skillet, heat oil over medium heat for 30 seconds. Add onion, celery and mushrooms and cook, stirring, until celery is tender, about 5 minutes. Add tarragon and pepper and cook, stirring, for 1 minute. Remove from heat and set aside.

2. In a bowl large enough to accommodate salmon and vegetables, beat eggs and lemon juice. Add salmon with bones and juice and break into small pieces with a fork. Add reserved mushroom mixture, parsley and bread crumbs and mix until blended. If mixture still seems wet, add more bread crumbs 1 tbsp (15 mL) at a time, until liquid is absorbed.

3. Fold a 2-foot (60 cm) piece of foil in half lengthwise. Place on bottom and up the sides of slow cooker stoneware (see Tips, left). Shape salmon mixture into a loaf and place in middle of foil strip on bottom of slow cooker stoneware.

4. Cover and cook on Low for 4 to 5 hours or on High for 2 to 2½ hours, or until loaf is set. Slide the loaf off the foil onto a platter and slice. Top with a dollop of tomato sauce, if using.

VARIATION

Dill Salmon Loaf

Substitute ½ tsp (2 mL) dried dillweed or thyme for tarragon and ½ cup (125 mL) chopped dill for parsley.

Mindful Morsels

Adding tomato sauce does more than enhance the flavor of this loaf. Tomato sauce is rich in lycopene (see Natural Wonders, page 213), a powerful antioxidant.

Natural Wonders

OMEGA-3 FATTY ACIDS

Salmon is an excellent source of omega-3 fatty acids, which are in short supply in the food that North Americans regularly eat. Even though our bodies can't manufacture these fatty acids, they are essential to good health. Without them the membranes of our cells are weakened, which may make us vulnerable to a wide range of health problems, from dry skin and brittle nails to depression and joint pain, not to mention more serious diseases. Studies show that an adequate supply of omega-3 fatty acids can reduce the risk of coronary artery disease, slightly lower blood pressure and strengthen the immune system. Researchers are also studying the possibility that consumption of omega-3 fatty acids may protect against some forms of cancer and help reduce the symptoms of autoimmune diseases such as multiple sclerosis, psoriasis, lupus and rheumatoid arthritis. Although the U.S. does not have a recommended daily value for this nutrient, the 2002 Report of Recommendations for Healthy Eating from the National Academies' Institute of Medicine recommends that men get 1.6 grams of omega-3s and women 1.1 grams every day, and the World Health Organization suggests that 3 grams are appropriate.

Nutrients Per Serving	
Calories	247
Protein	17.9 g
Carbohydrates	14.7 g
Fat (Total)	12.9 g
Saturated Fat	2.9 g
Monounsaturated Fat	5.2 g
Polyunsaturated Fat	2.1 g
Dietary Fiber	1.7 g
Sodium	467 mg
Cholesterol	111 mg

Excellent source of vitamins B12 and K and phosphorus.

Good source of vitamin B6, folacin, calcium, magnesium, potassium and iron.

Source of vitamins A and C.

See photo, page 122

Onion-Braised Shrimp

This is a great dish for a buffet, an Indian-style meal with numerous small plates or a light dinner. The substantial quantity of onions, which are cooked until they begin to caramelize and release their sugars, produces a dish that is pleasantly sweet. I like to serve this over brown basmati rice, accompanied by warm Indian bread such as naan.

MAKES 4 SERVINGS

TIP

❖ If you don't have a fresh chile, use ½ tsp (2 mL) cayenne pepper, instead. Dissolve it in the lemon juice before adding to the slow cooker.

❖ The quantity of pepper in the recipe produces a mildly spicy result, but the sweetness of the onions can balance more heat, if desired. Heat seekers can add an extra half of a fresh chile, finely chopped or more cayenne pepper. You can add up to ½ tsp (2 mL) cayenne pepper in addition to the fresh red chile. Just be sure to dissolve the powdered pepper in the lemon juice before adding to the slow cooker.

MAKE AHEAD

This dish can be partially prepared before it is cooked. Complete Steps 1 and 2. Cover and refrigerate overnight or for up to 2 days. When you're ready to cook, continue with Step 3.

● **Works in slow cookers from 3½ to 6 quarts**

1 tsp	coriander seeds	5 mL
1 tbsp	olive oil	15 mL
4	onions, finely chopped	4
2	cloves garlic, minced	2
1 tbsp	minced gingerroot	15 mL
1 tsp	turmeric	5 mL
1 tsp	salt, or to taste	5 mL
½ tsp	cracked black peppercorns	2 mL
1	can (14 oz/398 mL) diced tomatoes, including juice (see Tips, right)	1
1	long red chile pepper, seeded and finely chopped (see Tips, left)	1
1 tbsp	freshly squeezed lemon juice	15 mL
1 lb	peeled cooked shrimp, thawed if frozen	500 g
½ cup	plain yogurt	125 mL
2 tbsp	finely chopped cilantro leaves	25 mL

1. In a dry skillet over medium heat, toast coriander seeds, stirring, until fragrant, about 3 minutes. Immediately transfer to a mortar or a spice grinder and grind. Set aside.

2. In same skillet, heat oil over medium heat for 30 seconds. Add onions and cook, stirring, until they turn golden and just begin to brown, about 7 minutes. Add garlic, gingerroot, turmeric, salt, peppercorns and reserved coriander and cook, stirring, for 1 minute. Add tomatoes with juice and stir well. Transfer to slow cooker stoneware.

See photo, page 123

3. Cover and cook on Low for 6 hours or on High for 3 hours, until mixture is hot and bubbly. Stir in chile pepper and lemon juice. Add shrimp and stir well. Cover and cook on High for 20 minutes, until shrimp are heated through. Stir in yogurt. Garnish with cilantro and serve.

❖ **If your supermarket has 19 oz (540 mL) cans of diced tomatoes, by all means substitute that size in this recipe.**

Mindful Morsels

Most of the sodium in a serving of this dish (573 mg) comes from the added salt. The remainder of the sodium comes from the shrimp and the canned tomatoes. To lower the amount of sodium, reduce the quantity of salt or omit it entirely.

Nutrients Per Serving	
Calories	244
Protein	27.1 g
Carbohydrates	19.4 g
Fat (Total)	6.7 g
Saturated Fat	1.5 g
Monounsaturated Fat	3.1 g
Polyunsaturated Fat	1.2 g
Dietary Fiber	3.0 g
Sodium	914 mg
Cholesterol	175 mg

Natural Wonders
ONIONS

Along with garlic and leeks, onions belong to the Allium family. They are loaded with compounds containing sulfur, which is what makes your eyes water. But these compounds are also responsible for many of the vegetable's health benefits, and one rule of thumb suggests that the more pungent the onion, the healthier it is. These compounds, along with the quercetin found in onions, are active cancer fighters. Recent research also indicates that eating onions on a regular basis raises levels of beneficial high-density lipoproteins (HDL) and lowers harmful triglycerides. Other studies show onion consumption helps to prevent high blood pressure, thereby reducing the risk of heart attack or stroke. In fact, recent analysis identifies onions as one of a select few vegetables and fruits that you should eat to significantly reduce your risk of heart disease.

Excellent source of vitamins C and B12, phosphorus, potassium and iron.

Good source of vitamins A and B6, folacin, calcium, magnesium and zinc.

Source of vitamin K.

Contains a moderate amount of dietary fiber.

Bistro Fish Soup

Although it is described as soupe de poisson *in France, where it is a mainstay of bistro culture, this ambrosial concoction is more closely related to a stew. It makes a satisfying main course accompanied by crusty rolls and a green salad.*

MAKES
8 TO 10 SERVINGS

TIPS

❖ **If you prefer a more pronounced garlic flavor, brush the baguette with garlic-infused oil.**

❖ **If you don't have a mini-chopper, you can chop the roasted red pepper very finely and grate the garlic or put it through a press. Combine in a bowl with the mayonnaise and hot pepper sauce.**

MAKE AHEAD

This recipe can be partially prepared before it is cooked. Complete Step 1. Cover and refrigerate overnight or for up to 2 days. When you're ready to cook, continue with Steps 2 and 3.

● **Large (minimum 6 quart) slow cooker**

2 tbsp	olive oil	25 mL
3	large leeks, white part with a bit of green, cleaned and thinly sliced	3
1	onion, diced	1
1	bulb fennel, trimmed, cored and chopped, or 6 stalks celery, chopped	1
4	sprigs parsley or chervil	4
4	cloves garlic, minced	4
1 tsp	fennel seeds, crushed	5 mL
1/2 tsp	each salt and cracked black peppercorns	2 mL
1	can (28 oz/796 mL) tomatoes, including juice, coarsely chopped	1
6 cups	vegetable stock	1.5 L
2 lbs	fish bones and pieces	1 kg
2	potatoes (about 1 lb/500 g), diced	2
1 tbsp	Pernod, optional	15 mL
1/2 cup	parsley leaves, finely chopped	125 mL
	Crostini (see Tips, right)	

ROUILLE

1/4 cup	mayonnaise	50 mL
1	roasted red pepper, peeled and chopped	1
2	cloves garlic, minced	2
	Hot pepper sauce	
	Finely chopped parsley	

1. In a skillet, heat oil over medium heat for 30 seconds. Add leeks, onion and fennel and cook, stirring, until fennel is softened, about 6 minutes. Add parsley, garlic, fennel seeds, peppercorns and salt and cook, stirring, for 1 minute. Add tomatoes with juice and broth and bring to a boil. Transfer to slow cooker stoneware.

2. Add fish trimmings and potatoes and stir well. Cover and cook on Low for 8 to 10 hours or on High for 4 to 5 hours, until vegetables are very tender. Place a sieve over a large bowl or saucepan. Working in batches, ladle the soup into the sieve, removing and discarding any visible bones. Using a wooden spoon, push the solids through a sieve. Add Pernod, if using, to the strained soup. Add parsley and stir well.

3. *Rouille:* In a mini-chopper, combine mayonnaise, red pepper, garlic and hot pepper sauce to taste. Process until smooth. To serve, ladle hot soup into individual bowls and float a crostini on top of each serving. Garnish with parsley and top with a dollop of rouille.

❖ **To make crostini: Brush 8 to 10 baguette slices with olive oil on both sides. Toast under preheated broiler, turning once, until golden, about 2 minutes per side.**

Mindful Morsels
If you are concerned about sodium make Basic Vegetable Stock (see recipe, page 34) to reduce the amount of sodium to 403 mg.

Natural Wonders
OLIVE OIL
If you make your own mayonnaise using olive oil, almost all of the fat in this recipe comes from olive oil. Olive oil is one of the few fats that has been linked with good health for a relatively long time. In 1958, Dr. Ancel Keys began a study which revealed a link between lower rates of heart disease and a diet rich in fruits, vegetables, fish, poultry, nuts, pasta and olive oil. Surprisingly, more than 35 percent of the calories in this "Mediterranean" diet came from fat, on par with the North American diet, which was linked with a high rate of heart disease. The difference was the kind of fat consumed. The North American diet was high in saturated fat, whereas most of the fat in the Mediterranean diet was heart healthy monounsaturated and polyunsaturated fats, the kinds found in olive oil. Since then other studies have confirmed that olive oil protects against heart disease. Recent research indicates that it is also high in antioxidants and helps our bodies absorb key vitamins, among other benefits.

Nutrients Per Serving	
Calories	220
Protein	7.8 g
Carbohydrates	26.4 g
Fat (Total)	9.7 g
Saturated Fat	1.2 g
Monounsaturated Fat	5.8 g
Polyunsaturated Fat	2.2 g
Dietary Fiber	3.5 g
Sodium	990 mg
Cholesterol	13 mg

Excellent source of vitamins C and K.

Good source of vitamin B6, potassium, folacin and magnesium.

Source of vitamin A, phosphorus and iron.

Contains a moderate amount of dietary fiber.

Thai-Style Coconut Fish Curry

This luscious dish has everything going for it: a centerpiece of succulent fish, a sauce of creamy coconut accented with zesty Asian flavors and an abundance of tasty vegetables to complement the mix. Serve this over brown basmati rice to add fiber and complete the meal.

MAKES 8 SERVINGS

MAKE AHEAD
This dish can be partially prepared ahead of time. Complete Step 1. Cover and refrigerate for up to 2 days. When you're ready to cook, complete Step 2.

• **Works in slow cookers from 3½ to 6 quarts**

1 tbsp	olive or extra virgin coconut oil	15 mL
2	onions, finely chopped	2
4	cloves garlic, minced	4
1 tbsp	minced gingerroot	15 mL
1 tsp	finely grated lime zest	5 mL
1 cup	vegetable stock	250 mL
½ cup	fish stock or clam juice	125 mL
2 tbsp	freshly squeezed lime juice	25 mL
2 tsp	Thai green curry paste	10 mL
1 cup	coconut milk	250 mL
2 tbsp	fish sauce	25 mL
2 lbs	firm white fish, such as snapper, skin removed, cut into bite-size pieces, if desired	1 kg
2 cups	drained rinsed canned bamboo shoot strips	500 mL
2 cups	sweet green peas, thawed if frozen	500 mL
1	red bell pepper, diced	1
½ cup	finely chopped cilantro leaves	125 mL
	Toasted sesame seeds, optional	

1. In a skillet, heat oil over medium heat for 30 seconds. Add onions and cook, stirring, until softened, about 3 minutes. Add garlic, gingerroot and lime zest and cook, stirring, for 1 minute. Add vegetable and fish stock and stir well. Transfer to slow cooker stoneware. Cover and cook on Low for 6 to 8 hours or on High for 3 to 4 hours.

2. In a bowl, combine lime juice and curry paste. Add to slow cooker stoneware and stir well. Stir in coconut milk, fish sauce, fish, bamboo shoots, green peas and red pepper. Cover and cook on High for 20 to 30 minutes, until fish flakes easily when pierced with a fork and mixture is hot. Garnish with cilantro and toasted sesame seeds, if using.

VARIATION

Substitute 12 oz (375 g) peeled cooked shrimp for half of the fish.

Mindful Morsels

Sesame seeds are a good source of calcium. Sprinkling each serving of this curry with 1 tbsp (15 mL) toasted sesame seeds adds about 90 mg of calcium.

Natural Wonders

THE IMPORTANCE OF BALANCE

It makes sense to regularly consume a high-quality protein that is low in saturated fat, such as fish. But it's also sensible to balance a serving of fish with a helping of vegetables. Not only does it extend the range of nutrients you consume, it also improves the ratio of carbohydrates to protein in your diet, which may help your body to maintain calcium. In the process of digesting protein, your body releases acid and draws calcium from your bones to neutralize it. The problem is, if you consume too much protein — as North Americans are inclined to do — you may end up leeching calcium from your bones. The Nurses' Health Study found that women who consumed more than 95 grams of protein a day over a 12-year period were 20 percent more likely to have broken their wrist than those whose consumption averaged less than 68 grams a day. Comparing women who ate red meat more than five times a week with those who ate red meat less than once a week produced a similar conclusion.

Nutrients Per Serving	
Calories	243
Protein	24.0 g
Carbohydrates	12.1 g
Fat (Total)	11.5 g
Saturated Fat	6.1 g
Monounsaturated Fat	2.9 g
Polyunsaturated Fat	1.5 g
Dietary Fiber	3.1 g
Sodium	516 mg
Cholesterol	52 mg

Excellent source of vitamins C, B6 and B12 and phosphorus.

Good source of vitamins A and K, magnesium, potassium, folacin and zinc.

Source of iron.

Contains a moderate amount of dietary fiber.

See photo, page 130

Sweet Potato Coconut Curry with Shrimp

I love the combination of sweet and spicy flavors in this luscious dish. Serve this over brown basmati rice and add a platter of steamed spinach sprinkled with toasted sesame seeds to complete the meal.

MAKES 4 SERVINGS

TIP

❖ **If you are adding the almond garnish, try to find slivered almonds with the skin on. They add color and nutrients to the dish.**

MAKE AHEAD

This dish can be partially prepared before it is cooked. Complete Step 1. Cover and refrigerate overnight or for up to 2 days. When you're ready to cook, continue with Steps 2 and 3.

• **Works in slow cookers from 3½ to 6 quarts**

1 tbsp	olive or extra virgin coconut oil	15 mL
2	onions, finely chopped	2
4	cloves garlic, minced	4
1 tbsp	minced gingerroot	15 mL
1 cup	vegetable stock	250 mL
2	sweet potatoes, peeled and cut into 1-inch (2.5 cm) cubes	2
2 tsp	Thai green curry paste	10 mL
1 tbsp	freshly squeezed lime juice	15
½ cup	coconut milk	125 mL
1 lb	cooked peeled shrimp, thawed if frozen	500 g
¼ cup	toasted slivered almonds, optional	50 mL
¼ cup	finely chopped cilantro leaves	50 mL

1. In a skillet, heat oil over medium heat for 30 seconds. Add onions and cook, stirring, until softened, about 3 minutes. Add garlic and gingerroot and cook, stirring, for 1 minute. Add vegetable stock. Transfer to slow cooker stoneware.

2. Add sweet potatoes and stir well. Cover and cook on Low for 6 to 8 hours or on High for 3 to 4 hours, until sweet potatoes are tender.

3. In a small bowl, combine curry paste and lime juice. Add to slow cooker stoneware and stir well. Stir in coconut milk and shrimp. Cover and cook on High for 20 minutes, until shrimp are hot. Transfer to a serving dish. Garnish with almonds, if using, and cilantro and serve.

See photo, page 131

Mindful Morsels

Low in saturated fat, almonds are a source of vitamin E and contain a trace of the mineral selenium.

Natural Wonders

SHRIMP

Like all shellfish, shrimp contain B vitamins such as B6, B12 and niacin, as well as the essential minerals magnesium and zinc. Shrimp are also a source of low-fat, high-quality protein. Four ounces (125 g) of shrimp contain only 124 calories and less than half a gram of saturated fat, while supplying 26 grams of high-quality protein. Many people avoid shrimp because they contain quite a bit of sodium and are high in cholesterol. But the cholesterol in food is not as much of a problem as previously thought (see page 149) and shrimp contain almost no saturated fat. In one study, in which participants ate 300 grams of shrimp a day, researchers found that while their LDL ("bad") cholesterol increased by 7 percent, their HDL ("good") cholesterol went up by 12 percent, producing a net benefit. The shrimp diet also lowered triglycerides by 13 percent. (High triglyceride levels have been linked with coronary artery disease.)

Nutrients Per Serving	
Calories	348
Protein	27.0 g
Carbohydrates	32.7 g
Fat (Total)	12.3 g
Saturated Fat	6.3 g
Monounsaturated Fat	3.8 g
Polyunsaturated Fat	1.4 g
Dietary Fiber	2.9 g
Sodium	587 mg
Cholesterol	221 mg

Excellent source of vitamins A, B6 and B12 and iron.

Good source of vitamin C, phosphorus, magnesium, potassium and zinc.

Contains a moderate amount of dietary fiber.

Louisiana Seafood Stew with Chicken and Sausage

This tasty dish is a variation on gumbo, with less stock and minus the heavy roux for thickening. Gumbo is a bit of a grab bag — within the flavor profile, you can add just about anything. The more health conscious you are the more you should downplay sausage and emphasize seafood. This is a rich dish — it just needs rice and a simple green salad to complete the meal.

MAKES 8 SERVINGS

TIPS

❖ If you don't like clams, you can substitute an equal quantity of shucked oysters with their liquid, cooked crabmeat or sliced turkey kielbasa.

❖ Regular blended chili powder works fine in this recipe, but if you prefer you can substitute ancho or New Mexico chili powder or a "gourmet" blend of your choice.

❖ Canned tomatoes vary in sizes. If your supermarket carries the 19 oz (540 mL) can of diced tomatoes, by all means substitute it in this recipe.

MAKE AHEAD

This dish can be partially prepared before it is cooked. Complete Steps 1 and 2. Cover and refrigerate overnight or for up to 2 days. When you're ready to cook, continue with Steps 3 and 4.

• Large (minimum 5 quart) slow cooker

1 to 2 tbsp	olive oil, divided (approx.)	15 to 25 mL
3 oz	sweet Italian sausage, casings removed and crumbled (about 1)	90 g
2	onions, diced	2
4	stalks celery, diced	4
4	cloves garlic, minced	4
1 tsp	each dried thyme and oregano leaves	5 mL
1/2 tsp	cracked black peppercorns	2 mL
1 tbsp	tomato paste	15 mL
1 tbsp	all-purpose flour	15 mL
3 cups	chicken stock	750 mL
1	can (14 oz/398 mL) diced tomatoes, including juice (see Tips, left)	1
1 lb	skinless boneless chicken thighs, cut into bite size pieces (about 8 thighs)	500 g
8 oz	peeled cooked shrimp, thawed if frozen	250 g
1	can (5 oz/142 g) clams, drained	1
1	each green and red bell pepper, diced	1
1/2 cup	finely chopped parsley leaves	125 mL
1 tsp	chili powder (see Tips, left)	5 mL
Pinch	cayenne pepper	Pinch
8 oz	sea scallops, halved	250 g
1 tbsp	butter	15 mL
1 tbsp	filé powder, optional (see Tips, right)	15 mL
	Hot pepper sauce	

1. In a skillet, heat 1 tbsp (15 mL) of the oil over medium heat. Add sausage and cook, stirring, until no longer pink inside, about 4 minutes. Transfer to slow cooker stoneware.

2. Add remaining oil to pan, if necessary. Add onions and celery and cook, stirring, until celery is tender, about 5 minutes. Add garlic, thyme, oregano and peppercorns and cook, stirring, for 1 minute. Stir in tomato paste. Add flour and cook, stirring, for 1 minute. Add chicken stock and tomatoes with juice and bring to a boil. Cook, stirring, until slightly thickened, about 3 minutes. Transfer to slow cooker stoneware.

3. Add chicken and stir well. Cover and cook on Low for 6 hours or on High for 3 hours, until juices run clear. Add shrimp, clams, green and red peppers and parsley and stir well. Cover and cook on High for 30 minutes, until peppers are tender and shrimp are heated through.

4. Meanwhile, combine chili powder and cayenne in a plastic bag. Add scallops and toss until coated with mixture. In a skillet over medium heat, melt butter. Add scallops and cook, stirring, just until they become opaque, about 4 minutes. Add to slow cooker stoneware and stir well. Add filé powder, if using, and stir well. Serve immediately. Pass the hot pepper sauce at the table.

❖ **Filé powder, made from dried sassafras leaves, is traditionally used for thickening gumbo. You can find it in specialty food shops.**

Mindful Morsels
Scallops are a good source of vitamin B12.

Natural Wonders
POTASSIUM
This recipe is an excellent source of the mineral potassium. If you are feeling fatigued or experiencing pain or muscle weakness, the problem may be a potassium deficiency. Potassium works with sodium to help your body maintain a proper fluid balance, and although potassium is present in many foods, it is vulnerable to being depleted from the body. A diet high in refined foods is linked with potassium loss, as is the overconsumption of coffee. Prolonged diarrhea or the use of diuretics can also lead to potassium deficiencies, and boiling vegetables in large amounts of water causes the potassium to drain off.

Nutrients Per Serving	
Calories	247
Protein	27.5 g
Carbohydrates	10.7 g
Fat (Total)	10.0 g
Saturated Fat	3.0 g
Monounsaturated Fat	3.9 g
Polyunsaturated Fat	1.6 g
Dietary Fiber	2.0 g
Sodium	708 mg
Cholesterol	128 mg

Excellent source of vitamins C, B6, B12 and K, potassium and iron.

Good source of vitamin A, phosphorus, magnesium and zinc.

Contains a moderate amount of dietary fiber.

Meat

Veal Goulash, see recipe overleaf

Veal Goulash

This version of goulash, a luscious Hungarian stew seasoned with paprika, is lighter than the traditional version made with beef. It is usually served over hot noodles, but fluffy mashed potatoes also make a sybaritic finish. Not only do the red bell peppers enhance the flavor, they also add valuable nutrients to the dish.

MAKES 8 SERVINGS

TIPS

❖ **There is a hint of caraway flavor in this version. If you prefer a stronger caraway flavor, increase the quantity of caraway seeds to as much as 2 tsp (10 mL).**

❖ **I like to use small whole cremini mushrooms in this stew, but if you can't find them, white mushrooms or larger cremini mushrooms, quartered or sliced, depending upon their size, work well, too.**

MAKE AHEAD

This dish can be partially prepared before it is cooked. Heat 1 tbsp (15 mL) of the oil and complete Step 2. Cover and refrigerate overnight or for up to 1 day. When you're ready to cook, either brown the veal as outlined in Step 1 or add it to the stoneware without browning. Stir well and continue with Steps 3 and 4.

• **Works in slow cookers from 3½ to 6 quarts**

2 tbsp	olive oil, divided	25 mL
2 lbs	trimmed stewing veal, cut into 1-inch (2.5 cm) pieces	1 kg
2	onions, finely chopped	2
4	cloves garlic, minced	4
1 tsp	caraway seeds (see Tips, left)	5 mL
½ tsp	cracked black peppercorns	2 mL
1 lb	mushrooms (see Tips, left)	500 g
2 tbsp	all-purpose flour	25 mL
1	can (14 oz/398 mL) diced tomatoes, including juice (see Tips, page 134)	1
1 cup	chicken stock (see Mindful Morsels, right)	250 mL
1 tbsp	sweet Hungarian paprika, dissolved in 2 tbsp (25 mL) water or chicken stock	15 mL
2	red bell peppers, diced	2
½ cup	finely chopped dill	125 mL
	Sour cream, optional	

1. In a skillet, heat 1 tbsp (15 mL) of the oil over medium-high heat for 30 seconds. Add veal, in batches, and cook, stirring, adding more oil as necessary, until browned, about 5 minutes per batch. Using a slotted spoon, transfer to slow cooker stoneware.

2. Reduce heat to medium. Add onions to pan and cook, stirring, until softened, about 3 minutes. Add garlic, caraway seeds and peppercorns and cook, stirring, for 1 minute. Add mushrooms and toss to coat. Add flour and cook, stirring, for 1 minute. Add tomatoes with juice and chicken stock and bring to a boil. Transfer to slow cooker stoneware. Stir well.

3. Cover and cook on Low for 8 hours or on High for 4 hours, until veal is tender.

4. Add paprika solution to slow cooker stoneware and stir well. Add red peppers and stir well. Cover and cook on High for 30 minutes, until peppers are tender. To serve, ladle into bowls and top each serving with 1 tbsp (15 mL) of the dill and a dollop of sour cream, if using.

Mindful Morsels

The nutritional analysis on this recipe was done using regular prepared chicken stock. If you are trying to reduce your sodium intake, use Homemade Chicken Stock (see recipe, page 35) or a reduced-sodium version.

Natural Wonders
RED BELL PEPPERS

Red bell peppers, also known as sweet red peppers, are low in calories (about 32 calories in one medium pepper) and are extremely nutritious. These tasty and versatile vegetables are rich in powerful antioxidants, such as beta-carotene and vitamin C, which help to keep your immune system healthy, among other benefits. In fact, ounce for ounce, red peppers contain more vitamin C than oranges! Vitamin C helps our bodies fight free radical damage and may help to prevent age-related ailments such as heart disease and diabetes. Its absence in the diet causes scurvy, a disease characterized by gum disease and fatigue. During the great age of exploration and the settlement of North America, scurvy was a serious concern, affecting sailors who were at sea for long periods of time and settlers who had exhausted their winter stores of vegetables and fruits by the time spring arrived.

Nutrients Per Serving	
Calories	207
Protein	25.5 g
Carbohydrates	11.3 g
Fat (Total)	6.8 g
Saturated Fat	1.4 g
Monounsaturated Fat	3.5 g
Polyunsaturated Fat	0.8 g
Dietary Fiber	2.4 g
Sodium	262 mg
Cholesterol	95 mg

Excellent source of vitamins C, B6 and B12, phosphorus, potassium and zinc.

Good source of vitamin A, magnesium and iron.

Contains a moderate amount of dietary fiber.

Beef and Barley with Rosemary and Orange

This hearty stew, with its deep rich flavors, makes a great family meal that is tasty enough to serve to company. The persillade adds a zesty finish, while allowing you to enjoy the health benefits of garlic free from worry about garlic breath because the parsley works to negate any offensive odor. Add a tossed green salad and crusty whole grain rolls.

MAKES 8 SERVINGS

TIP

❖ **If you're using small mushrooms, quarter them. Large ones may be sliced.**

MAKE AHEAD

This dish can be partially prepared before it is cooked. Complete Step 2. Cover and refrigerate overnight or for up to 2 days. When you're ready to cook, either brown the beef as outlined in Step 1 or add it to the stoneware without browning. Stir well and continue with Steps 3 and 4.

- Large (minimum 5 quart) slow cooker

2 tbsp	olive oil, divided	25 mL
2 lbs	trimmed stewing beef, cut into 1-inch (2.5 cm) cubes	1 kg
8 oz	mushrooms (see Tip, left)	250 g
3	onions, finely chopped	3
4	stalks celery, diced	4
4	carrots, peeled and diced	4
4	cloves garlic, minced	4
4	sprigs fresh rosemary or 2 tsp (10 mL) dried rosemary leaves, crumbled	4
1 tsp	cracked black peppercorns	5 mL
	Grated zest and juice of 1 orange	
1 cup	whole (hulled) or pot barley, rinsed	250 mL
3 cups	beef stock	750 mL
1½ cups	dry red wine	375 mL
	Salt, optional	

PERSILLADE (optional)

1 cup	finely chopped parsley	250 mL
4	cloves garlic, minced	4
1 tsp	balsamic vinegar	5 mL

1. In a skillet, heat 1 tbsp (15 mL) of the oil over medium-high heat. Add beef, in batches and cook, stirring, until browned, about 4 minutes per batch. Transfer to slow cooker stoneware.

2. Add remaining 1 tbsp (15 mL) of the oil to pan. Add mushrooms and toss until lightly seared, about 2 minutes. Transfer to slow cooker stoneware. Reduce heat to medium. Add onions, celery and carrots and cook, stirring, until carrots are softened, about 7 minutes. Add garlic, rosemary,

peppercorns and orange zest and cook, stirring, for 1 minute. Add barley and toss to coat. Add orange juice, beef stock and wine and bring to a boil. Season to taste with salt, if using. Transfer to slow cooker stoneware. Stir well.

3. Cover and cook on Low for 8 hours or on High for 4 hours, until meat is tender.

4. *Persillade (optional):* In a bowl, combine parsley, garlic and vinegar. Set aside at room temperature for 30 minutes to allow flavors to develop. Ladle stew onto plates and garnish with persillade, if using.

Mindful Morsels
To lower the sodium content of this recipe use reduced-sodium beef stock or make your own with no salt added.

Natural Wonders
SENSIBLE EATING

After years of debating the merits of low-carb or low-fat diets, studies are showing there is no magic bullet approach to weight loss and that the old-fashioned strategy of keeping calories under control by eating sensibly is most likely to produce sustainable results.

One study released in 2004 by the American Institute for Cancer Research (AICR), established some guidelines around sensible eating. It concluded that plant foods can play a major role in weight maintenance by lowering the "energy density" (i.e. caloric intake) of a meal. Researchers found that 72 percent of Americans eat meals containing a detrimentally high proportion of meats, poultry, fish and dairy foods and do not consume enough vegetables, fruits, whole grains and beans. As they see it, plant foods play an important role in weight loss because they are "energy dilute," high in fiber and water but low in calories. That means we don't need to consume a lot of calories to feel full. To lose weight gradually and keep it off, researchers recommend that a typical meal consist of one-third animal protein and two-thirds vegetables, fruits and/or whole grains.

Nutrients Per Serving	
Calories	358
Protein	29.6 g
Carbohydrates	32.9 g
Fat (Total)	12.1 g
Saturated Fat	3.5 g
Monounsaturated Fat	5.6 g
Polyunsaturated Fat	1.0 g
Dietary Fiber	4.6 g
Sodium	458 mg
Cholesterol	55 mg

Excellent source of vitamins A, B6 and B12, phosphorus, potassium, iron and zinc.

Good source of magnesium, folacin and vitamin K.

Source of vitamin C.

Contains a high amount of dietary fiber.

Greek-Style Beef with Eggplant

This ambrosial stew reminds me of moussaka without the topping, and it is far less work. Made with red wine and lycopene-rich tomato paste, it develops a deep and intriguing flavor. Serve this over hot bulgur (see Tip, below) and accompany with steamed broccoli and a tossed green salad for a delicious and nutrient-rich meal.

MAKES 6 TO 8 SERVINGS

TIP

❖ **To cook bulgur to accompany this recipe, combine 2 cups (500 mL) medium or fine bulgur and 4 cups (1 L) boiling water. Cover and set aside until water is absorbed and bulgur is tender to the bite, about 20 minutes.**

MAKE AHEAD

This dish can be partially prepared before it is cooked. Complete Steps 1 and 2, placing eggplant and meat mixtures in separate containers. Cover and refrigerate overnight or for up to 2 days. When you're ready to cook, combine mixtures in stoneware and complete Step 3.

- **Works in slow cookers from 3½ to 6 quarts**
- **Large rimmed baking sheet**

2	medium eggplant (each about 1 lb/500 g) peeled, halved and each half cut into quarters	2
2 tbsp	kosher salt	25 mL
2 tbsp	olive oil, divided	25 mL
1 lb	lean ground beef	500 g
4	onions, thinly sliced on the vertical	4
4	cloves garlic, minced	4
2 tsp	dried oregano leaves, crumbled	10 mL
1 tsp	ground cinnamon	5 mL
½ tsp	salt	2 mL
½ tsp	cracked black peppercorns	2 mL
1	can (5½ oz/156 mL) tomato paste	1
1 cup	dry red wine	250 mL
1 cup	packed parsley leaves, finely chopped	250 mL
	Grated Parmesan cheese	

1. In a colander over a sink, combine eggplant and kosher salt. Toss to ensure eggplant is well coated and set aside for 30 minutes to 1 hour. Meanwhile, preheat oven to 400°F (200°C). Rinse eggplant well under cold running water and drain. Pat dry with paper towel. Brush all over with 1 tbsp (15 mL) of the oil. Place on baking sheet and bake until soft and fragrant, about 20 minutes. Transfer to slow cooker stoneware.

2. In a skillet, heat remaining 1 tbsp (15 mL) of the oil over medium heat for 30 seconds. Add ground beef and onions and cook, stirring and breaking up with a spoon, until beef

is no longer pink, about 10 minutes. Add garlic, oregano, cinnamon, salt and peppercorns and cook, stirring for 1 minute. Add tomato paste and red wine and stir well. Transfer to slow cooker stoneware. Stir well.

3. Cover and cook on Low for 8 hours or on High for 4 hours, until mixture is bubbly and eggplant is tender. Stir in parsley and serve. Pass the Parmesan at the table.

Mindful Morsels
Eggplant is low in calories and contains small amounts of a wide variety of nutrients. It has a high antioxidant capacity.

Natural Wonders
VITAMIN K
I often use a fair bit of parsley in my recipes for two reasons: it's very tasty and it's loaded with nutrients. If you've ever thought about using parsley for more than a garnish, this recipe is a case in point. Each serving contains 48.8 mcg of vitamin K, 40.5 mcg of which comes from parsley. That's over half the recommended daily value of this important vitamin, which is found mainly in leafy greens and some vegetable oils such as olive oil. In fact, the more we learn about vitamin K, the more significant it becomes. Long recognized as an important blood-clotting agent, researchers have linked vitamin K intake with reduced rates of osteoporosis in older women and now think it plays an important role in bone health. Other research suggests that adequate consumption of this vitamin protects against cardiovascular disease.

Nutrients Per Serving	
Calories	225
Protein	13.9 g
Carbohydrates	17.8 g
Fat (Total)	11.7 g
Saturated Fat	3.7 g
Monounsaturated Fat	6.0 g
Polyunsaturated Fat	0.7 g
Dietary Fiber	4.8 g
Sodium	204 mg
Cholesterol	34 mg

Excellent source of vitamin K, potassium and zinc.

Good source of vitamins C, B12 and B6, folacin, phosphorus, magnesium and iron.

Source of vitamin A.

Contains a high amount of dietary fiber.

Stuffed Onions

Here's a tasty solution to the midweek dining blues — ground beef-and-bulgur-filled onions, topped with Parmesan and dill. Use any sweet onion — Vidalia, Spanish and red onions all work well. Just make sure they are as crisp and fresh as possible and that all will fit in the stoneware. Serve these with a tossed green salad, sprinkled with shredded carrots to add a sparkle of color, along with nutrients and flavor.

MAKES 6 SERVINGS

TIP

❖ **Use an apple corer to make the cavities for stuffing.**

MAKE AHEAD

This dish can be assembled before it is cooked. Complete Steps 1 through 3. Cool filling thoroughly, then continue with Step 4. Cover and refrigerate overnight or for up to 2 days. When you're ready to cook, continue with Step 5.

- **Large (minimum 6 quart) oval slow cooker**

1/2 cup	bulgur	125 mL
1/2 cup	boiling water	125 mL
6	large sweet onions	6
1 tbsp	olive oil	15 mL
12 oz	extra-lean ground beef	375 g
6	cloves garlic, minced	6
1 tsp	dried oregano leaves, crumbled	5 mL
1/2 tsp	salt	2 mL
1/2 tsp	cracked black peppercorns	2 mL
1/2 cup	dry white wine or chicken stock	125 mL
1	can (14 oz/398 mL) diced tomatoes, including juice (see Tips, page 134)	1
1/2 cup	grated Parmesan cheese	125 mL
1/2 cup	finely chopped dill or parsley	125 mL

1. In a bowl, combine bulgur and boiling water. Set aside for 20 minutes.

2. Cut off tops and bottoms of onions and peel. Hollow out the centers (see Tip, left) and discard. Drop prepared onions into a large pot of boiling water and blanch for 5 minutes. Drain and rinse in cold water. Place in slow cooker stoneware with the hollows pointing up.

3. In a skillet, heat oil over medium heat for 30 seconds. Add ground beef, garlic, oregano, salt and peppercorns and cook, stirring and breaking up with a spoon, until meat is no longer pink, about 5 minutes. Add white wine and tomatoes with juice and bring to a boil. Stir in bulgur.

4. Fill centers of onions with beef mixture, using a blunt object such as a kitchen knife to pack the filling in as tightly as possible. Pour remaining filling over onions.

5. Cover and cook on Low for 8 hours or on High for 4 hours, until onions are tender and mixture is hot and bubbly. To serve, place an onion on each plate. Sprinkle with Parmesan and garnish with dill.

Mindful Morsels

The next time you find yourself weeping while chopping onions, remember that the sulfur compounds that make your eyes water may also help to keep your blood pressure and, if you suffer from diabetes, blood sugar low.

Natural Wonders

BULGUR

Bulgur, parboiled wheat kernels that are dried and cracked, is an extremely nutritious whole grain. Not only is it high in dietary fiber, it also contains a panoply of minerals, including iron, zinc, phosphorus, manganese and magnesium. It also contains lignans, antioxidants that protect against heart disease, colon and breast cancer. A recent Dutch study indicates that long-term consumption of lignans may also improve cognitive function in older women and researchers are currently looking at the role that lignans might play in preventing hair loss. Because it releases its natural sugars slowly into the bloodstream (it has a low glycemic index) eating bulgur can also help to keep diabetes under control.

Bulgur contains no saturated fat but has a robust flavor and texture, which makes it a suitable substitute for some or all of the ground beef in a recipe. This makes it easy to improve the nutritional profile of a dish without sacrificing lip-smacking taste.

Nutrients Per Serving	
Calories	294
Protein	19.8 g
Carbohydrates	34.2 g
Fat (Total)	9.6 g
Saturated Fat	3.7 g
Monounsaturated Fat	4.3 g
Polyunsaturated Fat	0.5 g
Dietary Fiber	4.4 g
Sodium	508 mg
Cholesterol	38 mg

Excellent source of vitamin B6, phosphorus, potassium and zinc.

Good source of vitamins C and B12, calcium, folacin, magnesium and iron.

Source of vitamin A.

Contains a high amount of dietary fiber.

See photo, page 146

Greek-Style Veal Shanks with Feta and Caper Gremolata

Although I love osso buco, an Italian method for preparing veal shanks, from time to time I pine for a different approach to this succulent cut of meat. This version puts a Greek spin on the dish with flavorings of garlic, oregano, white wine, and a gremolata enhanced with feta and capers. Serve this over brown rice or hot orzo tossed with extra virgin olive oil, and add a platter of bitter greens, such as rapini, to complete the meal.

MAKES 6 SERVINGS

MAKE AHEAD

This dish can be partially prepared before it is cooked. Heat 1 tbsp (15 mL) of the oil and complete Step 2. Cover and refrigerate overnight or for up to 1 day. When you're ready to cook, complete Steps 1, 3 and 4.

• **Works in slow cookers from 3½ to 6 quarts**

6	veal shanks (each about 8 oz/250 g)	6
⅓ cup	all-purpose flour	75 mL
2 tbsp	olive oil, divided (approx.)	25 mL
3	leeks, white part only, cleaned and thinly sliced (see Tip, page 42)	3
12	cloves garlic, slivered	12
2 tsp	dried oregano leaves, crumbled	10 mL
½ tsp	cracked black peppercorns	2 mL
1 cup	dry white wine	250 mL
3 tbsp	tomato paste	45 mL
2 cups	chicken stock	500 mL
	Salt, optional	

GREMOLATA

½ cup	finely chopped parsley	125 mL
1 tbsp	drained capers, minced	15 mL
1 tbsp	finely grated lemon zest	15 mL
¼ cup	crumbled feta	50 mL

1. On a plate, coat veal shanks with flour, shaking off excess. In a skillet, heat 1 tbsp (15 mL) of the oil over medium-high heat. Add veal, in batches, and cook, stirring, adding more oil as necessary, until lightly browned on all sides, about 5 minutes per batch. Transfer to slow cooker stoneware.

2. Reduce heat to medium. Add leeks and cook, stirring, until softened, about 5 minutes. Add garlic, oregano and peppercorns and cook, stirring, for 1 minute. Add wine, tomato paste and chicken stock, stirring, and bring to a boil. Add salt to taste, if using. Transfer to slow cooker stoneware.

See photo, page 147

3. Cover and cook on Low for 12 hours or on High for 6 hours, until veal is very tender.

4. *Gremolata:* In a bowl, mix together parsley, capers and lemon zest. Add feta and stir until well integrated. Serve alongside veal.

Mindful Morsels

Oregano, like many herbs, contains flavonoids. Consumption of these powerful antioxidants has been linked with reduced rates of heart disease and stroke.

Natural Wonders

FOOD AND CHOLESTEROL

Like all animal foods, the meat in this recipe is a source of dietary cholesterol. The relationship between the cholesterol you consume in food and the cholesterol in your blood is not clear. Although dietary cholesterol has long been thought to be a major factor in raising the levels of LDL ("bad") cholesterol in blood, recent research indicates that the real culprits in this area are trans and saturated fats.

Blood cholesterol levels are also affected by factors such as family history, diabetes, body weight and shape and physical activity level. Research also shows that some people react more to the cholesterol in food than others. While it's worth keeping an eye on your blood cholesterol levels to ensure you aren't at risk, if you have no family history of cardiovascular disease and are not diabetic, keep your weight within a healthy range, exercise regularly and eat a balanced diet containing cholesterol-lowering nutrients, particularly soluble fiber, you probably don't need to be overly vigilant about the amount of dietary cholesterol you consume. You may want to bear in mind that the American Heart Association, which takes a conservative position on this issue, recommends that healthy adults consume less than 300 milligrams of dietary cholesterol a day.

Nutrients Per Serving	
Calories	359
Protein	38 g
Carbohydrates	14.4 g
Fat (Total)	15.7 g
Saturated Fat	5.5 g
Monounsaturated Fat	7.3 g
Polyunsaturated Fat	1.3 g
Dietary Fiber	2.6 g
Sodium	574 mg
Cholesterol	151 mg

Excellent source of vitamins B6, B12 and K, phosphorus, potassium, iron and zinc.

Good source of magnesium and folacin.

Source of vitamins A and C and calcium.

Contains a moderate amount of dietary fiber.

Lamb with Lentils and Chard

Rich with the flavors of the French countryside, this hearty stew is perfect for guests or a family meal. All it needs is a simple green salad, finished with a scattering of shredded carrots. I like to add whole grain bread to soak up the delicious sauce.

MAKES 10 SERVINGS

TIPS

❖ **If you can't find Swiss chard, use 2 packages (each 10 oz/300 g) fresh or frozen spinach. If using fresh spinach, remove the stems and chop before using. If it has not been pre-washed, rinse it thoroughly in a basin of lukewarm water. If using frozen spinach, thaw it first.**

❖ **Although this makes a large quantity, don't worry about leftovers. It reheats very well and may even be better the day after it is made.**

MAKE AHEAD

This dish can be partially prepared before it is cooked. Heat 1 tbsp (15 mL) of the oil and complete Step 2. Cover and refrigerate overnight or for up to 1 day. When you're ready to cook, either brown the lamb as outlined in Step 1 or add it to the stoneware without browning. Stir well and continue with Step 3.

• **Large (minimum 5 quart) slow cooker**

2 tbsp	olive oil, divided (approx.)	25 mL
2 lbs	trimmed stewing lamb, cut into 1-inch (2.5 cm) cubes	1 kg
2	onions, finely chopped	2
8	carrots, peeled and sliced	8
4	stalks celery, sliced	4
4	cloves garlic, minced	4
2 tsp	herbes de Provence	10 mL
1 tsp	salt	5 mL
1/2 tsp	cracked black peppercorns	2 mL
2	bay leaves	2
1 cup	vegetable or chicken stock	250 mL
1	can (28 oz/796 mL) tomatoes, including juice, coarsely chopped	1
2 cups	green or brown lentils, rinsed	500 mL
8 cups	chopped stemmed Swiss chard (about 2 bunches) (see Tips, left)	2 L

1. In a skillet, heat 1 tbsp (15 mL) of the oil over medium-high heat for 30 seconds. Add lamb, in batches, and cook, stirring, adding more oil as necessary, until browned, about 4 minutes per batch. Transfer to slow cooker stoneware.

2. Reduce heat to medium. Drain all but 1 tbsp (15 mL) of the fat from pan. Add onions, carrots and celery to pan and cook, stirring, until carrots are softened, about 7 minutes. Add garlic, herbes de Provence, salt and peppercorns and cook, stirring, for 1 minute. Add bay leaves, vegetable stock and tomatoes with juice and bring to a boil, Transfer to slow cooker stoneware. Stir in lentils.

3. Cover and cook on Low for 8 hours or on High for 4 hours, until mixture is bubbly and lamb and lentils are tender. Add chard, in batches, stirring each batch into the stew until wilted. Cover and cook on High for 20 to 30 minutes, until chard is tender. Discard bay leaves.

Mindful Morsels

A half cup (125 mL) serving of Swiss chard contains more than 150 percent of the recommended daily value of vitamin K.

Natural Wonders

VITAMIN B12

The lamb in this recipe is an excellent source of vitamin B12, which works in conjunction with other substances to help the body develop red blood cells and nerve cells, among other functions. Although the body stores B12, which means you don't need to consume it on a regular basis, recent studies suggest that it can be depleted more quickly than was previously thought. New research indicates that a B12 deficiency may affect a substantial number of infants in the developing world and as many as 22 percent of Americans over the age of 65. Those most at risk eat little or no meat, do not consume fortified foods and do not take supplements. One study of Boston mothers who followed a macrobiotic diet found that their breast milk contained insufficient levels of the vitamin, a long-term lack of which may be linked with chronic anxiety and depression and even lead to neurological damage. Meat, fish, eggs and milk are the most common sources of this vitamin, which vegans have difficulty obtaining through food sources.

Nutrients Per Serving	
Calories	332
Protein	30.5 g
Carbohydrates	35.5 g
Fat (Total)	8.2 g
Saturated Fat	2.2 g
Monounsaturated Fat	4.0 g
Polyunsaturated Fat	1.0 g
Dietary Fiber	7.9 g
Sodium	576 mg
Cholesterol	59 mg

Excellent source of vitamins A, B6, B12 and K, folacin, phosphorus, magnesium, potassium, iron and zinc.

Good source of vitamin C.

Source of calcium.

Contains a very high amount of dietary fiber.

Spanish-Style Pork and Beans

Here's a dish that is as delicious as the best Boston baked beans but even more nutritious. Salt pork or bacon is replaced with pork shoulder, trimmed of fat, and nutrient-dense kale is added just before the dish has finished cooking. Serve this with a tossed green salad sprinkled with shredded carrots. Add crusty rolls to complete the meal.

MAKES 10 SERVINGS

TIPS

❖ **When preparing kale, chop off the stem, then fold the leaf in half and remove the thickest part of the vein that runs up the center of the leaf.**

❖ **If you don't have kale you can substitute an equal quantity of spinach or Swiss chard.**

MAKE AHEAD

This dish can be partially prepared before it is cooked. Heat 1 tbsp (15 mL) of the oil and complete Step 2. Cover and refrigerate overnight or for up to 2 days. When you're ready to cook, either brown the pork as outlined in Step 1 or add it to the stoneware without browning. Stir well and continue with Steps 3 and 4.

• **Large (minimum 5 quart) slow cooker**

2 tbsp	olive oil, divided	25 mL
2 lbs	trimmed boneless pork shoulder, cut into bite-size pieces	1 kg
3	onions, finely chopped	3
4	cloves garlic, minced	4
2 tsp	dried oregano leaves, crumbled	10 mL
1 tsp	salt	5 mL
1/2 tsp	cracked black peppercorns	2 mL
1 cup	dry white wine or chicken stock	250 mL
2 tsp	sherry vinegar or white wine vinegar	10 mL
1	can (28 oz/796 mL) tomatoes, including juice, coarsely chopped	1
2	cans (each 14 to 19 oz/398 to 540 mL) white kidney beans, drained and rinsed, or 2 cups (500 mL) dried white kidney beans, soaked, cooked and drained (see Basic Beans, page 250)	2
2 tsp	hot or mild paprika dissolved in 2 tbsp (25 mL) dry white wine or water	10 mL
8 cups	coarsely chopped, stemmed kale, about 2 bunches (see Tips, left)	2 L

1. In a skillet, heat 1 tbsp (15 mL) of the oil over medium-high heat. Add pork, in batches, and cook, stirring, adding more oil as necessary, until browned, about 5 minutes per batch. Transfer to slow cooker stoneware.

2. Reduce heat to medium. Add onions to pan and cook, stirring, until softened, about 3 minutes. Add garlic, oregano, salt and peppercorns and cook, stirring, for 1 minute. Add wine and vinegar and cook, stirring, for 1 minute. Add

tomatoes with juice and bring to a boil. Transfer to slow cooker stoneware. Add beans and stir well.

3. Cover and cook on Low for 8 hours or on High for 4 hours, until pork is very tender (it should be falling apart).

4. Add paprika solution and stir well. Add kale, in batches, stirring well after each addition, until it begins to wilt. Cover and cook on High for 30 minutes, until kale is tender. Serve immediately.

Mindful Morsels

If you're watching your sodium intake, look for reduced-sodium canned beans or make your own with little or no salt added.

Natural Wonders
PORK

Contemporary farming has changed the way we think about pork. Once dismissed by health-conscious consumers as extremely fatty, pork has become almost 50 percent leaner than it was just a decade ago. This makes pork, eaten in moderation, a nutritious food choice. Even the fat in pork is healthier than traditional wisdom suggests. Only 45 percent of pork fat is saturated, and that part contains stearic acid, a fatty acid that scientists are interested in studying because they think it might help lower blood cholesterol. Like all meat, pork is high in protein, which helps the body to build and repair tissues and produce the antibodies necessary to battle infection. It also contains a wide range of nutrients, such as iron, pantothenic acid, zinc and vitamins B6 and B12. Pork is also one of the best food sources of thiamine, a B vitamin that supports your nervous system and helps to keep you energized.

Nutrients Per Serving	
Calories	277
Protein	25.8 g
Carbohydrates	23.4 g
Fat (Total)	9.5 g
Saturated Fat	2.6 g
Monounsaturated Fat	4.8 g
Polyunsaturated Fat	1.3 g
Dietary Fiber	6.9 g
Sodium	563 mg
Cholesterol	57 mg

Excellent source of vitamins A, C, B6 and K, phosphorus, potassium, iron and zinc.

Good source of vitamin B12, folacin and magnesium.

Source of calcium.

Contains a very high amount of dietary fiber.

Moroccan-Style Lamb with Raisins and Apricots

This classic tagine-style recipe, in which lamb is braised in spices and honey, is an appetizing combination of savory and sweet. I like to serve this over couscous, preferably whole wheat, which is the traditional accompaniment. It is also delicious served with fluffy quinoa, which adds a new world twist to this Middle Eastern dish.

MAKES 8 SERVINGS

TIP

❖ I prefer a peppery base in this dish to balance the sweetness of the apricots and raisins, so I usually use a whole teaspoon (5 mL) of cracked black peppercorns in this recipe. But I'm a pepper lover, so use your own judgment.

MAKE AHEAD

This dish can be partially prepared before it is cooked. Complete Step 1. Heat 1 tbsp (15 mL) of the oil and complete Step 3. Cover and refrigerate overnight or for up to 2 days. When you're ready to cook, either brown the lamb as outlined in Step 2 or add it to the stoneware without browning. Stir well and continue with Step 4.

● **Works in slow cookers from 3½ to 6 quarts**

1 tbsp	cumin seeds	15 mL
1 tsp	coriander seeds	5 mL
1 to 2 tbsp	olive oil	15 to 25 mL
2 lbs	trimmed stewing lamb, cut into 1-inch (2.5 cm) cubes	1 kg
1	onion, finely chopped	1
1 tbsp	minced gingerroot	15 mL
1 tsp	grated lemon zest	5 mL
1 tsp	salt	5 mL
½ tsp	cracked black peppercorns (approx.) (see Tip, left)	2 mL
1	piece (1 inch/2.5 cm) cinnamon stick	1
½ cup	chicken stock	125 mL
1 tbsp	freshly squeezed lemon juice	15 mL
1 tbsp	liquid honey	15 mL
	Salt, optional	
1 cup	dried apricots, chopped	250 mL
½ cup	raisins	125 mL
¼ cup	finely chopped cilantro leaves	50 mL

1. In a dry skillet over medium heat, toast cumin and coriander seeds, stirring, until fragrant and cumin seeds just begin to brown, about 3 minutes. Immediately transfer to a mortar or a spice grinder and grind. Set aside.

2. In same skillet, heat 1 tbsp (15 mL) of the oil over medium-high heat for 30 seconds. Add lamb, in batches, and cook, stirring, adding more oil if necessary, until browned, about 4 minutes per batch. Transfer to slow cooker stoneware.

3. Reduce heat to medium. Add onion to pan and cook, stirring, until softened. Add gingerroot, lemon zest, salt, peppercorns, cinnamon stick and reserved cumin and coriander and cook, stirring, for 1 minute. Add stock and bring to a boil. Transfer to slow cooker stoneware. Stir well.

4. Cover and cook on Low for 7 to 8 hours or on High for 3 to 4 hours, until lamb is tender. Add lemon juice and honey and stir well. Season to taste with salt, if using. Stir in apricots and raisins. Cover and cook on High for 20 minutes, until fruit is warmed through. Garnish with cilantro. Discard cinnamon stick.

Mindful Morsels

Naturally raised meat, although more costly, is better for your health. Some evidence suggests that grass-fed lamb has 14 percent less fat and 8 percent more protein than grain-fed lamb.

Natural Wonders

APRICOTS

In addition to providing a hint of exotic flavor, the apricots in this recipe deepen its nutritional value by adding fiber, vitamin A, potassium and iron. This tasty fruit also contains a wide variety of carotenoids, the consumption of which has been linked to various health benefits. Enjoying apricots in a stew has an added benefit because their beta-carotene becomes more available to the body when they are cooked.

Dried apricots are available year-round and make a very nutritious snack. Drying removes their high water content and concentrates the nutrients, which means that bite for bite, dried apricots are more nutritious than fresh. There's just one thing to watch for — most dried apricots are treated with sulfur dioxide, which maintains their bright orange color but can trigger allergic reactions or an attack of asthma in people sensitive to sulfur. I prefer to buy sulfur-free versions at a natural foods store.

Nutrients Per Serving	
Calories	246
Protein	20.7 g
Carbohydrates	22.5 g
Fat (Total)	8.7 g
Saturated Fat	2.7 g
Monounsaturated Fat	4.1 g
Polyunsaturated Fat	0.8 g
Dietary Fiber	2.3 g
Sodium	418 mg
Cholesterol	65 mg

Excellent source of vitamin B12 and zinc.

Good source of phosphorus, potassium, magnesium and iron.

Source of vitamins A and B6.

Contains a moderate amount of dietary fiber.

See photo, page 156

Ribs with Hominy and Kale

My version of pozole, this hearty stew is great to have on an early spring day when there is still a chill in the air but fresh radishes are appearing in the markets. A steaming bowl of pozole, garnished with fresh radishes, blends winter comfort food with the promise of spring.

MAKES 8 SERVINGS

TIPS

❖ Prepared hominy is available in well-stocked supermarkets or Latin American grocery stores. If you can't find it, chickpeas make an acceptable substitute.

❖ If you are using small Hass avocados, which in my opinion have the most flavor, use two in this recipe. Don't peel and dice avocados until you are ready to use them. Otherwise they will discolor.

MAKE AHEAD

This dish can be partially prepared before it is cooked. Heat 1 tbsp (15 mL) of the oil and complete Step 2. Cover and refrigerate overnight or for up to 2 days, When you're ready to cook, brown the ribs as outlined in Step 1 and add to stoneware. Stir well and continue with Steps 3 and 4.

● **Large (minimum 6 quart) slow cooker**

1 tbsp	olive oil	15 mL
2¹/₂ lbs	sliced country-style or side pork ribs, trimmed of fat	1.25 kg
2	onions, finely chopped	2
6	cloves garlic, minced	6
2 tsp	dried oregano leaves, preferably Mexican, crumbled	10 mL
¹/₂ tsp	cracked black peppercorns	2 mL
1 tbsp	cumin seeds, toasted (see Tips, page 49)	15 mL
2 cups	chicken or vegetable stock	500 mL
2 tbsp	tomato paste	25 mL
3	cans (each 15 oz/425 g) hominy, drained and rinsed (see Tips, left)	1
1 tbsp	ancho chili powder, dissolved in 2 tbsp (25 mL) lime juice	15 mL
1	jalapeño pepper or chipotle pepper in adobo sauce, minced	1
8 cups	chopped, stemmed kale (about 1 large bunch)	2 L
¹/₂ cup	finely chopped red or green onion	125 mL
¹/₂ cup	finely chopped cilantro	125 mL
1	avocado, peeled and diced, optional (see Tips, left)	1
	Sliced radishes, optional	
	Lime wedges	

1. In a skillet, heat oil over medium-high heat for 30 seconds. Add ribs, in batches, and brown on both sides, about 5 minutes per batch. Transfer to slow cooker stoneware.

See photo, page 157

2. In same skillet, reduce heat to medium and add onions to pan and cook, stirring, until softened, about 5 minutes. Add garlic, oregano, peppercorns and toasted cumin and cook, stirring, for 1 minute. Add chicken stock and tomato paste and bring to a boil. Transfer to slow cooker stoneware.

3. Add hominy and stir well. Cover and cook on Low for 8 hours or on High for 4 hours, until ribs are tender and falling off the bone.

4. Add chili powder solution and jalapeño pepper and stir well. Add kale, in batches, completely submerging each batch in the liquid before adding another. Cover and cook on High for 20 to 30 minutes, until kale is tender. To serve, ladle into bowls and garnish with onion, cilantro and avocado and/or radishes, if using. Pass lime wedges at the table.

Mindful Morsels

Kale is an excellent source of vitamin K. One serving of this dish provides almost 700 percent of the daily value of this vitamin. (For more about vitamin K, see page 143.)

Natural Wonders
PROTEIN

Meat is one of the best sources of high-quality protein. Protein plays a number of vital roles in bodily functions, from building and maintaining bones, muscles and skin to creating antibodies to fight against infection. High energy levels are also dependent upon having adequate supplies of this nutrient. In fact, new research suggests that we may need more protein than was previously thought. Recommendations on healthy eating suggest that adults should get between 10 and 35 percent of their calories from protein. However, a study reported in the *Journal of Bone and Mineral Research* linked low levels of protein with bone loss and suggested that dieting, exercise and aging all place more demands on the body for protein. These researchers recommended that at least 20 percent of calories be derived from protein.

Nutrients Per Serving	
Calories	343
Protein	20.7 g
Carbohydrates	27.5 g
Fat (Total)	17.0 g
Saturated Fat	5.0 g
Monounsaturated Fat	7.8 g
Polyunsaturated Fat	2.4 g
Dietary Fiber	5.3 g
Sodium	528 mg
Cholesterol	60 mg

Excellent source of vitamins A, C, B6 and K, folacin, potassium, iron and zinc.

Good source of magnesium and phosphorus.

Source of calcium.

Contains a high amount of dietary fiber.

Ribs 'n' Greens with Wheat Berries

This dish reminds me of one of my favorite dishes from the deep south, pot likker greens. In that down-home classic, steaming collards are cooked with a ham hock and seasoned with a splash of vinegar. Here, I've substituted pork ribs for the ham hock and added nutritious wheat berries to the pot. I like to serve this in large soup plates, accompanied by warm whole wheat rolls to soak up the tasty liquid. Pass a cruet of good vinegar at the table so diners can add its bitter finish to suit their tastes.

MAKES 8 SERVINGS

TIP

❖ **When cooked by conventional methods, wheat berries should be soaked overnight. I've never found this necessary when using the slow cooker.**

MAKE AHEAD

This dish can be partially prepared before it is cooked. Heat 1 tbsp (15 mL) of the oil and complete Step 2. Cover and refrigerate overnight or for up to 2 days. When you're ready to cook, brown the ribs as outlined in Step 1 and continue with Step 3.

• **Large (minimum 6 quart) slow cooker**

1 tbsp	olive oil	15 mL
2¹⁄₂ lbs	sliced country-style or side pork ribs, trimmed of fat	1.25 kg
2	onions, finely chopped	2
8	stalks celery, diced	8
2	cloves garlic, minced	2
1	piece (about 2 inches/5 cm) cinnamon stick	1
¹⁄₂ tsp	cracked black peppercorns	2 mL
2 cups	wheat berries, rinsed (see Tip, left)	500 mL
4 cups	chicken or vegetable stock	1 L
1 tbsp	paprika, dissolved in 2 tbsp (25 mL) white wine vinegar	15 mL
8 cups	thinly sliced (chiffonade) trimmed collard greens, (about 2 bunches) (see Tips, page 172)	2 L
	Balsamic or white wine vinegar	

1. In a skillet, heat oil over medium-high heat for 30 seconds. Add ribs, in batches, and brown on both sides, about 5 minutes per batch. Transfer to slow cooker stoneware.

2. In same skillet, reduce heat to medium and add onions and celery to pan and cook, stirring, until celery is softened, about 5 minutes. Add garlic, cinnamon stick and peppercorns and cook, stirring, for 1 minute. Add wheat berries and toss to coat. Add chicken stock and bring to a boil. Transfer to slow cooker stoneware.

3. Cover and cook on Low for 8 hours or on High for 4 hours, until ribs are tender and falling off the bone. Add paprika solution and stir well. Add collard greens, in batches, completely submerging each batch in the liquid before adding another. Cover and cook on High for 30 minutes, until collards are tender. Discard cinnamon stick. Pass the balsamic at the table.

Mindful Morsels

Wheat berries are unrefined kernels of whole wheat with a pleasingly nutty taste. They are high in fiber and rich in disease-fighting antioxidants, such as plant lignans, which are thought to protect against heart disease and breast cancer.

Natural Wonders

ABOUT FATS

At first glance, this recipe seems high in fat. But most of the fat is unsaturated, which experts now associate with healthful benefits. Unsaturated fat raises HDL ("good") cholesterol, while lowering LDL ("bad") cholesterol, the combination of which helps keep your arteries free of plaque.

For many years, major health organizations urged us to keep fat intake to 30 percent or less of the total calories we consumed because they believed the consumption of fat was linked with increased incidence of cardiovascular disease. Today, as we understand more about the various kinds of fat, these recommendations have become less stringent. Two large long-term studies conducted by Harvard researchers found no link between the overall percentage of calories from fat and any significant health outcome, including weight gain. The important factor was the kind of fat. While saturated fats did increase the risk of heart disease, trans fats were by far the worst offenders. These hydrogenated oils are found mainly in commercially prepared and processed foods such as hydrogenated margarine, baked goods and deep-fried foods.

Nutrients Per Serving	
Calories	383
Protein	22.1 g
Carbohydrates	38.8 g
Fat (Total)	16.2 g
Saturated Fat	4.9 g
Monounsaturated Fat	7.5 g
Polyunsaturated Fat	2.0 g
Dietary Fiber	7.4 g
Sodium	555 mg
Cholesterol	60 mg

Excellent source of vitamins B6 and K, phosphorus, magnesium, potassium and zinc.

Good source of vitamin A and iron.

Source of vitamin C and calcium.

Contains a very high amount of dietary fiber.

Buckwheat Meatballs in Tomato Sauce

More like a saucy meatloaf than traditional meatballs swimming in sauce, this tasty dish is as much at home over hot cooked rice or fluffy mashed potatoes as it is over pasta. I like to serve this with a platter of steamed bitter greens, such as rapini, drizzled with extra virgin olive oil and freshly squeezed lemon juice, but steamed broccoli also makes a nice accompaniment.

MAKES 8 SERVINGS

TIPS

❖ **Buckwheat groats are also known as kasha. If you prefer, you may substitute an equal quantity of bulgur. If using bulgur, combine it with the boiling water and set aside, until all the water is absorbed, about 20 minutes. Continue with Step 2.**

❖ **Do all your preparation for the sauce as well as the meatballs while the kasha cooks, so you'll be ready to start cooking as soon as it is completed.**

● **Works in slow cookers from 3½ to 6 quarts**

MEATBALLS

½ cup	buckwheat groats (see Tips, left)	125 mL
1 cup	boiling water	250 mL
1	onion, finely chopped	1
½ cup	finely chopped parsley	125 mL
1 tsp	salt	5 mL
¼ tsp	freshly ground black pepper	1 mL
¼ tsp	ground cinnamon	1 mL
1 lb	lean ground beef	500 g
1	egg, beaten	1
2 tbsp	olive oil, divided (approx.)	25 mL

TOMATO SAUCE

2	onions, finely chopped	2
4	cloves garlic, minced	4
1 tsp	dried oregano leaves, crumbled	5 mL
½ tsp	salt	2 mL
½ tsp	cracked black peppercorns	2 mL
1	can (28 oz/796 mL) tomatoes, including juice, coarsely chopped	1
1 cup	dry red wine	250 mL

1. *Meatballs:* In a saucepan, combine buckwheat groats and boiling water. Cover and cook over low heat until all the water has been absorbed, about 20 minutes. Remove from heat and set aside.

2. In a bowl, mix together onion, parsley, salt, pepper and cinnamon. Add ground beef and egg, and using your hands, mix until well combined. Using a wooden spoon (it will still be hot), mix in cooked buckwheat. Form into 24 meatballs, each about 1½ inches (4 cm) in diameter.

3. In a skillet, heat 1 tbsp (15 mL) of the oil over medium-high heat. Add meatballs, in batches, and brown well, about 5 minutes per batch. Transfer to slow cooker stoneware.

4. *Tomato Sauce:* Reduce heat to medium and add additional oil if necessary. Add onions to pan and cook, stirring, until softened, about 3 minutes. Add garlic, oregano, salt and peppercorns and cook, stirring, for 1 minute. Add tomatoes with juice and wine and bring to a boil.

5. Pour over meatballs. Cover and cook on Low for 7 hours or on High for 3½ hours, until hot and bubbly.

Mindful Morsels

Eating naturally raised meat is a healthy strategy. Grass-fed beef contains more omega-3 fatty acids and may have as much as five times the amount of conjugated linoleic acids (CLA) as grain-fed beef.

Natural Wonders
BUCKWHEAT

Despite its name, buckwheat is not a form of wheat and does not contain gluten, which makes it an ideal "grain" for people with gluten sensitivity. In fact, buckwheat is technically a fruit, one that contains many essential amino acids. A recent study suggests that a diet high in buckwheat may be beneficial in managing diabetes, and other research indicates this food is particularly effective in lowering cholesterol and keeping blood pressure under control. Buckwheat is high in flavonoids, particularly rutin, and the mineral magnesium. An easy way to add buckwheat to your diet is by serving soba noodles with meals. Traditionally a Japanese delicacy, these tasty noodles are often added to soups and stir-fries and are particularly delicious served cold and tossed with a simple oil and vinegar dressing.

Nutrients Per Serving	
Calories	233
Protein	14.9 g
Carbohydrates	17.1 g
Fat (Total)	12.2 g
Saturated Fat	3.8 g
Monounsaturated Fat	6.3 g
Polyunsaturated Fat	0.7 g
Dietary Fiber	2.7 g
Sodium	629 mg
Cholesterol	57 mg

Excellent source of vitamin K and zinc.

Good source of vitamins C, B6, B12, potassium, phosphorus, magnesium and iron.

Source of vitamin A.

Contains a moderate amount of dietary fiber.

Indian Beef with Cauliflower and Peppers

If you have a hankering for something that resembles a beef curry but is more nutritious, here's the recipe for you. I like to serve this over brown basmati rice, with a cucumber salad on the side.

MAKES 8 SERVINGS

TIPS

❖ **This quantity of black peppercorns provides a nicely zesty result. If you prefer a less peppery dish, reduce the quantity by half.**

❖ **In my opinion, cauliflower needs to be cooked quickly in rapidly boiling salted water. Cook it until it's tender to the bite, about 3 minutes after the water has returned to a boil, drain and add to the slow cooker.**

MAKE AHEAD

This dish can be partially prepared before it is cooked. Heat oil and complete Step 2. Cover and refrigerate overnight or for up to 2 days. When you're ready to cook, either brown the beef as outlined in Step 1 or add it to the stoneware without browning. Stir well and continue with Step 3.

• **Works in slow cookers from 3½ to 6 quarts**

1 tbsp	olive oil (approx.)	15 mL
2 lbs	trimmed stewing beef, cut into ½-inch (1 cm) cubes	1 kg
2	onions, finely chopped	2
1 tbsp	minced gingerroot	15 mL
2	cloves garlic, minced	2
1	piece (2 inches/5 cm) cinnamon stick	1
1 tsp	cracked black peppercorns (see Tips, left)	5 mL
2	bay leaves	2
2 tbsp	cumin seeds, toasted (see Tip, page 49)	25 mL
1 tbsp	coriander seeds	15 mL
1 cup	beef stock	250 mL
2 tbsp	tomato paste	25 mL
	Salt, optional	
1	red bell pepper, diced	1
1 to 2	long green chile peppers, minced	1 to 2
4 cups	cooked cauliflower florets (see Tips, left)	1 L
	Plain yogurt	
¼ cup	toasted slivered almonds	50 mL
½ cup	finely chopped cilantro leaves	125 mL

1. In a skillet, heat oil over medium-high heat for 30 seconds. Add beef, in batches and cook, stirring, adding additional oil if necessary, until browned, about 3 minutes per batch. Transfer to slow cooker stoneware.

2. Reduce heat to medium. Add additional oil to pan if necessary. Add onions to pan and cook, stirring, until softened, about 3 minutes. Add gingerroot, garlic, cinnamon stick, peppercorns, bay leaves and toasted cumin and coriander and cook, stirring, for 1 minute. Add beef stock and tomato paste and bring to a

boil, scraping up brown bits in the pan. Season to taste with salt, if using. Transfer to slow cooker stoneware. Stir well.

3. Cover and cook on Low for 6 to 8 hours or on High for 3 to 4 hours, until beef is tender. Discard bay leaves and cinnamon stick. Add red pepper and chile pepper and stir well. Stir in cooked cauliflower. Cover and cook on High for 20 minutes, until pepper is tender. To serve, garnish with a drizzle of yogurt, toasted almonds and cilantro.

VARIATION

Substitute 4 cups (1 L) broccoli florets for the cauliflower.

Mindful Morsels

When cooking beef, trim as much of the visible fat from the meat to reduce the calories and the amount of saturated fat you consume. About half the calories in untrimmed beef come from the fat.

Natural Wonders

CAULIFLOWER

A century ago Mark Twain called cauliflower "a cabbage with a college education." Today, he might describe it as one with a graduate degree in pharmacology. Like its close relative broccoli, cauliflower is a member of the Cruciferous family of vegetables, which was among the first groups of foods to be strongly identified as cancer fighters. Among its arsenal of phytochemicals, cauliflower contains sulforaphane, which helps the liver to neutralize toxic substances before they can become cancerous. Its other strong chemopreventor is indoles, which help to prevent cancers of the breast and prostate, in particular, by blocking estrogen receptors. And if that isn't enough, cauliflower is also rich in vitamin C, folacin and fiber, three nutrients that have been linked with protection against cardiovascular disease as well as cancer.

Nutrients Per Serving	
Calories	263
Protein	28.6 g
Carbohydrates	9.4 g
Fat (Total)	12.6 g
Saturated Fat	3.4 g
Monounsaturated Fat	5.9 g
Polyunsaturated Fat	1.3 g
Dietary Fiber	3.4 g
Sodium	200 mg
Cholesterol	55 mg

Excellent source of vitamins C and B12, phosphorus, potassium, iron and zinc.

Good source of vitamin B6, folacin and magnesium.

Source of vitamin A.

Contains a moderate amount of dietary fiber.

See photo, page 166

Mediterranean Beef Ragout

Succulent peppers, sweet or hot, are so much a part of Mediterranean cooking that it's interesting to recall they are indigenous to North America and didn't cross the Atlantic until Columbus brought them to Spain. Here they combine with cumin, olives and tomatoes to transform humble stewing beef into an Epicurean delight.

MAKES 8 SERVINGS

TIPS

❖ **Substitute an equal quantity of lemon thyme for the thyme, if you prefer.**

❖ **This produces a mildly flavored stew. If you like the taste of cumin, feel free to increase the quantity to as much as 2 tbsp (25 mL).**

❖ **If you don't have a mortar or a spice grinder, place the toasted cumin seeds on a cutting board and use the bottom of a wine bottle or measuring cup to grind them.**

❖ **For convenience use bottled roasted red peppers if you don't have the time or inclination to roast your own.**

MAKE AHEAD

This dish can be partially prepared before it is cooked. Heat oil and complete Step 3. Refrigerate overnight or for up to 2 days. When you're ready to cook, complete Steps 1, 2 and 4.

• **Works in slow cookers from 3½ to 6 quarts**

¼ cup	all-purpose flour	50 mL
1 tsp	dried thyme leaves, crumbled	5 mL
1 tsp	grated lemon zest, optional	5 mL
½ tsp	salt	2 mL
½ tsp	cracked black peppercorns	2 mL
2 lbs	trimmed stewing beef, cut into 1-inch (2.5 cm) cubes	1 kg
2 tbsp	olive oil, divided	25 mL
2	onions, chopped	2
4	cloves garlic, minced	4
1 tbsp	cumin seeds, toasted (see Tips, page 49)	15 mL
1 cup	beef stock	250 mL
½ cup	dry red wine	125 mL
1	can (14 oz/398 mL) diced tomatoes, including juice (see Tips, page 134)	1
2	bay leaves	2
2	roasted red bell peppers, thinly sliced, then cut into 1-inch (2.5 cm) pieces	2
½ cup	sliced pitted green olives	125 mL
½ cup	finely chopped parsley	125 mL

1. In a resealable plastic bag, combine flour, thyme, lemon zest, if using, salt and peppercorns. Add beef and toss until evenly coated. Set aside, shaking any excess flour from beef and reserving.

2. In a skillet, heat 1 tbsp (15 mL) of the oil over medium-high heat for 30 seconds. Add beef, in batches, and cook, stirring, adding more oil as necessary, until browned, about 4 minutes per batch. Transfer to slow cooker stoneware.

See photo, page 167

3. Reduce heat to medium. Add onions and garlic to pan and cook, stirring, until onions are softened, about 3 minutes. Sprinkle with toasted cumin and flour mixture and cook, stirring, for 1 minute. Add beef stock, wine, tomatoes with juice and bay leaves and bring to a boil. Cook, stirring, until slightly thickened, about 2 minutes. Add to slow cooker and stir well.

4. Cover and cook on Low for 8 hours or on High for 4 hours, until mixture is bubbly and beef is tender. Stir in roasted peppers, olives and parsley. Cover and cook on High for 15 minutes, until peppers are heated through. Discard bay leaves.

Mindful Morsels

On a daily basis we need to consume about 9 grams of protein for every 20 pounds of weight (1 gram per kilogram). Most vegetables are not a good source of protein because they lack the complete range of amino acids (see Natural Wonders, page 159).

Natural Wonders
OLIVES

Although they are high in sodium, olives add a burst of flavor to this tasty stew, in addition to beneficial nutrients. Olives are a good source of healthy monounsaturated fats and polyphenols, which protect cells from damage and inflammation. Polyphenols are powerful antioxidants that appear to protect against cardiovascular disease and may also play a role in preventing cancer. One study found that women who regularly consumed olive oil lowered their risk of breast cancer by 25 percent. A recent study published in the journal *Nature* identified an anti-inflammatory agent in olive oil, a natural painkiller which acts like ibuprofen. The anti-inflammatory components of olives may reduce the severity of osteoarthritis and rheumatoid arthritis, among other conditions.

Nutrients Per Serving	
Calories	270
Protein	27.4 g
Carbohydrates	10.5 g
Fat (Total)	13.0 g
Saturated Fat	3.6 g
Monounsaturated Fat	6.5 g
Polyunsaturated Fat	0.9 g
Dietary Fiber	1.6 g
Sodium	669 mg
Cholesterol	55 mg

Excellent source of vitamins C, B12 and K, potassium, iron and zinc.

Good source of vitamin B6, phosphorus and magnesium.

Source of vitamin A.

Chili con Carne

Because it contains beans, this chili doesn't qualify as a "Texas" version, but in my opinion, it is every bit as flavorful. It is also much more nutritious because it balances the quantity of red meat with other healthful ingredients such as onions, garlic, peppers, kidney beans, cumin and oregano. Add a nutrient-dense garnish, such as strips of roasted red pepper, and if you're eating for health, just be sure to keep the sour cream in check.

MAKES 8 SERVINGS

TIP

❖ **I've provided a range of fresh peppers in this recipe so you can select to suit your taste and their availability. The poblano and Anaheim chiles are mildly hot. Green bell peppers produce a milder, but equally pleasant chili.**

MAKE AHEAD

This dish can be partially prepared before it is cooked. Heat 1 tbsp (15 mL) of the oil and complete Step 2. Cover and refrigerate overnight or for up to 2 days. When you're ready to cook, brown the beef as outlined in Step 1. Stir well and continue with Step 3.

• **Works in slow cookers from 3½ to 6 quarts**

⅓ cup	all-purpose flour	75 mL
1 tsp	salt	5 mL
2 lbs	trimmed stewing beef, cut into 1-inch (2.5 cm) cubes	1 kg
2 tbsp	olive oil, divided (approx.)	25 mL
2	onions, finely chopped	2
4	cloves garlic, minced	4
1 tbsp	dried oregano leaves, crumbled	15 mL
1	piece (2 inches/5 cm) cinnamon stick	1
1 tsp	cracked black peppercorns	5 mL
2 tbsp	cumin seeds, toasted (see Tips, page 49)	25 mL
1 cup	beef stock	250 mL
1 cup	lager or pilsner beer	250 mL
2	cans (each 14 to 19 oz/398 to 540 mL) red kidney beans, rinsed and drained, or 2 cups (500 mL) dried red kidney beans, soaked, cooked and drained (see Basic Beans, page 250)	2
1 tbsp	ancho chili powder or ½ tsp (2 mL) cayenne dissolved in 2 tbsp (25 mL) lime juice	15 mL
1	jalapeño pepper or chipotle pepper in adobo sauce, minced	1
2	poblano or Anaheim chiles or green bell peppers, diced (see Tip, left)	2
	Finely chopped cilantro	
	Sour cream	
	Chopped red onion	
	Roasted red pepper strips	

1. In a resealable plastic bag, combine flour and salt. Add beef and toss until evenly coated, discarding excess flour mixture. In a skillet, heat 1 tbsp (15 mL) of the oil over medium-high heat for 30 seconds. Add beef, in batches, and cook, stirring, adding more oil as necessary, until browned, about 4 minutes per batch. Transfer to slow cooker stoneware.

2. Reduce heat to medium. Add onions to pan and cook, stirring, until softened, about 3 minutes. Add garlic, oregano, cinnamon stick, peppercorns and toasted cumin and cook, stirring, for 1 minute. Add stock and bring to a boil. Transfer to slow cooker stoneware. Add beer and beans and stir well.

3. Cover and cook on Low for 8 to 10 hours or on High for 4 to 5 hours, until beef is tender. Add chili powder solution, jalapeño pepper and poblano peppers and stir well. Cover and cook on High for 20 minutes, until fresh peppers are tender. Discard cinnamon stick. Serve with garnishes of your choice.

Nutrients Per Serving	
Calories	340
Protein	31.8 g
Carbohydrates	25.1 g
Fat (Total)	12.4 g
Saturated Fat	3.5 g
Monounsaturated Fat	5.8 g
Polyunsaturated Fat	1.1 g
Dietary Fiber	7.0 g
Sodium	735 mg
Cholesterol	55 mg

Mindful Morsels
You can reduce the amount of sodium in this dish by using canned beans with no salt added or cooking dried beans from scratch or reducing the quantity of salt used to flavor the beef.

Natural Wonders
ZINC
Like all meat, beef is a good source of zinc. Among its functions, zinc stimulates enzyme activity, helps wounds heal, boosts the immune system and supports growth during key periods of development. For instance, zinc improves pregnancy outcomes and helps children develop reasoning skills and eye-hand coordination. One recent study showed that zinc supplementation improved teenagers' attentiveness at school. Adolescents, particularly girls, who are more inclined to be vegetarians, may not be getting enough of this important mineral. The best food sources of zinc are oysters and red meat. Poultry, fish, whole grains, legumes, nuts and seeds, particularly pumpkin seeds, also contain varying amounts of zinc.

Excellent source of vitamin B12, phosphorus, potassium, iron and zinc.

Good source of vitamins C and B6, folacin and magnesium.

Source of vitamin A.

Contains a very high amount of dietary fiber.

Carbonnade with Collards

Carbonnade, a stew made of beef, onions and beer, is a favorite dish in Belgium. It is hearty bistro food, often flavored with bacon and brown sugar. Although it is great comfort food, carbonnade can be a tad bland and extremely rich. I prefer this lighter version with a hint of spice rather than sweetness, and the addition of flavorful and nutrient-dense collard greens. Serve this over noodles or mashed potatoes for a meal that is destined to become a family favorite.

MAKES 8 SERVINGS

TIPS

❖ I prefer to use sweet paprika in this recipe, but if you like a bit of heat, use hot paprika, instead, reducing the quantity to 2 tsp (10 mL).

❖ One way of preparing collard greens for use in a stew is to cut them into a chiffonade. Remove any tough veins toward the bottom of the leaves and up the center of the lower portion of the leaf. Stack about 6 in a pile. Roll them up like a cigar, then slice as thinly as you can. Repeat until all the greens are sliced.

MAKE AHEAD

Heat 1 tbsp (15 mL) of the oil and complete Step 2. Cover and refrigerate overnight or for up to 2 days. When you're ready to cook, either brown the beef as outlined in Step 1 or add it to the stoneware without browning. Stir well and continue with Step 3.

• **Works in slow cookers from 3½ to 6 quarts**

2 tbsp	olive oil, divided (approx.)	25 mL
2 lbs	trimmed stewing beef, cut into 1-inch (2.5 cm) cubes	1 kg
3	onions, thinly sliced on the vertical	3
4	cloves garlic, minced	4
1 tsp	dried thyme leaves, crumbled	5 mL
1 tsp	salt	5 mL
½ tsp	cracked black peppercorns	2 mL
2 tbsp	all-purpose flour	25 mL
1 tbsp	tomato paste	15 mL
2 cups	dark beer	500 mL
½ cup	chicken stock	125 mL
2	bay leaves	2
1 tbsp	paprika, dissolved in 2 tbsp (25 mL) cider vinegar (see Tips, left)	15 mL
8 cups	thinly sliced (chiffonade) stemmed collard greens (about 2 bunches) (see Tips, left)	2 L

1. In a skillet, heat 1 tbsp (15 mL) of the oil over medium-high heat for 30 seconds. Add beef, in batches, and cook, stirring, adding more oil as necessary, until browned, about 5 minutes per batch. Transfer to slow cooker stoneware.

2. Reduce heat to medium. Add onions to pan and cook, stirring, until softened, about 3 minutes. Add garlic, thyme, salt and peppercorns and cook, stirring, for 1 minute. Add flour and cook, stirring, until lightly browned, about 2 minutes. Stir in tomato paste. Add beer, chicken stock and bay leaves and bring

to a boil. Cook, stirring, for 1 minute, scraping up all brown bits in the pan. Transfer to slow cooker stoneware. Stir well.

3. Cover and cook on Low for 8 hours or on High for 4 hours, until meat is tender. Add paprika solution and stir well. Add collard greens, in batches, completely submerging each batch in the liquid before adding another. Cover and cook on High for 30 minutes, until collards are tender. Discard bay leaves.

Mindful Morsels
Garlic is more than a flavor-enhancer for many dishes. It may also help to keep LDL ("bad") cholesterol under control and protect against certain types of cancer.

Natural Wonders
A BALANCED DIET

Low Carb? High Protein? Low Fat? These days there are so many trendy diets it's hard to know what to eat. One approach, taken by the National Academies' Institute of Medicine is to recognize that protein, carbohydrate and fat (the macronutrients) substitute for one another to meet the body's energy needs. In a report sponsored by U.S. and Canadian government agencies, with the assistance of corporate partners, scientists recommended flexible ranges rather than fixed daily values for the macronutrients. Noting that extremely low-fat diets can decrease levels of HDL ("good") cholesterol and that high-fat diets can lead to obesity, researchers advised that fats (mainly unsaturated) should provide from 20 to 35 percent of calories. They also suggested that protein provide from 10 to 35 percent and carbohydrates from 45 to 65 percent of the calories regularly consumed. The report recommended that children as well as adults consume at least 130 grams of carbohydrates daily, while limiting the amount of added sugars (those found in prepared foods such as candy bars and soft drinks) to less than 25 percent of total calories consumed. A serving of this tasty stew, accompanied by noodles or mashed potatoes, works toward achieving the kind of balance the report recommends.

Nutrients Per Serving	
Calories	266
Protein	27.2 g
Carbohydrates	12.5 g
Fat (Total)	11.8 g
Saturated Fat	3.4 g
Monounsaturated Fat	5.6 g
Polyunsaturated Fat	0.9 g
Dietary Fiber	2.2 g
Sodium	428 mg
Cholesterol	55 mg

Excellent source of vitamins B12 and K, potassium and zinc.

Good source of vitamins A and B6, phosphorus, magnesium and iron.

Source of vitamin C and calcium.

Contains a moderate amount of dietary fiber.

Beef and Chickpea Curry with Spinach

This combination of beef and chickpeas in an Indian-inspired sauce is particularly delicious. I like to serve this with brown basmati rice, not only because I like its pleasant nutty flavor but also because it contains a significant amount of fiber. Complete this dinner with a platter of sliced tomatoes drizzled with olive oil and balsamic vinegar, in season, or a green salad.

MAKES 4 SERVINGS

TIPS

❖ **If using fresh spinach, be sure to remove the stems, and if it has not been pre-washed, rinse it thoroughly in a basin of lukewarm water.**

❖ **The nutritional analysis on this recipe has been done using regular canned chickpeas, which are relatively high in sodium. If you are concerned about your sodium consumption, use canned chickpeas with no added salt or cook dried chickpeas from scratch, with no salt added (see Basic Beans, page 250).**

MAKE AHEAD

This dish can be partially prepared before it is cooked. Heat 1 tbsp (15 mL) of the oil and complete Step 2. Cover and refrigerate overnight or for up to 2 days. When you're ready to cook, either brown the beef as outlined in Step 1 or add it to the stoneware without browning. Stir well and continue with Step 3.

● **Works in slow cookers from 3½ to 6 quarts**

1 tbsp	olive oil	15 mL
1 lb	trimmed stewing beef, cut into ½-inch (2 cm) cubes	500 g
2	onions, finely chopped	2
4	cloves garlic, minced	4
1 tbsp	minced gingerroot	15 mL
½ tsp	cracked black peppercorns	2 mL
1	piece (1 inch/2.5 cm) cinnamon stick	1
1	bay leaf	1
1 cup	beef stock	250 mL
1	can (14 to 19 oz/398 to 540 mL) chickpeas, drained and rinsed, or 1 cup (250 mL) dried chickpeas, soaked, cooked and drained (see Basic Beans, page 250)	1
1 tsp	curry powder, dissolved in 2 tsp (10 mL) freshly squeezed lemon juice	5 mL
1 lb	fresh spinach, stems removed, or 1 package (10 oz/300 g) spinach leaves, thawed if frozen (see Tips, left)	500 g
	Plain yogurt, optional	

1. In a skillet, heat oil over medium-high heat for 30 seconds. Add beef, in batches, and cook, stirring, adding additional oil if necessary, until browned, about 4 minutes per batch. Transfer to slow cooker stoneware.

2. Reduce heat to medium. Add onions to pan and cook, stirring, until softened, about 3 minutes. Add garlic, gingerroot, peppercorns, cinnamon stick and bay leaf and cook, stirring, for 1 minute. Add beef stock and bring to a boil. Transfer to slow cooker stoneware.

3. Add chickpeas and stir well. Cover and cook on Low for 8 hours or on High for 4 hours, until beef is tender. Add curry powder solution and stir well. Add spinach, in batches, stirring until each batch is submerged in the curry. Cover and cook on High for 20 minutes, until spinach is wilted. Discard cinnamon stick and bay leaf. Ladle into bowls and drizzle with yogurt, if using.

Mindful Morsels

Meat is one of the best food sources of vitamin B12 (see Natural Wonders, page 151).

Natural Wonders

MORE ABOUT FAT

Did you know that half of the fat in beef is monounsaturated, the heart-healthy fat found in olive oil? And although the other half is saturated, almost one-third of that is stearic acid, which does not affect blood cholesterol levels. While health professionals agree it's a good idea to reduce our consumption of saturated fat, some saturated fats are not as bad for us as others. The saturated fats in dairy products have the most negative effect on blood cholesterol levels. Even so, dairy products (along with beef) contain conjugated linoleic acid (CLA), a fatty acid with some compelling properties. Researchers are currently investigating CLA's ability to strengthen the immune system and its possible role in helping to prevent cancer. It may help to normalize blood glucose levels, lowering the risk of type-2 diabetes. It may also help to keep blood cholesterol levels under control.

Nutrients Per Serving	
Calories	353
Protein	32.7 g
Carbohydrates	27.4 g
Fat (Total)	12.7 g
Saturated Fat	3.6 g
Monounsaturated Fat	5.8 g
Polyunsaturated Fat	1.2 g
Dietary Fiber	6.4 g
Sodium	551 mg
Cholesterol	55 mg

Excellent source of vitamins A, B6, B12 and K, folacin, phosphorus, magnesium, potassium, iron and zinc.

Source of vitamin C and calcium.

Contains a very high amount of dietary fiber.

Pasta & Grains

Barley and Wild Rice Pilaf, see recipe overleaf

Barley and Wild Rice Pilaf

Serve this tasty pilaf as a nutritious side or turn it into a light main course with the addition of a salad of sliced tomatoes or mixed greens tossed in a vinaigrette made with your best cold-pressed extra virgin olive oil. For optimal nutrition (and flavor) always use oils that are cold-pressed when making salad dressings or for drizzling over a finished dish.

MAKES
4 TO 6 SERVINGS

TIPS

❖ **The folded tea towels absorb the moisture that accumulates during cooking, preventing it from dripping on the pilaf, which would make it soggy.**

❖ **If using a smaller slow cooker the cooking time will decrease to 5 to 6 hours on Low or 2½ to 3 hours on High.**

MAKE AHEAD

This dish can be partially prepared before it is cooked. Complete Step 1. Cover and refrigerate overnight or for up to 2 days. When you're ready to cook, continue with Step 2.

- **Large (minimum 5 quart) slow cooker (see Tips, left)**

1 tbsp	olive oil	15 mL
1	onion, finely chopped	1
4	cloves garlic, minced	4
2 tsp	dried rosemary leaves, crumbled	10 mL
½ tsp	cracked black peppercorns	2 mL
1	can (28 oz/796 mL) tomatoes, drained and coarsely chopped	1
½ cup	wild rice	125 mL
½ cup	whole (hulled) or pot barley, rinsed (see Mindful Morsels, 65)	125 mL
2 cups	vegetable or chicken stock or water	500 mL
¼ cup	toasted pine nuts	50 mL

1. In a skillet, heat oil over medium heat for 30 seconds. Add onion and cook, stirring, until softened, about 3 minutes. Add garlic, rosemary and peppercorns and cook, stirring, for 1 minute. Add tomatoes and bring to a boil. Transfer to slow cooker stoneware.

2. Add rice, barley and vegetable stock and stir well. Place two clean tea towels, each folded in half (so you will have four layers) over top of stoneware (see Tips, left). Cover and cook on Low for 8 hours or on High for 4 hours. Sprinkle with pine nuts and serve hot.

Mindful Morsels

Because it is more commonly available, the nutrient analysis on this recipe was done using pearled barley, which is more processed and less nutritious than the whole (hulled) or pot barley called for.

Nutrients Per Serving	
Calories	198
Protein	5.8 g
Carbohydrates	31.9 g
Fat (Total)	6.3 g
Saturated Fat	1.0 g
Monounsaturated Fat	3.0 g
Polyunsaturated Fat	1.9 g
Dietary Fiber	4.2 g
Sodium	461 mg
Cholesterol	0 mg

Natural Wonders
COMPLEX CARBOHYDRATES

This recipe is relatively high in carbohydrates, most of which come from healthy whole grains (wild rice and barley). Most nutritionists agree that complex carbohydrates, such as whole grains, should be the dietary staples of healthy eating. North Americans get about half their calories from carbohydrates. The problem is, about half those carb calories come from refined foods, such as white bread, fast food snacks and baked goods. Research links a steady diet of refined carbs with an increase in diabetes and cardiovascular disease, among other concerns. On the other hand, a diet rich in good carbs, such as fruits, vegetables and whole grains, can significantly benefit your health. For instance, participants in the Harvard Nurses' Study who ate three servings of whole grains, or more, a day reduced their risk of heart attack by 35 percent. So it's not surprising that the Harvard School of Public Health recommends "whenever possible, replace highly processed grains, cereals and sugars with minimally processed whole-grain products."

Good source of magnesium, potassium, iron and zinc.

Source of vitamins A, C, B6 and K and phosphorus.

Contains a high amount of dietary fiber.

Celery Root and Mushroom Lasagna

If you're tired of the same old thing, try this delightfully different lasagna, which combines celery root and mushrooms with more traditional tomatoes and cheese. To complete the unusual but appetizing flavors, add a sprinkle of toasted walnuts.

MAKES
6 TO 8 SERVINGS

TIP

❖ **Make this using whole wheat lasagna noodles or oven-ready noodles, if you prefer. If using oven-ready noodles, do not toss with olive oil and use only 1 tbsp (15 mL) of oil when softening the vegetables.**

MAKE AHEAD

This dish can be partially prepared before it is cooked. Complete Steps 1 through 4. Cover and refrigerate overnight. In the morning, continue with Step 5.

- **Large (minimum 5 quart) oval slow cooker**
- **Greased slow cooker stoneware**

9	brown rice lasagna noodles (see Tip, left)	9
2 tbsp	olive oil, divided	25 mL
4 cups	shredded, peeled celery root (about 1 medium celery root)	1 L
2 tbsp	freshly squeezed lemon juice	25 mL
1	large sweet onion, such as Spanish or Vidalia, finely chopped	1
1 lb	cremini mushrooms, stems removed and sliced	500 g
4	cloves garlic, minced	4
1 tbsp	fresh thyme leaves or 1 tsp (5 mL) dried thyme leaves, crumbled	15 mL
1 tbsp	fresh rosemary leaves, finely chopped, or 1 tsp (5 mL) dried rosemary leaves, crumbled	15 mL
4 cups	tomato sauce, divided	1 L
2 cups	ricotta cheese	500 mL
2 cups	shredded lower-fat mozzarella cheese	500 mL
1/2 cup	toasted chopped walnuts, optional	125 mL

1. Cook lasagna noodles in a pot of boiling salted water, until slightly undercooked, or according to package instructions, undercooking by 2 minutes. Drain, toss with 1 tbsp (15 mL) of the oil and set aside.

2. In a bowl, toss celery root with lemon juice. Set aside.

3. In a skillet, heat remaining 1 tbsp (15 mL) of the oil over medium heat for 30 seconds. Add onion and mushrooms and cook, stirring, for 2 minutes. Add garlic, thyme and rosemary and cook, stirring, for 1 minute. Add celery root and 2 cups

(500 mL) of the tomato sauce and bring to a boil. Remove from heat.

4. Spread 1 cup (250 mL) of the tomato sauce over bottom of prepared slow cooker stoneware. Cover with 3 noodles. Spread with half of the ricotta, half of the mushroom mixture and one-third of the mozzarella. Repeat. Cover with final layer of noodles. Pour remaining 1 cup (250 mL) of the tomato sauce over top. Sprinkle with remaining mozzarella.

5. Cover and cook on Low for 6 hours or on High for 3 hours, until mushrooms are tender and mixture is hot and bubbly. Garnish with toasted walnuts, if using.

Mindful Morsels

This recipe was tested using whole milk ricotta cheese and prepared tomato sauce. Reduce the quantity of saturated fat by using a reduced-fat cheese. To reduce the amount of sodium, use reduced sodium sauce, or make your own with no salt added (see Basic Tomato Sauce, page 212).

Natural Wonders
CREMINI MUSHROOMS

In many recipes I prefer to use cremini mushrooms rather than white mushrooms for their more intense flavor. While Asian mushrooms, such as shiitakes, have long been recognized as having medicinal value, in recent years researchers have been investigating the potential benefits of button mushrooms, including cremini, and the results are promising. A good source of the B vitamin niacin, cremini mushrooms may also help to protect against breast cancer by keeping the body's estrogen levels in check. Cremini mushrooms are also an excellent source of the mineral selenium, which acts as an antioxidant, apparently protecting against colon cancer and heart disease and easing the symptoms of asthma and arthritis.

Nutrients Per Serving	
Calories	401
Protein	20.7 g
Carbohydrates	44.3 g
Fat (Total)	17.4 g
Saturated Fat	8.9 g
Monounsaturated Fat	6.4 g
Polyunsaturated Fat	1.0 g
Dietary Fiber	5.1 g
Sodium	1,091 mg
Cholesterol	46 mg

Excellent source of vitamins A and B6, calcium, phosphorus and potassium.

Good source of magnesium, iron and zinc.

Source of vitamins C and K.

Contains a high amount of dietary fiber.

Basic Polenta

Polenta, which is cornmeal cooked in seasoned liquid, is extremely nutritious and goes well with many different foods. It is usually served as a side dish. To add variety to your diet, consider topping polenta with sauces traditionally served with pasta.

MAKES 6 SERVINGS

TIP

❖ **Depending upon your preference, you can cook polenta directly in the slow cooker stoneware or in a 6-cup (1.5 L) baking dish. If you are cooking directly in the stoneware, I recommend using a small (maximum 3½ quart) slow cooker, lightly greased. If you are using a baking dish, you will need a large (minimum 5 quart) oval slow cooker.**

MAKE AHEAD

This dish can be partially prepared before it is cooked. Complete Step 1. Transfer to a container, cover and refrigerate overnight or for up to 2 days. When you're ready to cook, continue with Step 2.

• **Works in slow cookers from 3½ to 6 quarts**

4 cups	chicken or vegetable stock or water	1 L
1 tsp	salt	5 mL
¼ tsp	freshly ground black pepper	1 mL
1¼ cups	coarse yellow cornmeal, preferably stone-ground	300 mL

1. In a saucepan over medium heat, bring stock, salt and pepper to a boil. Add cornmeal in a thin stream, stirring constantly.

2. *Direct method:* Transfer mixture to prepared slow cooker stoneware (see Tip, left). Cover and cook on Low for 1½ hours.

3. *Baking dish method:* Transfer mixture to prepared baking dish (see Tip, left). Cover with foil and secure with a string. Place dish in slow cooker stoneware and pour in enough boiling water to come 1 inch (2.5 cm) up the sides of the dish. Cover and cook on Low for 1½ hours.

VARIATION

Creamy Polenta

Substitute 2 cups (500 mL) milk for 2 cups (500 mL) of the liquid in the recipe above. If desired, stir in ½ cup (125 mL) finely chopped fresh parsley and/or 2 tbsp (25 mL) freshly grated Parmesan cheese, after the cornmeal has been added to the liquid.

Mindful Morsels

This polenta was made with 1 tsp (5 mL) of salt and regular prepared stock, which adds 382 mg of sodium per serving. To reduce the amount of sodium, do not add salt or make the polenta with water, reduced-sodium stocks or make your own homemade stock with no salt added.

Nutrients Per Serving	
Calories	116
Protein	2.4 g
Carbohydrates	24.5 g
Fat (Total)	0.5 g
Saturated Fat	0.1 g
Monounsaturated Fat	0.1 g
Polyunsaturated Fat	0.2 g
Dietary Fiber	1.5 g
Sodium	1,035 mg
Cholesterol	0 mg

Natural Wonders

GLYCEMIC INDEX

If you follow nutrition news, you've likely heard about the Glycemic Index (GI). Although it's rather complicated, in actual practice the GI is a method for assessing aspects of the dietary value of high carbohydrate foods by measuring the speed at which they are converted to blood sugar. High GI foods (bad) release glucose quickly, prompting a strong insulin response and providing short-lived bursts of energy. Those that are low on the GI (good) release glucose more slowly, providing sustained energy.

One determinant of a food's glycemic rating may be the degree to which its carbohydrates have been processed. For instance, the more finely ground a grain, the higher its glycemic rating. Conversely, the more fiber it contains, the lower its position on the GI. The GI rating of foods can be used as a dieting tool because foods that are low on the glycemic index tend to keep you from feeling hungry longer. By helping to keep blood glucose levels under control, a diet containing an abundance of low GI foods is also a valuable tool for managing diabetes. Low GI foods include soy products, beans and fruit. At 69 on the GI scale, cornmeal, like many whole grains, is a medium GI food.

Creamy Polenta with Corn and Chiles

In my opinion, polenta is a quintessential comfort food. I love it as side dish, where it is particularly apt at complementing robust stews, or as a main course topped with a traditional pasta sauce. This version, which contains the luscious combination of corn and chiles, also works as a main course on its own. I like to serve it with a tossed salad, sliced tomatoes with vinaigrette or some marinated roasted peppers.

MAKES 6 SERVINGS

- Works best in a small (3½ quart) slow cooker
- Greased slow cooker stoneware

3 cups	skim milk	750 mL
2	cloves garlic, minced	2
1 tsp	finely chopped fresh rosemary leaves or ½ tsp (2 mL) dried rosemary leaves, crumbled	5 mL
½ tsp	salt	2 mL
	Freshly ground black pepper	
¾ cup	coarse yellow cornmeal, preferably stone-ground	175 mL
1 cup	corn kernels	250 mL
1 cup	shredded Monterey Jack cheese	250 mL
½ cup	freshly grated Parmesan cheese	125 mL
1	can (4.5 oz/127 mL) diced mild green chiles	1

1. In a large saucepan over medium heat, bring milk, garlic, rosemary, salt and black pepper to taste to a boil. Gradually add polenta, in a steady stream, whisking to remove all lumps. Continue whisking until mixture begins to thicken and bubbles like lava, about 5 minutes. Add corn, Jack and Parmesan cheeses and chiles and mix well. Transfer to slow cooker stoneware.

2. Cover and cook on Low for 2 hours, until mixture is firm and just beginning to brown around the edges.

Mindful Morsels

If you're concerned about your calcium intake, including dairy products in your diet makes sense. One serving of this polenta contains about 40 percent of the daily value of this essential mineral, virtually all of which comes from the milk and cheese

Natural Wonders

CORN

Although we tend to think of corn as a vegetable, it is actually a grain, and a healthful one at that. When researchers tested the antioxidant activity of some grains, corn had the highest ranking by far. Cornmeal is produced when the kernels are dried and ground. Most of the cornmeal sold in supermarkets is fine-ground and enriched, which means that in the process of refining, most of the B vitamins, fiber, iron and healthful phytochemicals, are removed from the grain, although iron may subsequently be returned through fortification. The most nutritious and tastiest form of the grain is stone-ground, which is processed the old-fashioned way, with water-powered millstones. Stone-ground cornmeal, which is available in well-stocked supermarkets and natural food stores, retains the bran and the germ during processing and has more texture and flavor than steel-ground varieties. Whole grain yellow cornmeal contains more than twice as much magnesium, phosphorus and zinc and significantly more potassium and selenium than the de-germed variety. But because the germ contains healthful fats, among other nutrients, whole grain cornmeal spoils relatively quickly and should be stored in the refrigerator or freezer.

Nutrients Per Serving	
Calories	241
Protein	14.7 g
Carbohydrates	26.2 g
Fat (Total)	8.9 g
Saturated Fat	5.4 g
Monounsaturated Fat	2.5 g
Polyunsaturated Fat	0.4 g
Dietary Fiber	1.7 g
Sodium	693 mg
Cholesterol	26 mg

Excellent source of calcium and phosphorus.

Good source of magnesium and zinc.

Source of vitamin C.

See photo, page 186

Caramelized Onion Sauce with Whole Wheat Pasta

I love the bittersweet flavor of caramelized onions but on the stovetop caramelizing onions is a laborious process of slow, constant stirring. Made in the slow cooker, caramelized onions require almost no attention. Serve this luscious sauce over whole wheat pasta, polenta or even a bowl of steaming grits to add fiber and nutrients. Complete the meal with a tossed green salad topped with shredded carrots for a splash of healthy color.

MAKES 6 SERVINGS

TIPS

❖ **If you're pressed for time you can soften the onions on the stovetop. Heat the oil over medium heat for 30 seconds in a large skillet. Add the onions and cook, stirring, until they soften, about 5 minutes. Transfer to the stoneware and continue with Step 2.**

❖ **If you prefer a smoother sauce, combine the arugula with 1 cup (250 mL) of the tomato sauce in a food processor and pulse several times until the arugula is finely chopped and integrated into the sauce. Add to the onion mixture along with the remaining sauce.**

• **Works in slow cookers from 3½ to 6 quarts**

2 tbsp	olive oil	25 mL
6	onions, cut in half from stem to root and thinly sliced on the vertical (about 3 lbs/1.5 kg)	6
1 tsp	granulated sugar	5 mL
1 tsp	cracked black peppercorns	5 mL
4	anchovy fillets, finely chopped, or 1 tbsp (15 mL) white or red miso	4
3 cups	tomato sauce	750 mL
2	bunches arugula, stems removed and chopped (see Tips, left)	2
8 oz	whole wheat pasta	250 g

1. In slow cooker stoneware, combine olive oil and onions. Stir well to coat onions thoroughly. Cover and cook on High for 1 hour, until onions are softened (see Tip, left).

2. Add sugar and peppercorns and stir well. Place two clean tea towels, each folded in half (so you will have four layers) over top of stoneware to absorb the moisture. Cover and cook on High for 4 hours, stirring two or three times to ensure that the onions are browning evenly and replacing towels each time.

3. Remove towels, add anchovies and stir well to ensure they are well coated with oil and integrated into the onions. Add tomato sauce and arugula and stir well to blend. Cover and cook on High for 30 minutes, until mixture is hot and flavors have blended.

4. Meanwhile, cook pasta in a pot of boiling salted water until tender or according to package directions. Serve topped with sauce.

See photo, page 187

Mindful Morsels

This recipe is relatively high in sodium because it was tested using regular prepared tomato sauce. If you are concerned about your intake of sodium, use reduced-sodium tomato sauce or make your own with no salt added (see Basic Tomato Sauce, page 212).

Natural Wonders
WHOLE WHEAT PASTA

Switching from white pasta to a whole wheat version is an easy way to add fiber and other nutrients to your diet. The nutrient value of pasta is determined by the flour it is made from and most pasta is made from semolina and/or farina, which are refined white flours, from which the healthful bran and germ layers of the wheat have been removed. In North America, manufacturers restore some of the lost nutrients in the form of supplements, but much of the fiber, along with other valuable nutrients, has been lost. Pasta made from whole wheat durum semolina contains about two and a half times as much fiber as pasta made from white durum semolina. Whole wheat, which includes the bran and the germ, also contains many other nutrients. In fact, recent research is exploring the antioxidants in wheat, which appear to contain high levels of cancer-fighting phytochemicals. If you haven't tried whole wheat pasta recently but didn't care for its chewy texture and more robust flavor in the past, it might be time to give it another try. In response to consumer demands, pasta makers have been working hard to improve the taste and texture of these products, with considerable success.

Nutrients Per Serving	
Calories	305
Protein	11.7 g
Carbohydrates	57.2 g
Fat (Total)	6.2 g
Saturated Fat	0.9 g
Monounsaturated Fat	3.6 g
Polyunsaturated Fat	1.0 g
Dietary Fiber	8.9 g
Sodium	962 mg
Cholesterol	2 mg

Excellent source of vitamins B6 and K, magnesium and potassium.

Good source of vitamins A and C, folacin, phosphorus, iron and zinc.

Source of calcium.

Contains a very high amount of dietary fiber.

Vegetable Cobbler with Millet Crust

Not only is this tasty cobbler loaded with flavor, the distinctive millet crust makes it a delightfully different treat. Add a sliced tomato salad, in season, or a tossed green salad topped with shredded carrots to add color and nutrients.

MAKES 8 SERVINGS

TIPS

❖ **If using canned beans in this recipe be sure to rinse them thoroughly under cold running water to remove as much sodium as possible.**

❖ **You can substitute 1 tbsp (15 mL) dried rosemary leaves, crumbled, for the fresh.**

MAKE AHEAD

This dish can be partially prepared before it is cooked. Complete Step 2. Cover and refrigerate overnight or for up to 2 days. When you're ready to cook, continue with Steps 1 and 3.

• **Large (minimum 6 quart) slow cooker**

TOPPING

1 cup	millet (see Tips, page 26)	250 mL
3 cups	water	750 mL
	Salt and freshly ground black pepper	
1/2 cup	freshly grated Parmesan, optional	125 mL

COBBLER

1 tbsp	olive oil	15 mL
1	chunk (3 oz/90 g) pancetta, diced (see Tips, right)	1
2	onions, finely chopped	2
4	carrots, peeled and diced	4
4	stalks celery, diced	4
2 tbsp	fresh rosemary leaves, finely chopped	25 mL
4	cloves garlic, minced	4
1/2 tsp	cracked black peppercorns	2 mL
1	can (28 oz/796 mL) tomatoes, including juice, coarsely chopped	1
	Salt, optional	
1	can (14 to 19 oz/398 to 540 mL) white beans, drained and rinsed (see Tip, left), or 1 cup (250 mL) dried white beans, soaked, cooked and drained	1
12 oz	frozen sliced green beans (about 2 cups/500 mL)	375 g

1. In a saucepan over medium heat, toast millet, stirring constantly, until it crackles and releases its aroma, about 5 minutes. Add water, and salt and black pepper to taste, and bring to a boil. Reduce heat to low, cover and cook until millet is tender and all the water is absorbed, about 20 minutes. Stir in Parmesan, if using, and set aside.

2. *Cobbler:* Meanwhile, in a large skillet, heat oil over medium heat for 30 seconds. Add pancetta and cook, stirring, until crispy, about 3 minutes. Add onions, carrots and celery and cook, stirring, until vegetables are softened, about 7 minutes. Add rosemary, garlic and peppercorns and cook, stirring, for 1 minute. Add tomatoes with juice and bring to a boil. Add salt to taste, if using. Transfer to stoneware.

3. Add white beans and green beans and stir well. Spread millet evenly over the top. Cover and cook on Low for 8 to 10 hours or on High for 4 to 5 hours, until hot and bubbly.

❖ **I find that the small bit of pancetta (Italian-style cured pork) in this recipe adds so much flavor that it's worth including in keeping with "limited" consumption.**

Mindful Morsels

Limit your consumption of cured pork products, such as ham, bacon and pancetta, because they are high in sodium and may contain unhealthy nitrates.

Nutrients Per Serving	
Calories	285
Protein	11.2 g
Carbohydrates	40.2 g
Fat (Total)	9.6 g
Saturated Fat	4.4 g
Monounsaturated Fat	5.4 g
Polyunsaturated Fat	1.7 g
Dietary Fiber	8.8 g
Sodium	507 mg
Cholesterol	12 mg

Natural Wonders

WHOLE GRAINS

Although we've long known that whole grains are good for us, until recently we haven't realized how healthy they actually are. Recent research by Dr. Rui Hai Liu of Cornell University shows that the phytonutrients in whole grains are much more powerful than previously recognized. Traditionally, scientists have only studied the "free" forms of phytochemicals, such as phenolics, which are quickly absorbed by the bloodstream. Dr. Liu and his colleagues found almost all the phenolics in whole grains are in "bound" form, which means they must be digested before they can be absorbed. Consequently, the antioxidant activity of whole grains has been greatly underestimated. This may explain why clinical trials using isolated supplements, such as fiber, have not consistently shown a reduction in colon cancer, although populations eating high-fiber whole grains have lower rates of the disease. Dr. Liu believes that the wholeness of the food is exactly what gives it cancer-fighting power. The healthful benefits of whole grains are derived from the interaction of all the nutrients they contain.

Excellent source of vitamins A and K and magnesium.

Good source of vitamins C and B6, calcium, phosphorus, potassium, folacin, iron and zinc.

Contains a very high amount of dietary fiber.

Pumpkin and Rice Casserole with Mushrooms

This simple casserole makes a nice weeknight dinner. Serve it with a green salad or sliced tomatoes in season. It can also be used as a hearty side dish.

MAKES 6 SERVINGS

MAKE AHEAD
This dish can be partially prepared before it is cooked. Complete Step 1. Cover and refrigerate overnight or up to 2 days. When you're ready to cook, continue with Step 2.

● **Large (minimum 5 quart) slow cooker**

1 tbsp	olive oil	15 mL
2	onions, diced	2
2	stalks celery, diced	2
2	carrots, peeled and diced	2
2	cloves garlic, minced	2
1 tsp	dried thyme leaves, crumbled	5 mL
1/2 tsp	salt	2 mL
1/2 tsp	cracked black peppercorns	2 mL
12 oz	cremini mushrooms, trimmed and quartered	375 g
2 cups	long-grain brown rice	500 mL
1	can (28 oz/796 mL) diced tomatoes, including juice	1
2 cups	vegetable stock	500 mL
4 cups	cubed (1/2 inch/1 cm) peeled pumpkin or orange or yellow squash	1 L
1	chipotle pepper in adobo sauce, minced	1
2 cups	shredded reduced-fat Monterey Jack cheese, optional	500 mL

1. In a large skillet, heat oil over medium heat for 30 seconds. Add onions, celery and carrots and cook, stirring, until carrots are softened, about 7 minutes. Add garlic, thyme, salt and peppercorns and cook, stirring, for 1 minute. Add mushrooms and toss to coat. Add rice and toss to coat. Add tomatoes with juice and vegetable stock and bring to a boil. Transfer to slow cooker stoneware. Stir in pumpkin.

2. Place one clean tea towel, folded in half (so you will have two layers) across the top of slow cooker stoneware, to absorb moisture. Cover and cook on Low for 7 to 8 hours or on High for 4 hours, until rice is tender and liquid is absorbed. Remove tea towel. Stir in chile pepper and sprinkle cheese over top of mixture, if using. Cover and cook on High for 20 to 25 minutes, until flavors meld and cheese is melted.

Mindful Morsels

Like carrots, carotenoid-rich pumpkin helps to keep your eyes healthy.

Natural Wonders
FRUITS AND VEGETABLES

Low in saturated fat and rich in a variety of nutritious vegetables, this casserole really fits the bill as healthy eating. If you're serious about preventing heart disease, add some fresh fruit or berries for dessert. Researchers at Tufts University who followed a group of men for 18 years found that increasing fruit and vegetable consumption while simultaneously reducing the amount of saturated fat they consumed provided more protection against dying from heart disease than either strategy alone.

Nutrients Per Serving	
Calories	343
Protein	9.6 g
Carbohydrates	68.5 g
Fat (Total)	4.6 g
Saturated Fat	0.8 g
Monounsaturated Fat	2.4 g
Polyunsaturated Fat	1.0 g
Dietary Fiber	8.0 g
Sodium	780 mg
Cholesterol	0 mg

Excellent source of vitamins A, B6, phosphorus, magnesium and potassium.

Good source of vitamins C and K, folacin and zinc.

Source of calcium.

Contains a very high amount of dietary fiber.

Shrimp 'n' Grits

I first tasted this delectable combination many years ago in Charleston, South Carolina, and I haven't been able to get enough of it since. Serve this to guests for a special lunch with a crisp green salad or fresh asparagus in season. Or just it enjoy it with your family, as I often do.

MAKES 4 SERVINGS

TIP

❖ **Whole grain stone-ground grits (the tastiest and most nutritious kind) take a long time to cook. Preparing them on the stovetop requires about 2 hours of attention and frequent stirring. If, like me, you're a grits lover, having a slow cooker is very advantageous. Once you put them in the stoneware and turn the appliance on, you can forget about them until they are done.**

- Works best in a small (3½ quart) slow cooker
- Lightly greased slow cooker stoneware

GRITS

4 cups	water	1 L
1 tbsp	olive oil	15 mL
½ tsp	salt	2 mL
½ tsp	freshly ground black pepper	2 mL
1 cup	grits (not instant, preferably stone-ground) (see Tip, left)	250 mL
1 tbsp	olive oil	15 mL
2	cloves garlic, minced	2
1 lb	medium shrimp, peeled and deveined	500 g
¼ tsp	cayenne pepper	1 mL
1 tbsp	freshly squeezed lemon juice	15 mL
2 cups	tomato sauce	500 mL

1. *Grits:* In a saucepan over medium heat, bring water, olive oil, salt and pepper to boil. Gradually add grits, stirring constantly until smooth and blended. Continue cooking and stirring until grits are slightly thickened, about 4 minutes. Transfer to prepared stoneware. Cover and cook on High for 4 hours or on Low for 8 hours, until set.

2. In a skillet, heat oil over medium heat. Add garlic and cook, stirring, for 1 minute. Add shrimp and cook, stirring, until shrimp firm up and turn pink, about 3 minutes. Sprinkle with cayenne and toss. Add lemon juice and toss. Add tomato sauce and bring to a boil.

3. To serve, spoon grits onto a warm platter and top with shrimp sauce.

Mindful Morsels

This recipe is high in sodium, most of which comes from the prepared tomato sauce. If you are concerned about your sodium intake, use reduced-sodium tomato sauce or, better still, make your own with no salt added (see Basic Tomato Sauce, page 212). You can also omit the added salt when preparing the grits.

Natural Wonders

A HEALTHY DIET

As Dr. Walter Willet, chair of the Department of Nutrition at the Harvard School of Public Health, says in his excellent book *Eat, Drink and Be Healthy*, "No single food will make or break good health." Research confirms it is the overall quality of your diet that matters. A pattern of healthy eating includes plenty of high-fiber plant-based foods such as fruits, vegetables, including legumes, and whole grains. Evidence suggests that consumption of red meat and processed meats should be limited. Not only has heavy consumption of red meat and processed meats been linked with an increased risk of colon cancer, a Tufts University study found that people who consumed a "meat and potatoes" diet were six times more likely to gain weight as they aged, compared with those who ate more fruits, vegetables and whole grains. Over the long term, keeping your weight under control and following a healthy diet appears to lower the risk of cancer and other chronic diseases.

Nutrients Per Serving	
Calories	333
Protein	22.5 g
Carbohydrates	41.6 g
Fat (Total)	8.9 g
Saturated Fat	1.3 g
Monounsaturated Fat	5.3 g
Polyunsaturated Fat	1.4 g
Dietary Fiber	2.5 g
Sodium	1,156 mg
Cholesterol	129 mg

Good source of vitamins A, B6, B12 and K, magnesium, potassium, iron and phosphorus.

Source of vitamin C.

Contains a moderate amount of dietary fiber.

See photo, page 196

Pasta with Syracuse Sauce

Serve this rich and delicious sauce over hot whole wheat pasta or polenta for a great Italian-themed meal. Add a simple green salad and crusty whole grain rolls to complete the meal.

MAKES 6 SERVINGS

TIP

❖ **You can't taste the anchovies in this sauce, but they add depth to the flavor. If you're a vegetarian, you can omit the anchovies and enhance the flavor of this sauce by adding 1 tbsp (15 mL) white or red miso along with the parsley.**

MAKE AHEAD

This dish can be partially prepared before it is cooked. Complete Steps 1, 2 and 3. Cover and refrigerate overnight or for up to 2 days. When you're ready to cook, continue with Step 4.

• **Works in slow cookers from 3½ to 6 quarts**

1	large eggplant, peeled and cut into 2-inch (5 cm) cubes	1
1 tsp	salt	5 mL
2 tbsp	olive oil, divided (approx.)	25 mL
2	onions, finely chopped	2
4	cloves garlic, minced	4
4	anchovy fillets, finely chopped, optional (see Tip, left)	4
1	can (28 oz/796 mL) tomatoes, including juice, coarsely chopped	1
1 tbsp	tomato paste	15 mL
2	roasted red bell peppers, diced	2
½ cup	black olives, pitted and chopped (about 20 olives)	125 mL
½ cup	finely chopped parsley leaves	125 mL
2 tbsp	capers, drained and minced	25 mL
	Cooked whole wheat pasta or polenta	

1. In a colander over a sink, combine eggplant and salt. Toss and let stand for 30 minutes. Rinse thoroughly under cold running water. Lay a clean tea towel on a work surface. Working in batches over the sink and using your hands, squeeze liquid out of the eggplant. Transfer to the tea towel. When batches are complete, roll the towel up and press down to remove remaining liquid.

2. In a nonstick skillet, heat 1 tbsp (15 mL) of the oil over medium heat for 30 seconds. Add sweated eggplant, in batches, and cook until browned, adding more oil as necessary. Transfer to slow cooker stoneware.

3. Add onions to pan, adding oil, if necessary, and cook, stirring, until softened, about 3 minutes. Add garlic and anchovies, if using, and cook, stirring, for 1 minute. Add

See photo, page 197

tomatoes with juice and tomato paste and bring to a boil. Transfer to slow cooker stoneware.

4. Place a clean tea towel folded in half (so you will have two layers) over top of the stoneware to absorb moisture. Cover and cook on Low for 8 hours or on High for 4 hours, until hot and bubbly. Add roasted red peppers, olives, parsley and capers. Stir well. Cover and cook on High for 20 minutes, until heated through. To serve, ladle over hot cooked pasta or polenta.

Mindful Morsels

A serving of this sauce contains 117 percent of the daily value of vitamin C. Over half comes from the red peppers.

Natural Wonders
ANTIOXIDANTS

While enjoying this tasty sauce think of it as a potent antioxidant cocktail that is helping your body defend itself against aging, cancer, heart disease and numerous other diseases. Antioxidants are a group of nutrients that protect your body against the harmful effects of free radicals, much like rust-proofing protects your car from rust. The best-known antioxidants are vitamins C and E and beta-carotene, but minerals such as selenium and manganese also pack significant antioxidant punch. Scientists are only beginning to learn about these fascinating compounds, and new ones are constantly being discovered. While consumption of cruciferous vegetables, such as broccoli and cauliflower, has been linked with reduced risk of cancer, the antioxidants in other vegetables also seem to have a protective effect. For instance, eggplant is rich in phenolic compounds, onions contain the flavonoid, quercetin, and tomatoes and bell peppers contain lycopene, all of which appear to have anti-carcinogenic properties. Interestingly, research suggests that the antioxidants in food work together as part of the whole food. Some recent studies indicate that taking antioxidants as single agents does not produce similar benefits.

Nutrients Per Serving	
Calories	127
Protein	3.0 g
Carbohydrates	17.7 g
Fat (Total)	6.2 g
Saturated Fat	0.9 g
Monounsaturated Fat	4.3 g
Polyunsaturated Fat	0.7 g
Dietary Fiber	4.5 g
Sodium	448 mg
Cholesterol	0 mg

Excellent source of vitamins C and K.

Good source of vitamins A and B6 and potassium.

Source of iron.

Contains a high amount of dietary fiber.

Greek-Style Beans and Barley

Here's a tasty casserole the whole family can enjoy. Add a simple green or shredded carrot salad for a great weekday meal.

MAKES 6 SERVINGS

TIPS

❖ **If possible use golden or yellow zucchini, which has more flavor than the green version. If you're not peeling it, scrub the skin thoroughly with a vegetable brush.**

❖ **If you prefer, complete Step 3 while the zucchini sweats. When finished, wipe skillet clean and complete Step 2.**

MAKE AHEAD

This dish can be partially prepared before it is cooked. Complete Steps 1 through 3. Cover and refrigerate separately overnight or for up to 2 days. When you're ready to cook, continue with Step 4.

• **Works in slow cookers from 3½ to 6 quarts**

2	zucchini, thinly sliced into ½-inch (1 cm) slices (see Tips, left)	2
½ tsp	salt	2 mL
2 tbsp	olive oil, divided	25 mL
4	cloves garlic, minced	4
	Freshly ground black pepper	
2	onions, finely chopped	2
2 tsp	dried oregano leaves, crumbled	10 mL
½ tsp	cracked black peppercorns	2 mL
1	can (28 oz/796 mL) tomatoes, including juice, coarsely chopped	1
2 tbsp	tomato paste	25 mL
2 cups	vegetable stock	500 mL
1 cup	whole (hulled) or pot barley (see Mindful Morsels, page 65)	250 mL
3 cups	frozen sliced green beans	750 mL
	Crumbled feta cheese, optional	

1. In a colander over a sink, combine zucchini and salt. Toss well and set aside for 30 minutes to allow zucchini to sweat. Rinse thoroughly. Pat dry with paper towel.

2. In a skillet, heat 1 tbsp (15 mL) of the oil over medium heat for 30 seconds. Add zucchini and cook, stirring, for 3 minutes. Add garlic and cook, stirring, until zucchini softens and just begins to brown, about 4 minutes. Season to taste with freshly ground black pepper. Transfer to a bowl, cover and refrigerate.

3. In same skillet, heat remaining oil over medium heat for 30 seconds. Add onions and cook, stirring, until softened, about 3 minutes. Add oregano and peppercorns and cook, stirring, for 1 minute. Add tomatoes with juice, tomato paste and vegetable stock and bring to a boil. Transfer to slow cooker stoneware.

4. Add barley and green beans and stir well. Cover and cook on Low for 6 hours or on High for 3 hours, until barley is tender. Add reserved zucchini and stir well. Cover and cook on High for 15 minutes, until zucchini is heated through. Sprinkle with crumbled feta to taste, if using.

VARIATION

Greek-Style Bean and Potato Stew

Omit vegetable stock and tomato paste. Substitute 2 medium potatoes, peeled and diced, for the barley. Serve over orzo, whole wheat couscous, rice or another grain.

Mindful Morsels

Zucchini is a member of the summer squash family. While not a nutrient-dense vegetable, it does contain small amounts of nutrients such as manganese, vitamin C, magnesium and potassium.

Natural Wonders

FROZEN VEGETABLES

There's no question that freshly picked locally grown vegetables provide optimum nutrition and taste, but sometimes frozen vegetables may be preferable to fresh. During winter, for instance, fresh produce is likely to have traveled several days before it arrives in your city. Then it sits in a store until purchased and once again in your refrigerator until it is used, all the while losing nutrients and flavor. On the other hand, vegetables picked at the peak of ripeness and quickly frozen are likely to have as many nutrients as their "fresh" counterparts and taste just as good. Green beans are a case in point. I always have a bag in the freezer so I can add them to recipes. They contain valuable nutrients: vitamins K and C, a selection of the B vitamins, including folacin, and the minerals manganese, iron and magnesium. They also contain fiber.

Nutrients Per Serving	
Calories	227
Protein	5.0 g
Carbohydrates	42.9 g
Fat (Total)	5.3 g
Saturated Fat	0.8 g
Monounsaturated Fat	3.4 g
Polyunsaturated Fat	0.8 g
Dietary Fiber	6.6 g
Sodium	472 mg
Cholesterol	0 mg

Excellent source of potassium.

Good source of vitamins C, B6 and K, folacin, magnesium, iron and zinc.

Source of vitamin A and phosphorus.

Contains a very high amount of dietary fiber.

Barley and Sweet Potato Chili

This unusual chili has great flavor and with the addition of optional toppings, such as sliced roasted pepper strips (either bottled or freshly roasted) and cilantro, it can be enhanced and varied to suit many tastes. I like to serve this with a simple green salad topped with sliced avocado.

MAKES 6 SERVINGS

TIPS

❖ **Use your favorite chili powder blend in this recipe or, if you prefer, ground ancho, New Mexico or guadillo peppers.**

❖ **I prefer the slightly smoky flavor that a chipotle pepper in adobo sauce lends to this recipe, but it's not to everyone's taste. If you're unfamiliar with the flavor, add just half a pepper and a bit of the sauce. If you're a heat seeker, use a whole one and increase the quantity of adobo sauce.**

MAKE AHEAD

This dish can be partially prepared before it is cooked. Complete Steps 1 and 2. Cover and refrigerate overnight or for up to 2 days. When you're ready to cook, continue with Step 3.

• **Large (minimum 5 quart) slow cooker**

1 tbsp	cumin seeds	15 mL
1 tbsp	olive oil	15 mL
2	onions, finely chopped	2
2	cloves garlic, minced	2
1 tsp	dried oregano leaves, crumbled	5 mL
1 tsp	salt	5 mL
1/2 tsp	cracked black peppercorns	2 mL
1/2 cup	whole (hulled) or pot barley (see Mindful Morsels, 65)	125 mL
1	can (28 oz/796 mL) tomatoes, including juice, coarsely crushed	1
1 cup	vegetable stock	250 mL
2	medium sweet potatoes, peeled and cut into 1-inch (2.5 cm) cubes	2
1	can (14 to 19 oz/398 to 540 mL) red kidney or black beans, drained and rinsed, or 1 cup (250 mL) dried red kidney or black beans, soaked, cooked and drained (see page 250)	1
1 tbsp	chili powder, dissolved in 2 tbsp (25 mL) lime juice (see Tips, left)	15 mL
1	jalapeño pepper, minced, or 1/2 to 1 chipotle pepper in adobo sauce, minced (see Tips, left)	1
1	green bell pepper, diced, optional	1
	Sliced roasted bell peppers, optional	
	Finely chopped cilantro	

1. In a large dry skillet over medium heat, toast cumin seeds, stirring, until fragrant and they just begin to brown, about 3 minutes. Immediately transfer to a mortar or spice grinder and grind. Set aside.

2. In same skillet, heat oil over medium heat for 30 seconds. Add onions and cook, stirring, until softened, about 3 minutes. Add garlic, oregano, salt, peppercorns and reserved cumin and cook, stirring, for 1 minute. Add barley and stir well. Add tomatoes with juice and bring to a boil. Transfer to slow cooker stoneware. Add vegetable stock, sweet potatoes and beans.

3. Cover and cook on Low for 6 to 8 hours or on High for 3 to 4 hours, until barley and sweet potatoes are tender. Stir in chili powder solution, jalapeño pepper and bell pepper, if using. Cover and cook on High for 20 to 30 minutes, until flavors have melded and bell pepper is tender. To serve, ladle into soup plates and garnish with roasted pepper strips, if using, and cilantro.

Mindful Morsels

The nutrient analysis on this recipe was done using pearl barley. To add fiber and nutrients, be sure to use the whole (also known as hulled) barley called for in the recipe.

Natural Wonders
WHOLE GRAINS

Dr. Walter Willet, Chairman of the Department of Nutrition at the Harvard School of Public Health, has noted that regular consumption of whole grains is as important to good health as maintaining a healthy weight and avoiding unhealthy fats. Whole grains contain fiber and many valuable nutrients, which enriched grain products are lacking. The committee that updated the U.S. Dietary Guidelines pointed out that whole grains contain at least 18 nutrients, including B vitamins, magnesium, iron, zinc, vitamin E, phytoestrogens and antioxidants. After a decade of studying the health impact of refined and whole grain foods, Dr. Willet and his colleagues concluded that a diet rich in whole grain foods promotes good health and protects against a variety of chronic diseases.

Nutrients Per Serving	
Calories	217
Protein	6.5 g
Carbohydrates	42.6 g
Fat (Total)	3.4 g
Saturated Fat	0.5 g
Monounsaturated Fat	1.9 g
Polyunsaturated Fat	0.7 g
Dietary Fiber	7.3 g
Sodium	866 mg
Cholesterol	0 mg

Excellent source of vitamin A.

Good source of vitamins C and B6, magnesium, folacin, potassium and iron.

Source of phosphorus.

Contains a very high amount of dietary fiber.

Tamale Pie with Chili Millet Crust

This tasty pie is a great dish for après ski or to come home to after a brisk day outdoors. Add a tossed green salad, crusty rolls and pass the salsa at the table.

MAKES 8 SERVINGS

TIPS

❖ **If you don't care for much heat use the jalapeño pepper. Heat seekers may prefer a whole chipotle in adobo sauce.**

❖ **To toast cumin seeds: Place seeds in a skillet over medium heat, stirring, until fragrant and they just begin to brown, about 3 minutes. Immediately transfer to a mortar or spice grinder and grind.**

MAKE AHEAD

This dish can be partially prepared before it is cooked. Complete Step 1. Cover and refrigerate overnight or for up to 2 days. When you're ready to cook, continue with Steps 2 through 4.

• **Large (minimum 6 quart) slow cooker**

1 tbsp	olive oil	15 mL
2	onions, finely chopped	2
4	stalks celery, thinly sliced	4
4	cloves garlic, minced	4
2 tsp	dried oregano leaves, crumbled	10 mL
1 tsp	salt	5 mL
1/2 tsp	cracked black peppercorns	2 mL
1 tbsp	cumin seeds, toasted (see Tips, left)	15 mL
2	cans (each 14 to 19 oz/398 to 540 mL) black or pinto beans, drained and rinsed (see Mindful Morsels, right)	2
1	can (28 oz/796 mL) tomatoes, drained and coarsely chopped	1
2 cups	frozen corn kernels	500 mL
1	green bell pepper, diced	1
1	jalapeño pepper or chipotle pepper in adobo sauce, diced (see Tips, left)	1
	Salsa, optional	

TOPPING

1 cup	millet	250 mL
3 cups	water	750 mL
	Salt and freshly ground black pepper	
1 cup	reduced-fat shredded Monterey Jack cheese	250 mL
1	can (4.5 oz/127 mL) chopped mild green chiles, including juice	1

1. In a skillet, heat oil over medium heat for 30 seconds. Add onions and celery and cook, stirring, until celery is softened, about 5 minutes. Add garlic, oregano, salt, peppercorns and toasted cumin and cook, stirring, for 1 minute. Add beans and tomatoes and bring to a boil. Transfer to stoneware.

2. Add corn and stir well. Cover and cook on Low for 3 hours or on High for 1½ hours.

3. *Topping:* In a saucepan over medium heat, toast millet, stirring constantly, until it crackles and releases its aroma, about 5 minutes. Add water, salt and black pepper to taste, and bring to a boil. Reduce heat to low, cover and cook until millet is tender and all of the water is absorbed, about 20 minutes. Stir in cheese and chiles with juice and set aside.

4. Add bell pepper and jalapeño pepper to slow cooker stoneware and stir well. Spread millet topping evenly over pie. Place two clean tea towels, each folded in half (so you will have four layers) over top of stoneware to absorb moisture. Cover and cook on High for 1½ to 2 hours, until topping is set.

Mindful Morsels

The nutrient analysis on this recipe was done using canned beans, which are high in sodium. If you are concerned about your sodium intake, cook your own (see Basic Beans, page 250) with no salt added.

Natural Wonders
VEGETABLE PROTEIN

Traditional thinking held that the best — i.e. "complete" — protein came from meat and that vegetarian diets were less nutritious. Now we know this isn't true. Some vegetable proteins, such as quinoa and soy, are complete. And it has become clear that combining a variety of vegetables and/or whole grains (for instance, the beans and millet in this recipe) can produce a complete protein.

Complete proteins contain all nine of the essential amino acids provided by food. Meat, fish and dairy products qualify but most vegetables and grains do not. Until relatively recently, nutritionists thought it was necessary to consume all the essential amino acids at one meal, but after studying vegetarians it became clear that eating a variety of vegetables and whole grains throughout the day will provide your body with an adequate supply of these essential nutrients.

Nutrients Per Serving	
Calories	294
Protein	14.5 g
Carbohydrates	48.7 g
Fat (Total)	5.8 g
Saturated Fat	1.8 g
Monounsaturated Fat	2.3 g
Polyunsaturated Fat	1.0 g
Dietary Fiber	10.4 g
Sodium	976 mg
Cholesterol	8 mg

Excellent source of vitamin C, folacin and magnesium.

Good source of vitamins B6 and K, potassium, phosphorus, iron and zinc.

Source of vitamin A.

Contains a very high amount of dietary fiber.

See photo, page 206

Squash with Quinoa and Apricots

Banish the blahs with this robust combination of fruits, vegetables and a nutritious whole grain seasoned with ginger, orange and a hint of cinnamon. In season, accompany with a serving of watercress tossed in a simple vinaigrette.

MAKES 8 SERVINGS

TIPS

❖ **If you prefer, use frozen chopped butternut squash in this recipe. Reduce the quantity to 2 cups (500 mL).**

❖ **Be sure to rinse the quinoa thoroughly before using because some quinoa has a resinous coating called saponin, which needs to be rinsed off. To ensure your quinoa is saponin-free, before cooking fill a bowl with warm water and swish the kernels around, then transfer to a sieve and rinse thoroughly under cold running water.**

MAKE AHEAD

This dish can be partially prepared before it is cooked. Complete Steps 1 and 2. Cover and refrigerate overnight or for up to 2 days. When you're ready to cook, continue with Steps 3 and 4.

• **Works in slow cookers from 3½ to 6 quarts**

1 tbsp	cumin seeds	15 mL
1 tbsp	olive oil	15 mL
2	onions, finely chopped	2
2	cloves garlic, minced	2
1 tbsp	minced gingerroot	15 mL
2 tsp	finely grated orange zest	10 mL
1	piece (2 inches/5 cm) cinnamon stick	1
1 tsp	turmeric	5 mL
1 tsp	salt	5 mL
½ tsp	cracked black peppercorns	2 mL
1 cup	vegetable stock	250 mL
½ cup	orange juice	125 mL
4 cups	cubed (1 inch/2.5 cm) peeled squash (see Tips, left)	1 L
2	apples, peeled, cored and sliced	2
½ cup	chopped dried apricots	125 mL
1½ cups	quinoa, rinsed	375 mL

1. In a large dry skillet over medium heat, toast cumin seeds, stirring, until fragrant and they just begin to brown, about 3 minutes. Immediately transfer to a mortar or spice grinder and grind. Set aside.

2. In same skillet, heat oil over medium heat for 30 seconds. Add onions and cook, stirring, until softened, about 3 minutes. Add garlic, gingerroot, orange zest, cinnamon stick, turmeric, salt, peppercorns and reserved cumin seeds and cook, stirring, for 1 minute. Add vegetable stock and orange juice and bring to a boil. Transfer to slow cooker stoneware.

See photo, page 207

3. Add squash, apples and apricots to stoneware and stir well. Cover and cook on Low for 6 hours or on High for 3 hours, until vegetables are tender.

4. In a pot, bring 3 cups (750 mL) of water to a boil. Add quinoa in a steady stream, stirring to prevent lumps from forming, and return to a boil. Cover, reduce heat to low and simmer for 15 minutes until tender and liquid is absorbed. Add to slow cooker and stir well. Serve immediately.

Mindful Morsels

Apricots contain vitamins A and C and fiber, as well as the phytochemicals beta-carotene and lycopene. When buying dried apricots be sure to source them at a natural foods store to ensure they have not been treated with sulphates. They may not look as pretty, but it's unlikely they will produce an allergic reaction.

Natural Wonders

QUINOA

Quinoa is extremely nutritious — so nutritious, in fact, that it's been called a "supergrain." Originally grown in the Andes this "grain of the Incas" has recently been rediscovered. It is one of the few vegetable sources of complete protein, including lysine, not commonly found in grains. It is an excellent source of iron (¼ cup/50 mL uncooked quinoa, a typical serving, provides about 4 mg of iron) and is a source of fiber. Quinoa also contains potassium, folacin and a range of B vitamins, as well as magnesium and zinc. Like all whole grains, it is a source of beneficial phytochemicals. Quinoa contains saponins, which appear to reduce the risk of cancer and heart disease.

Nutrients Per Serving	
Calories	231
Protein	5.9 g
Carbohydrates	45.8 g
Fat (Total)	4.1 g
Saturated Fat	0.5 g
Monounsaturated Fat	1.9 g
Polyunsaturated Fat	1.0 g
Dietary Fiber	5.4 g
Sodium	425 mg
Cholesterol	0 mg

Excellent source of vitamin A, magnesium potassium and iron.

Good source of vitamin C and phosphorus.

Source of vitamin B6.

Contains a high amount of dietary fiber.

Mushroom Tomato Sauce

One way of adding variety to your diet is by expanding the kinds of grains you use with sauces traditionally served with pasta. I like to serve this classic sauce over polenta or grits, as well as whole wheat pasta. Accompanied by a tossed green salad, it makes a great weeknight meal.

MAKES 6 SERVINGS

TIP

❖ **For an easy and delicious meal, make this sauce ahead of time and refrigerate. Prepare 1 batch of Basic or Creamy Polenta (see page 182), and just before they are ready to serve, reheat Mushroom Tomato Sauce. To serve, spoon polenta onto a warm plate and top with the sauce. Sprinkle with grated Parmesan, if desired.**

MAKE AHEAD

This dish can be partially prepared before it is cooked. Complete Step 1. Cover and refrigerate overnight or for up 2 days. When you're ready to cook, continue with Step 2.

• **Works in slow cookers from 3½ to 6 quarts**

1 tbsp	olive oil	15 mL
1	onion, finely chopped	1
2	stalks celery, diced	2
4	cloves garlic, minced	4
1 tbsp	finely chopped fresh rosemary or 2 tsp (10 mL) dried rosemary leaves, crumbled	15 mL
1 tsp	salt	5 mL
½ tsp	cracked black peppercorns	2 mL
8 oz	cremini mushrooms, sliced	250 g
½ cup	dry white wine or chicken or vegetable stock	125 mL
1 tbsp	tomato paste	15 mL
1	can (28 oz/796 mL) tomatoes, including juice, coarsely chopped	1
	Crushed red pepper flakes, optional	
	Whole wheat pasta, polenta or grits	
	Freshly grated Parmesan cheese, optional	

1. In a skillet, heat oil over medium heat for 30 seconds. Add onion and celery and cook, stirring, until celery is softened, about 5 minutes. Add garlic, rosemary, salt and peppercorns and cook, stirring, for 1 minute. Add mushrooms and toss to coat. Add wine and cook for 1 minute. Stir in tomato paste and tomatoes with juice and bring to a boil. Transfer to slow cooker stoneware.

2. Place a tea towel folded in half (so you will have two layers) over top of the stoneware to absorb moisture. Cover and cook on Low for 6 hours or on High for 3 hours, until hot and bubbly. Stir in pepper flakes, if using. Serve over cooked whole wheat pasta, polenta or grits. Garnish with Parmesan to taste, if using.

VARIATIONS

Vegetarian Bolognese

In a bowl, combine 1 cup (250 mL) bulgur and 2 cups (500 mL) boiling water. Set aside for 20 minutes until water is absorbed. Add to sauce along with tomatoes.

Classic Bolognese

Cook 1 lb (500 g) extra-lean ground beef, until no longer pink, along with onion. If desired, add 2 tbsp (25 mL) whipping (35%) cream, after the sauce has finished cooking.

Double Mushroom Tomato Sauce

Soak 1 package (½ oz/14 g) dried porcini mushrooms in 1 cup (250 mL) hot water for 20 minutes. Drain, pat dry and chop finely. Discard soaking liquid. Add mushrooms to pan along with peppercorns and use stock rather than wine.

Mindful Morsels

Rosemary contains flavonoids as well as substances that may help stimulate the immune system, increase circulation and improve digestion.

Natural Wonders

HYPERTENSION

Over the past decade, hypertension rates in the United States increased by about 8 percent, and the disease now affects about one-third of U.S. adults age 18 and older. Given the rising rates of childhood obesity, hypertension is also becoming a concern for young people.

Hypertension is a major risk factor for heart disease and stroke. It can also lead to kidney damage. You can reduce your chances of developing the disease by becoming physically active, losing excess weight, limiting your consumption of alcoholic beverages and cutting back on salt and other forms of sodium. A healthy diet can also increase the odds that you will be able to keep your blood pressure under control. The Dietary Approaches to Stop Hypertension (DASH) study found that a diet rich in fruits, vegetables and low-fat dairy products, which restricted the total amount of fat, particularly saturated fat, could significantly lower blood pressure.

Nutrients Per Serving	
Calories	67
Protein	2.5 g
Carbohydrates	10.5 g
Fat (Total)	2.6 g
Saturated Fat	0.4 g
Monounsaturated Fat	1.7 g
Polyunsaturated Fat	0.3 g
Dietary Fiber	2.3 g
Sodium	597 mg
Cholesterol	0 mg

Good source of vitamin C and potassium.

Source of vitamins A, B6 and K.

Contains a moderate amount of dietary fiber.

Basic Tomato Sauce

Not only is this sauce tasty and easy to make, it is also much lower in sodium than prepared sauces. It keeps covered for up to 1 week in the refrigerator and can be frozen for up to 6 months.

MAKES ABOUT 8 CUPS (2 L)

TIP

❖ **If you are in a hurry, you can soften the vegetables on the stovetop. Heat oil in a skillet for 30 seconds. Add onions and carrots and cook, stirring, until carrots are softened, about 7 minutes. Add garlic, thyme and peppercorns and cook, stirring, for 1 minute. Transfer to slow cooker stoneware. Add tomatoes with juice and continue with Step 2.**

• **Works in slow cookers from 3½ to 6 quarts**

1 tbsp	olive oil	15 mL
2	onions, finely chopped	2
2	carrots, peeled and diced	2
4	cloves garlic, minced	4
1 tsp	dried thyme leaves, crumbled	5 mL
½ tsp	cracked black peppercorns	2 mL
2	cans (each 28 oz/796 mL) tomatoes, including juice, coarsely chopped	2
	Salt, optional	

1. In slow cooker stoneware, combine olive oil, onions and carrots. Stir well to ensure vegetables are coated with oil. Cover and cook on High for 1 hour, until vegetables are softened. Add garlic, thyme and peppercorns. Stir well. Stir in tomatoes with juice.

2. Place a tea towel folded in half (so you have two layers) over top of stoneware to absorb moisture. Cover and cook on Low for 6 to 8 hours or on High for 3 to 4 hours, until sauce is thickened and flavors are melded. Season to taste with salt, if using.

Natural Wonders

TOMATOES

Low in calories, tomatoes are extremely nutritious. They contain vitamins A and C, potassium and folacin and are loaded with phytochemicals. Tomatoes contain carotenoids: beta-carotene, alpha-carotene, lutein and lycopene, a powerful antioxidant with cancer-fighting properties. Tomato sauce is one of the best ways to consume lycopene because cooking tomatoes, especially with oil, makes this nutrient more available to the body. A number of studies link the consumption of tomato products with a significantly reduced risk (about one-third) of prostate cancer. Consumption of lycopene may also help prevent colon, stomach, breast and lung cancers. Since your body can't produce lycopene, you need to eat foods rich in this phytonutrient to obtain the benefits, and because lycopene is fat soluble, it needs to be consumed with a bit of dietary fat to be absorbed by your body.

Nutrients Per 2 Cups (500 mL)	
Calories	149
Protein	5.0 g
Carbohydrates	27.5 g
Fat (Total)	4.1 g
Saturated Fat	0.6 g
Monounsaturated Fat	2.6 g
Polyunsaturated Fat	0.6 g
Dietary Fiber	5.2 g
Sodium	621 mg
Cholesterol	0 mg

Excellent source of vitamins A, C, B6 and K.

Good source of folacin, magnesium and iron.

Source of calcium and phosphorus.

Contains a high amount of dietary fiber.

Just Veggies

Mixed Vegetables in Spicy Peanut Sauce, see recipe overleaf

Mixed Vegetables in Spicy Peanut Sauce

Here's one way to get kids to eat their vegetables, so long as they don't have peanut allergies — cook them in a spicy sauce made from peanut butter and add a garnish of chopped roasted peanuts. All you need to add is some steaming rice or brown rice noodles.

MAKES 8 SERVINGS

TIP

❖ **If you prefer, substitute fresh green beans for the frozen. Blanch in boiling water for 4 minutes after the water returns to a boil and add to the slow cooker along with the cabbage.**

MAKE AHEAD

This dish can be partially prepared before it is cooked. Complete Step 1. Cover and refrigerate overnight or for up to 2 days. When you're ready to cook, continue with Steps 2 and 3.

• **Works in slow cookers from 3½ to 6 quarts**

1 tbsp	olive oil	15 mL
2	onions, finely chopped	2
6	medium carrots, peeled and thinly sliced (about 4 cups/1 L)	6
4	stalks celery, diced (about 2 cups/500 mL)	4
2 tbsp	minced gingerroot	25 mL
4	cloves garlic, minced	4
½ tsp	cracked black peppercorns	2 mL
1 cup	vegetable stock	250 mL
3 cups	frozen sliced green beans (see Tip, left)	750 mL
½ cup	smooth natural peanut butter	125 mL
2 tbsp	soy sauce	25 mL
2 tbsp	freshly squeezed lemon juice	25 mL
1 tbsp	pure maple syrup	15 mL
2 tsp	Thai red curry paste	10 mL
4 cups	shredded Napa cabbage	1 L
2 cups	bean sprouts	500 mL
½ cup	finely chopped green onions, white part only	125 mL
½ cup	chopped dry roasted peanuts	125 mL

1. In a large skillet, heat oil over medium heat for 30 seconds. Add onions, carrots and celery and cook, stirring, until softened, about 7 minutes. Add gingerroot, garlic and peppercorns and cook, stirring, for 1 minute. Transfer to slow cooker stoneware. Add vegetable stock and stir well.

2. Add green beans and stir well. Cover and cook on Low for 6 hours or on High for 3 hours, until vegetables are tender.

3. In a bowl, beat together peanut butter, soy sauce, lemon juice, maple syrup and red curry paste until blended. Add to slow cooker stoneware and stir well. Add Napa cabbage, in batches, stirring until each batch is submerged in liquid. Cover and cook for 10 minutes, until heated through. Stir in bean sprouts. Garnish each serving with a sprinkle of green onions, then peanuts.

VARIATION

Add 2 cups (500 mL) cooked broccoli florets along with the cabbage.

Mindful Morsels

One Harvard study found that women who ate a handful of nuts or 2 tbsp (25 mL) of peanut butter at least five times a week were 20 percent less likely to develop type-2 diabetes.

Natural Wonders

DIETARY FIBER

This recipe is very high in dietary fiber, the ingredient in food that helps to keep you regular, among other benefits. Because it absorbs significant amounts of water as it passes through your digestive system, fiber softens stool and helps to speed up the elimination of waste products, both of which have significant health benefits. Fiber also helps to keep blood cholesterol low. A number of studies link a high intake of dietary fiber with a lower risk of heart disease. One Harvard study of more than 4,000 men found those whose diets were high in fiber reduced their risk of heart disease by 40 percent compared with men who consumed little fiber. A typical North American consumes about 15 grams of fiber a day, far less than experts recommend. A report from the National Academies' Institute of Medicine published in 2002 established guidelines for fiber consumption. Men aged 50 and under should consume 38 grams of fiber a day and women in the same age bracket should consume 25 grams. Those over 50 should consume 30 and 21 grams, respectively.

Nutrients Per Serving	
Calories	253
Protein	9.8 g
Carbohydrates	24.1 g
Fat (Total)	15.4 g
Saturated Fat	2.7 g
Monounsaturated Fat	7.8 g
Polyunsaturated Fat	4.1 g
Dietary Fiber	6.2 g
Sodium	520 mg
Cholesterol	0 mg

Excellent source of vitamins A, B6 and K, folacin and magnesium.

Good source of vitamin C, potassium, phosphorus, iron and zinc.

Source of calcium.

Contains a very high amount of dietary fiber.

Ratatouille

Ratatouille makes a great accompaniment to roast meat or, if you're a vegetarian, served over baked tofu. I also think it's delicious on its own with some warm whole grain bread.

MAKES 8 SERVINGS

TIPS

❖ I use Italian San Marzano tomatoes in this recipe. They are richer and thicker and have more tomato flavor than domestic varieties. If you are using a domestic variety, add 1 tbsp (15 mL) tomato paste along with the tomatoes.

❖ Be sure to rinse the salted eggplant thoroughly after sweating. Otherwise it may retain salt and your ratatouille will be too salty.

MAKE AHEAD

This dish can be partially prepared before it is cooked. Complete Steps 1 through 3. Cover and refrigerate stoneware and zucchini mixture separately overnight. The next day, continue with Step 4.

- Large (minimum 5 quart) slow cooker
- Preheat oven to 400°F (200°C)
- Rimmed baking sheet, ungreased

2	medium eggplant (each about 12 oz/375 g), peeled and cut into 1-inch (2.5 cm) cubes	2
2 tbsp	kosher or coarse sea salt	25 mL
3 tbsp	olive oil, divided	45 mL
4	medium zucchini (about 1 1/2 lbs/ 750 g total), peeled and thinly sliced	4
2	cloves garlic, minced	2
2	onions, thinly sliced	2
1 tsp	herbes de Provence	5 mL
1/2 tsp	salt	2 mL
1/2 tsp	cracked black peppercorns	2 mL
8 oz	mushrooms, sliced	250 g
1	can (28 oz/796 mL) tomatoes, including juices, coarsely chopped	1
2	green bell peppers, cubed (1/2 inch/1 cm)	2
1/2 cup	chopped parsley or basil leaves	125 mL

1. In a colander over a sink, combine eggplant and salt. Toss to ensure eggplant is well coated and let stand for 30 minutes to 1 hour. Rinse thoroughly under cold running water. Lay a clean tea towel on a work surface. Working in batches over the sink and using your hands, squeeze liquid out of eggplant. Transfer to the tea towel. When batches are complete, roll the towel up and press down to remove remaining liquid. Transfer eggplant to prepared baking sheet and toss with 1 tbsp (15 mL) of the olive oil. Spread evenly on baking sheet. Cover with foil and bake in preheated oven until soft and fragrant, about 15 minutes. Remove from oven and transfer to slow cooker stoneware.

2. Meanwhile, heat 1 tbsp (15 mL) of the oil over medium-high heat. Add zucchini and cook, stirring, for 6 minutes. Add garlic and cook, stirring, until zucchini is soft and browned, about 1 minute. Transfer to a bowl. Cover and refrigerate.

3. Reduce heat to medium. Add remaining 1 tbsp (15 mL) oil. Add onions and cook, stirring, until softened, about 3 minutes. Add herbes de Provence, salt and peppercorns and cook, stirring, about 1 minute. Add mushrooms and toss until coated. Stir in tomatoes and bring to a boil. Transfer to stoneware.

4. Cover and cook on Low for 6 to 8 hours or on High for 3 to 4 hours, until vegetables are tender. Add green peppers, reserved zucchini mixture and parsley and stir well. Cover and cook on High for 25 minutes, until peppers are tender and zucchini is heated through.

Mindful Morsels

Researchers are studying nasunin, an antioxidant found in eggplant, which appears to protect cells and joints from free radical damage. If so, nasunin consumption would reduce the risk of cancer and rheumatoid arthritis.

Natural Wonders

ZUCCHINI

Zucchini is a member of the summer squash family. While not a nutrient-dense vegetable, it does contain small amounts of a variety of nutrients, such as manganese, vitamin C, magnesium and potassium. Zucchini contains oxalates, which some think may contribute to the formation of kidney stones in sensitive individuals. If you have kidney or gallbladder problems it may be wise to monitor your consumption of zucchini and other summer squash.

Nutrients Per Serving	
Calories	121
Protein	3.1 g
Carbohydrates	17.5 g
Fat (Total)	5.6 g
Saturated Fat	0.8 g
Monounsaturated Fat	3.8 g
Polyunsaturated Fat	0.7 g
Dietary Fiber	5.1 g
Sodium	300 mg
Cholesterol	0 mg

Excellent source of vitamins C and K and potassium.

Good source of vitamin B6, folacin and magnesium.

Source of vitamin A, phosphorus and iron.

Contains a high amount of dietary fiber.

Sweet Potato Shepherd's Pie

I love the meaty texture of bulgur, the sweetness of the parsnips and the hint of pungent rosemary in this tasty dish. Serve this with a tossed green salad to complete the meal.

MAKES 8 SERVINGS

TIPS

❖ Use your fingers to crumble the rosemary as you add it to the pan. Not only does this make the leaves smaller so they are better integrated into the dish, it releases the enticing flavor of the herb.

❖ Small whole cremini mushrooms work best in this recipe, but if you can't find them, use larger ones, quartered.

MAKE AHEAD

This recipe can be partially prepared before it is cooked. Complete Steps 1 though 3. Cover and refrigerate the sweet potato topping separately from the stoneware overnight. When ready to cook, continue with Step 4.

- **Large (minimum 5 quart) slow cooker**
- **Greased slow cooker stoneware**

TOPPING

4	medium sweet potatoes, peeled and sliced (about 2 lbs/1 kg)	4
1 tbsp	butter	15 mL
	Salt and freshly ground black pepper	

PIE

1 cup	bulgur	250 mL
2 cups	boiling water	500 mL
1 tbsp	olive oil	15 mL
2	onions, finely chopped	2
4 to 5	large carrots, peeled and sliced (about 1 1/2 lbs/750 g)	4 to 5
4 to 5	large parsnips, peeled and sliced (about 1 1/2 lbs/750 g)	4 to 5
4	cloves garlic, minced	4
2 tsp	dried rosemary leaves, crumbled (see Tips, left), or 1 tbsp (15 mL) fresh rosemary leaves, minced	10 mL
1 tsp	salt	5 mL
1/2 tsp	cracked black peppercorns	2 mL
8 oz	cremini mushrooms (see Tips, left)	250 g
1 tbsp	all purpose flour	15 mL
1 cup	vegetable stock	250 mL
1/4 cup	tomato paste	50 mL
1 cup	shredded Swiss cheese, optional	250 mL

1. *Topping:* In a pot of boiling salted water, cook sweet potatoes until tender, about 20 minutes. Mash, stir in butter and season to taste with salt and pepper. Set aside.

2. *Pie:* In a bowl, combine bulgur and boiling water. Set aside for 20 minutes until water is absorbed.

3. In a skillet, heat oil over medium heat for 30 seconds. Add onions, carrots and parsnips and cook, stirring, until vegetables are softened, about 6 minutes. Add garlic, rosemary, salt and peppercorns and cook, stirring, for 1 minute. Add mushrooms and toss to coat. Add flour and cook, stirring, for 1 minute. Stir in stock and tomato paste. Bring to boil. Transfer to prepared stoneware.

4. Add soaked bulgur and stir well. Spread topping evenly over mushroom mixture. Place a tea towel folded in half (so you will have two layers) over top of stoneware to absorb moisture. Cover and cook on Low for 7 to 8 hours or on High for 3½ to 4 hours, until vegetables are tender. Sprinkle with Swiss cheese, if using. Cover and cook on High for 15 minutes, until cheese is melted.

❖ **If you prefer a meat-based version of this recipe, after preparing the topping, omit the bulgur and sauté 1 lb (500 g) extra-lean ground beef in 1 tbsp (15 mL) olive oil until it is no longer pink. Drain off any fat. Transfer to slow cooker stoneware. Proceed with Step 3.**

Mindful Morsels
The cheese in the topping is a source of calcium, which helps to keep osteoporosis at bay and blood pressure under control.

Natural Wonders
SALAD
Completing a meal with salad is an excellent way to ensure that you consume an adequate amount of valuable fiber. But it's also a technique for adding nutrients to your diet. Among other nutrients, romaine lettuce contains vitamins A and C and folacin. Adding dark leafy greens, such as spinach and parsley, bumps up the vitamin K content, and a sprinkling of toasted whole sesame seeds helps to provide much-needed calcium. Add sliced bell peppers, chopped scallions, a few radishes — whatever captures your fancy — and you have a bowl brimming with a colorful array of vitamins, minerals and antioxidants that will work together to keep you healthy.

Nutrients Per Serving	
Calories	314
Protein	7.1 g
Carbohydrates	65.8 g
Fat (Total)	4.2 g
Saturated Fat	1.3 g
Monounsaturated Fat	1.8 g
Polyunsaturated Fat	0.6 g
Fiber	9.4 g
Sodium	734 mg
Cholesterol	5 mg

Excellent source of vitamins A, C and B6, magnesium and potassium.

Good source of vitamin K, folacin, phosphorus, iron and zinc.

Source of calcium.

Contains a very high amount of dietary fiber.

Spinach, Sun-Dried Tomato and Cheddar Cheesecake

Rich, dense and delicious, you don't need much of this quiche-like dish to satisfy any longings for a cheese-flavored fix. Serve this with a lettuce and scallion salad topped with shredded carrots and chopped parsley to round out the nutrient mix.

**MAKES
4 TO 6 SERVINGS**

- **Large (minimum 5 quart) oval slow cooker**
- **7-inch (17.5 cm) well-greased springform pan, or 7-inch (17.5 cm) 6 cup (1.5 L) soufflé dish, lined with greased heavy foil**

CRUST

1 cup	cheese-flavored cracker crumbs (about 24 crackers)	250 mL
2 tbsp	unsalted butter, melted	25 mL

FILLING

1 cup	evaporated 2% milk	250 mL
3	eggs	3
1 tsp	paprika	5 mL
1/2 tsp	salt	2 mL
	Freshly ground black pepper	
1	package (10 oz/300 g) frozen spinach, thawed, drained, squeezed dry and finely chopped	1
1/3 cup	finely chopped drained oil-packed sun-dried tomatoes	75 mL
1 cup	shredded Cheddar cheese	250 mL

1. *Crust:* In a bowl, mix together crumbs and butter. Press mixture into the bottom of prepared pan. Place in freezer until ready to use.

2. *Filling:* In a bowl, whisk milk and eggs until blended. Whisk in paprika, salt and black pepper. Stir in spinach and tomatoes. Fold in cheese. Pour over chilled crust. Cover entire pan (to prevent leaks) tightly with foil. Place pan in slow cooker stoneware and pour in enough boiling water to come 1 inch (2.5 cm) up the sides.

3. Cover and cook on High for 3 to 4 hours or until firm.

Mindful Morsels

Dairy products contain conjugated linoleic acid (CLA), a fatty acid that has numerous health benefits.

Natural Wonders

CALCIUM

Not only are the milk and cheese in this dish good sources of calcium, the spinach is also a source of this essential mineral. Nowadays most of us are aware of how much our bodies need calcium to maintain healthy bones and keep osteoporosis at bay. But this essential mineral also supports a wide range of important body functions, from your nervous system to how your muscles function. Recent research also suggests it may help to prevent many ailments, from high blood pressure and PMS to inflammatory bowel disease. A recent study involving more than 45,000 American women found a link between calcium intake and a reduced risk of colon cancer.

The problem is, most North Americans consume about half the calcium they need. The daily value is 1,000 mg for men and women aged 19 to 50 and 1,200 mg for those between the ages of 51 and 70. It's wise to add more calcium-rich foods, such as leafy greens, dairy products or calcium-fortified daily alternatives and sesame seeds to your diet.

Nutrients Per Serving	
Calories	282
Protein	13.4 g
Carbohydrates	17.2 g
Fat (Total)	18.3 g
Saturated Fat	8.4 g
Monounsaturated Fat	6.5 g
Polyunsaturated Fat	1.0 g
Dietary Fiber	1.8 g
Sodium	541 mg
Cholesterol	126 mg

Excellent source of vitamins A and K and calcium.

Good source of folacin, phosphorus, magnesium, potassium and zinc.

Source of vitamin C.

See photo, page 224

New Age Succotash

I call this dish "new age" because it uses edamame, or soybeans, instead of traditional lima beans. I've also bumped up the flavor with paprika, and finished with a smattering of mouth-watering roasted red peppers, usually not included in the dish. I like to serve this with steamed asparagus, in season.

MAKES 8 SERVINGS

MAKE AHEAD

This dish can be partially prepared before it is cooked. Complete Step 1. Cover and refrigerate overnight or for up to 2 days. When you're ready to cook, continue with Step 2.

• **Works in slow cookers from 3½ to 6 quarts**

1 tbsp	olive oil	15 mL
2	onions, finely chopped	2
4	stalks celery, diced	4
2	carrots, peeled and diced	2
4	cloves garlic, minced	4
1	sprig fresh rosemary or 2 tsp (10 mL) dried rosemary leaves, crumbled	1
1 tsp	salt	5 mL
½ tsp	cracked black peppercorns	2 mL
1	can (28 oz/796 mL) tomatoes, including juice, coarsely chopped	1
1½ cups	vegetable stock	375 mL
4 cups	frozen shelled edamame	1 L
4 cups	frozen corn kernels	1 L
2 tsp	paprika, dissolved in 2 tbsp (25 mL) water	10 mL
2	roasted red bell peppers, diced	2
½ cup	finely chopped parsley leaves	125 mL

1. In a skillet, heat oil over medium heat for 30 seconds. Add onions, celery and carrots and cook, stirring, until softened, about 7 minutes. Add garlic, rosemary, salt and peppercorns and cook, stirring, for 1 minute. Stir in tomatoes with juices and vegetable stock and bring to a boil. Transfer to slow cooker stoneware.

2. Add edamame and corn. Stir well. Cover and cook on Low for 8 to 10 hours or on High for 4 to 5 hours, until mixture is hot and bubbly. Stir in paprika solution, roasted red peppers and parsley. Cover and cook on High for 15 minutes, until heated through.

See photo, page 225

VARIATIONS

Barley Succotash

For a more substantial dish, add ½ cup (125 mL) whole (hulled) or pot barley along with the edamame.

Spicy Succotash

For a livelier dish, stir in 1 can (4.5 oz/127 mL) mild green chiles along with the red peppers.

Mindful Morsels

A serving of this dish contains more than 4 grams of omega-3 fatty acids, most of which comes from the soybeans.

Natural Wonders

SOY

If you follow nutrition news, you've been hearing a lot about soy. One day it's being touted as a panacea for almost all that ails us, the next we're being told to avoid it at all costs. What are confused consumers to do?

In general terms, the concerns around soy focus on how soy products are made, and soy supplements versus whole soy foods. For instance, soy oil, which is highly processed, contains trans fats. Evidence suggests that taking isoflavones (a phytochemical contained in soy) in supplement form may have a negative effect on hormone-dependent breast cancer, and there is some evidence to suggest that soy itself may contain compounds that encourage existing breast cancers to grow. Moreover, many of the claims related to soy's supposed ability to ease women's transition to menopause and reduce the risk of osteoporosis have not been proven.

However, one thing there is little doubt about is that soybeans themselves are extremely nutritious. Soybeans provide a complete protein and are an excellent source of potassium, folacin and niacin, a good source of thiamin and a source of riboflavin and zinc. They are low in saturated fat, cholesterol-free, and a source of omega-3 fatty acids (see pages 97 and 121 for more on omega-3 fatty acids).

Nutrients Per Serving	
Calories	324
Protein	20.9 g
Carbohydrates	42.9 g
Fat (Total)	11.1 g
Saturated Fat	1.3 g
Monounsaturated Fat	2.4 g
Polyunsaturated Fat	5.3 g
Dietary Fiber	9.8 g
Sodium	717 mg
Cholesterol	0 mg

Excellent source of vitamins A, C and K, folacin, phosphorus, magnesium, potassium and iron.

Good source of vitamin B6, calcium and zinc.

Contains a very high amount of dietary fiber.

Squash and Black Bean Chili

Flavored with cumin and chili powder, with a hint of cinnamon, this luscious chili makes a fabulous weeknight meal. Add a tossed green salad and some whole grain rolls, relax and enjoy.

MAKES 6 SERVINGS

TIPS

❖ **Try substituting coconut oil for the olive oil. It adds a hint of coconut flavor to this chili that is quite appealing.**

❖ **Add the chipotle pepper if you like heat and a bit of smoke.**

MAKE AHEAD

This dish can be partially prepared before it is cooked. Complete Step 1. Cover and refrigerate overnight or for up to 2 days. When you're ready to cook, continue with Step 2.

• **Works in slow cookers from 3½ to 6 quarts**

1 tbsp	olive oil	15 mL
2	onions, finely chopped	2
4	cloves garlic, minced	4
2 tsp	chili powder	10 mL
1 tsp	dried oregano leaves	5 mL
1 tsp	salt	5 mL
1 tsp	cumin seeds, toasted (see Tips, page 49)	5 mL
1	piece (3 inches/7.5 cm) cinnamon stick	1
1	can (28 oz/796 mL) tomatoes, including juice, coarsely chopped	1
1	can (14 to 19 oz/398 to 540 mL) black beans, drained and rinsed, or 1 cup (250 mL) dried black beans, soaked, cooked and drained (see Basic Beans, page 250)	1
4 cups	cubed (1 inch/2.5 cm) peeled butternut squash	1 L
2	green bell peppers, diced	2
1	can (4.5 oz/127 mL) chopped mild green chiles	1
1	finely chopped chipotle pepper in adobo sauce, optional	1
	Finely chopped fresh cilantro leaves	

1. In a skillet, heat oil over medium heat for 30 seconds. Add onions to pan and cook, stirring, until softened, about 3 minutes. Add garlic, chili powder, oregano, salt, toasted cumin and cinnamon stick and cook, stirring, for 1 minute. Add tomatoes with juice and bring to a boil. Transfer to slow cooker stoneware. Add beans and squash and stir well.

2. Cover and cook on Low for 8 hours or on High for 4 hours, until squash is tender. Add bell peppers, chiles and chipotle

pepper, if using. Cover and cook on High for 20 minutes, until bell pepper is tender. Discard cinnamon stick. When ready to serve, ladle into bowls and garnish with cilantro.

VARIATION

Squash and Black Bean Chili con Carne
Add 1 lb (500 g) lean ground beef along with the onions. Cook, stirring, until meat is no longer pink, about 6 minutes. Drain off fat and continue with Step 2.

Mindful Morsels

The beans in this recipe contain non-heme iron, the kind obtained from vegetarian sources. Although not as effectively absorbed by the body as heme iron (which is found in meat), non-heme iron can be consumed along with a source of vitamin C or a small quantity of meat to improve absorption.

Nutrients Per Serving	
Calories	171
Protein	6.6 g
Carbohydrates	33.5 g
Fat (Total)	3.1 g
Saturated Fat	0.4 g
Monounsaturated Fat	1.8 g
Polyunsaturated Fat	0.6 g
Dietary Fiber	8.1 g
Sodium	976 mg
Cholesterol	0 mg

Natural Wonders
PHYTOCHEMICALS AND CANCER

The vegetables in this dish contain a wide range of phytochemcials — carotenoids, isoflavones and lycopene, among others — which may help your body fight certain types of cancer. Studies show that people who regularly consume an abundance of fruits and vegetables may reduce their risk of cancers of the esophagus, stomach, colon, lung and ovaries, among others. And there is evidence to suggest that specific vegetables help to protect against different types of cancer. For instance, the lycopene in tomatoes appears to reduce the risk of prostate cancer and/or its progression. Carrots and dark leafy green vegetables have been linked with lower rates of lung cancer, and cruciferous vegetables, such as broccoli, cabbage and cauliflower, appear to reduce the risk of colon cancer. More research is needed before we fully understand the relationship between cancer and the consumption of fruits and vegetables, but in the meantime, it's advisable to eat the recommended 5 to 9 servings a day.

Excellent source of vitamins A, C and B6 and potassium.

Good source of vitamin K, folacin, magnesium and iron.

Source of calcium and phosphorus.

Contains a very high amount of dietary fiber.

Spinach Dal with Millet

Dal, which is usually made with split yellow peas, is one of my favorite ethnic comfort foods. Usually served as one of several small dishes at an Indian meal, dal is very versatile. I often enjoy it as a main course, accompanied by a tossed salad. It also makes a delicious side to accompany grilled or roasted chicken or meat.

MAKES 8 SERVINGS

TIPS

❖ If using fresh spinach, be sure to remove the stems, and if it has not been pre-washed, rinse it thoroughly in a basin of lukewarm water.

❖ To toast cumin and coriander seeds: Place seeds in a dry skillet over medium heat and toast, stirring, until fragrant and cumin seeds just begin to brown, about 3 minutes. Immediately transfer to a mortar or a spice grinder and grind.

MAKE AHEAD

This dish can be partially prepared before it is cooked. Complete Step 1. Cover and refrigerate overnight or for up to 2 days. When you're ready to cook, continue with Step 2.

• Large (minimum 5 quart) slow cooker

1 tbsp	olive oil	15 mL
2	onions, finely chopped	2
4	cloves garlic, minced	4
1 tbsp	minced gingerroot	15 mL
1 tsp	turmeric	5 mL
1/2 tsp	cracked black peppercorns	2 mL
2	bay leaves	2
1 tbsp	cumin seeds, toasted (see Tips, left)	15 mL
2 tsp	coriander seeds, toasted	10 mL
1	can (28 oz/796 mL) tomatoes, including juice, coarsely chopped	1
3 cups	vegetable stock	750 mL
1 cup	red lentils, rinsed	250 mL
1 cup	millet (see Tips, left)	250 mL
1/4 tsp	cayenne, dissolved in 2 tbsp (25 mL) freshly squeezed lemon juice	1 mL
	Salt, optional	
1 lb	fresh spinach, stems removed, or 1 package (10 oz/300 g) fresh or frozen spinach, thawed and drained if frozen (see Tips, left)	500 g
	Coconut milk or plain yogurt, optional	
1/4 cup	finely chopped cilantro leaves	50 mL

1. In a skillet, heat oil over medium heat. Add onions and cook, stirring, until softened, about 3 minutes. Add garlic and gingerroot and cook, stirring, for 1 minute. Add turmeric, peppercorns, bay leaves and toasted cumin and coriander and cook, stirring, for 1 minute. Add tomatoes with juice and bring to a boil. Transfer to slow cooker stoneware.

2. Add vegetable stock, lentils and millet and stir well. Cover and cook on Low for 10 hours or on High for 5 hours, until lentils are tender. Stir in cayenne solution and add salt to taste, if necessary. Add spinach, in batches, stirring after each batch until all the leaves are submerged in the liquid. Cover and cook on High for 20 minutes, until spinach is tender. Discard bay leaves. Transfer to a large serving bowl, drizzle with coconut milk, if using, and garnish with cilantro.

Mindful Morsels

A serving of this dal is an excellent source of fiber. The lentils provide 3 grams and the millet 2.3 grams of this valuable nutrient.

Natural Wonders

FOLACIN

It's long been known that pregnant women with a folacin deficiency are more likely to give birth prematurely or to have a baby with a low birth weight or a neural tube defect. As a result, food manufacturers have been supplementing grain products with this nutrient for several years. But new information from the Harvard Nurses' Study suggests that an adequate supply of folacin has more broad-ranging effects. Consumption of folacin helps to prevent high blood pressure and keeps homocysteine levels under control, protecting blood vessels from plaque. There also appears to be a link between folacin intake and a reduced risk of colon cancer, especially for women with a family history of the disease. And Finnish researchers found a link between the consumption of folacin and a reduced risk of depression. Folacin is not easily obtained in a typical North American diet. Good food sources are leafy greens, legumes such as lentils, globe artichokes, broccoli, asparagus and orange juice.

Nutrients Per Serving	
Calories	243
Protein	11.6 g
Carbohydrates	43.9 g
Fat (Total)	3.3 g
Saturated Fat	0.5 g
Monounsaturated Fat	1.6 g
Polyunsaturated Fat	0.8 g
Dietary Fiber	7.8 g
Sodium	543 mg
Cholesterol	0 mg

Excellent source of vitamins A and K, folacin, magnesium, potassium and iron.

Good source of vitamins C and B6, phosphorus and zinc.

Source of calcium.

Contains a very high amount of dietary fiber.

Vegetable Chili

Here's a chili that is loaded with flavor and nutrients. Garnish with any combination of roasted red peppers, diced avocado, finely chopped red onions and cilantro. Add a simple green salad and some whole grain bread for a great weekday meal.

MAKES 8 SERVINGS

TIPS

❖ **If you don't have leeks, substitute 2 yellow onions, finely chopped.**

❖ **If you prefer a more peppery chili use up to 1 tsp (5 mL) of cracked black peppercorns in this recipe.**

❖ **You can substitute your favorite chili powder blend for the ancho or New Mexico chili powder.**

MAKE AHEAD

This dish can be partially prepared before it is cooked. Complete Steps 1 through 4. Cover and refrigerate separately overnight or for up to 2 days. When you're ready to cook, continue with Step 5.

● **Large (minimum 5 quart) slow cooker**

4 cups	thinly sliced zucchini (about 1 lb/500 g)	1 L
1/2 tsp	salt	2 mL
2 tbsp	olive oil, divided	25 mL
4	cloves garlic, minced	4
2	large leeks, white and green parts only, cleaned and thinly sliced (see Tips, left)	2
4	stalks celery, diced	4
4	carrots, peeled and diced	4
2 tsp	dried oregano leaves, crumbled	10 mL
1/2 tsp	cracked black peppercorns (see Tips, left)	2 mL
1 tbsp	cumin seeds, toasted (see Tips, page 49)	15 mL
1	can (28 oz/796 mL) tomatoes, including juice, coarsely chopped	1
1	can (14 to 19 oz/398 to 540 mL) kidney or pinto beans drained and rinsed, or 1 cup (250 mL) dried kidney or pinto beans, soaked, cooked and drained (see Basic Beans, page 250)	1
1 cup	bulgur	250 mL
1 tbsp	ancho or New Mexico chili powder, dissolved in 2 tbsp (25 mL) freshly squeezed lemon juice (see Tips, left)	15 mL
2	green bell peppers, diced	2
1	jalapeño or chipotle pepper in adobo sauce, diced	1
	Sour cream, optional	

1. In a colander over a sink, combine zucchini and salt. Set aside to sweat for 20 minutes. Rinse thoroughly under cold running water and pat dry with paper towels. Set aside.

2. In a skillet, heat 1 tbsp (15 mL) of the oil over medium heat for 30 seconds. Add zucchini and cook, stirring, for 3 minutes. Add garlic and cook, stirring, until zucchini softens and just begins to brown, about 4 minutes. Transfer to a bowl, cover and refrigerate.

3. In a skillet, heat remaining 1 tbsp (15 mL) of the oil over medium heat. Add leeks, celery and carrots and cook, stirring, until carrots are softened, about 7 minutes. Add oregano, peppercorns and toasted cumin and cook, stirring, for 1 minute. Add tomatoes and bring to a boil. Transfer to stoneware.

4. Stir in beans. Cover and cook on Low for 6 hours or on High for 3 hours, until vegetables are tender.

5. In a bowl, combine bulgur and 1 cup (250 mL) boiling water. Set aside for 30 minutes, until water is absorbed. Meanwhile, add chili pepper solution to stoneware and stir well. Add bell peppers, jalapeño and reserved zucchini. Stir well. Cover and cook on High for 20 to 30 minutes, until peppers are tender. Stir in bulgur. Ladle chili into bowls.

Mindful Morsels
One serving of this chili provides more than 100 percent of the RDV of vitamin A.

Natural Wonders
CELERY
While not an excellent source of any nutrient, celery contains vitamin K, folacin and potassium, along with some valuable phytochemicals that scientists are now studying. Celery contains courmarins, which may help to protect against cancer, and the seeds contain phthalides, which seem to help keep blood pressure under control.

Nutrients Per Serving	
Calories	204
Protein	7.2 g
Carbohydrates	37.9 g
Fat (Total)	4.5 g
Saturated Fat	0.6 g
Monounsaturated Fat	2.75 g
Polyunsaturated Fat	0.8 g
Dietary Fiber	9.3 g
Sodium	480 mg
Cholesterol	0 mg

Excellent source of vitamins A, B6, C and K, magnesium and potassium.

Good source of folacin, phosphorus and iron.

Source of calcium.

Contains a very high amount of dietary fiber.

See photo, page 234

Mushroom and Chickpea Stew with Roasted Red Pepper Coulis

I've served this delicious stew to nonvegetarians who have scraped the bowl. Topped with the luscious coulis, it is quite divine. Add whole grain rolls and a green salad or steamed asparagus, in season.

MAKES 6 SERVINGS

MAKE AHEAD
This dish can be partially prepared before it is cooked. Complete Steps 1 and 2. Cover and refrigerate overnight or for up to 2 days. When you're ready to cook, continue with Steps 3 and 4.

• **Works in slow cookers from 3½ to 6 quarts**

1 tbsp	cumin seeds	15 mL
1 tbsp	olive oil	15 mL
2	onions, finely chopped	2
2	carrots, peeled and diced	2
4	stalks celery, thinly sliced or 1 bulb fennel, trimmed, cored and thinly sliced on the vertical	4
4	cloves garlic, minced	4
1 tsp	turmeric	5 mL
1 tsp	salt	5 mL
½ tsp	cracked black peppercorns	2 mL
8 oz	cremini mushrooms, thinly sliced	250 g
1	can (28 oz/796 mL) tomatoes, including juice, coarsely chopped	1
1	can (14 to 19 oz/398 to 540 mL) chickpeas, drained and rinsed, or 1 cup (250 mL) dried chickpeas, soaked, cooked and drained (see Basic Beans, page 250)	1

RED PEPPER COULIS

2	roasted red bell peppers	2
3	oil-packed sun-dried tomatoes, drained and chopped	3
2 tbsp	extra virgin olive oil	25 mL
1 tbsp	balsamic vinegar	15 mL
10	fresh basil leaves, optional	10

1. In a large dry skillet over medium heat, toast cumin seeds, stirring, until fragrant and they just begin to brown, about 3 minutes. Immediately transfer to a mortar or a spice grinder and grind. Set aside.

See photo, page 235

2. In same skillet, heat oil over medium heat for 30 seconds. Add onions, carrots and celery and cook, stirring, until vegetables are tender, about 7 minutes. Add garlic, turmeric, salt, peppercorns and reserved cumin and cook, stirring, for 1 minute. Add mushrooms and toss until coated. Add tomatoes with juice and bring to a boil. Transfer to slow cooker stoneware.

3. Add chickpeas and stir well. Cover and cook on Low for 6 hours or on High for 3 hours, until hot and bubbly.

4. *Roasted Red Pepper Coulis:* In a food processor, combine roasted peppers, sun-dried tomatoes, oil, vinegar, and basil, if using. Process until smooth. Ladle stew into bowls and top with coulis.

Mindful Morsels

Most of the sodium in a serving of this recipe comes from the added salt (383 mg), the canned tomatoes (198 mg) and the canned chickpeas (136 mg).

Natural Wonders
COMBINING FIBER-RICH FOODS

If you're concerned about your blood cholesterol levels, enjoy dishes that contain a variety of high-fiber and cholesterol-lowering foods. A new study shows that combining fiber-rich foods may boost their individual effect. The study, conducted by Canadian researchers, showed that a high-fiber diet combined with other foods known to have cholesterol-lowering properties, such as tofu, can control blood cholesterol levels as effectively as drugs. The diet included vegetables such as okra and eggplant, soy protein, legumes, nuts and plant sterol-enriched margarine, and it was more than three times as effective in lowering cholesterol as a diet low in saturated fat, a traditional approach. Moreover, it was almost as effective as a low (saturated) fat diet combined with a cholesterol-lowering drug, called a statin. Since statins may have unpleasant side-effects, a dietary approach to managing cholesterol has obvious benefits.

Nutrients Per Serving	
Calories	202
Protein	6.5 g
Carbohydrates	30.5 g
Fat (Total)	7.5 g
Saturated Fat	1.0 g
Monounsaturated Fat	4.9 g
Polyunsaturated Fat	1.0 g
Dietary Fiber	6.5 g
Sodium	848 mg
Cholesterol	0 mg

Excellent source of vitamins A, C, B6 and K and potassium.

Good source of folacin, magnesium and iron.

Source of calcium and phosphorus.

Contains a very high amount of dietary fiber.

Winter Vegetable Casserole

Here's a great dish to make during the dark days of winter. The combination of root vegetables, seasoned with caraway seeds, produces a great-tasting dish that is seasonally appropriate — I like to imagine my pioneer ancestors sitting down to a similar meal. I serve this with rye bread and steamed broccoli, but creamed spinach works well, too.

MAKES 6 SERVINGS

TIPS

❖ **Celery root oxidizes quickly on contact with air. Tossing it with lemon juice keeps it from discoloring.**

❖ **If your supermarket carries 19 oz (540 mL) cans of diced tomatoes, by all means substitute for the 14 oz (398 mL) called for in the recipe.**

MAKE AHEAD

This dish can be partially prepared before it is cooked. Complete Step 2. Cover and refrigerate overnight or for up to 2 days. When you're ready to cook, continue with Steps 1 and 3.

• **Large (minimum 5 quart) slow cooker**

1	large celery root, peeled and shredded	1
1 tbsp	freshly squeezed lemon juice	15 mL
1 tbsp	olive oil	15 mL
2	leeks, white and light green parts only, cleaned and thinly sliced (see Tip, page 42)	2
4	carrots, peeled and sliced	4
4	parsnips, peeled and sliced	4
2	cloves garlic, minced	2
1 tsp	caraway seeds	5 mL
1 tsp	salt	5 mL
1/2 tsp	cracked black peppercorns	2 mL
1	can (14 oz/398 mL) diced tomatoes, including juice (see Tips, left)	1
2 cups	vegetable stock	500 mL
1/2 cup	whole (hulled) or pot barley (see Mindful Morsels, page 65)	125 mL
1/2 cup	finely chopped parsley leaves	125 mL

1. In a bowl, toss celery root and lemon juice. Set aside.

2. In a large skillet, heat oil over medium heat for 30 seconds. Add leeks, carrots and parsnips and cook, stirring, until vegetables have softened, about 7 minutes. Add garlic, caraway seeds, salt and peppercorns and cook, stirring for 1 minute. Add tomatoes with juice, vegetable stock and barley and bring to a boil.

3. Spread celery root over bottom of slow cooker. Add vegetable mixture and stir well. Cover and cook on Low for 6 hours or on High for 3 hours, until vegetables and barley are tender. Sprinkle with parsley and serve.

Mindful Morsels

Although it tastes like celery, celery root, or celeriac, is actually a member of the parsley family. Low in calories and fat-free, it contains no cholesterol. It is a source of vitamins C and B6 and potassium and contains small amounts of folacin, calcium and iron.

Natural Wonders
SUPPLEMENTS VS THE REAL THING

A serving of this dish is an excellent source of vitamin C, a powerful antioxidant that reduces the risk of heart disease and certain cancers, among other benefits. Vitamin C is one of the most commonly consumed supplements, but, like all vitamins, it is preferable to obtain it from foods.

Nature doesn't produce nutrients in isolated form, the way they appear in supplements, but in combinations that work together synergistically to promote health and prevent disease. Moreover, foods contain so many nutrients it would be impossible to reproduce all of them in a supplement. Although we still have a lot to learn about how nutrients work, studies are sending early warning signals about supplements. For instance, concern has been raised about vitamin E, beta-carotene and isoflavones in supplement form. New research is beginning to show that the protective effect of phytochemicals is produced by the intakes found in foods, not the larger doses provided by supplements. And food tastes so much better, too.

Nutrients Per Serving	
Calories	252
Protein	5.5 g
Carbohydrates	53.7 g
Fat (Total)	3.4 g
Saturated Fat	0.4 g
Monounsaturated Fat	1.9 g
Polyunsaturated Fat	0.5 g
Dietary Fiber	9.1 g
Sodium	951 mg
Cholesterol	0 mg

Excellent source of vitamins A, C, B6 and K, folacin, magnesium and potassium.

Good source of phosphorus and iron.

Source of calcium.

Contains a very high amount of dietary fiber.

Indian Peas and Beans

Simple, yet delicious, this Indian-inspired dish makes a great weeknight dinner, served with Indian bread and a cucumber salad. It also makes a nice addition to a multidish Indian meal.

MAKES 6 SERVINGS

TIP

❖ **Can sizes vary from location to location. If your supermarket carries 19 oz (540 mL) cans of diced tomatoes, by all means substitute for the 14 oz (398 mL) called for in the recipe.**

MAKE AHEAD

This dish can be partially prepared before it is cooked. Complete Steps 1 through 3. Cover and refrigerate overnight or for up to 2 days. When you're ready to cook, continue with Step 4.

• **Works in slow cookers from 3½ to 6 quarts**

1 cup	yellow split peas, rinsed	250 mL
1 tbsp	cumin seeds	15 mL
2 tsp	coriander seeds	10 mL
1 tbsp	olive oil or extra virgin coconut oil	15 mL
2	onions, finely chopped	2
4	cloves garlic, minced	4
1 tbsp	minced gingerroot	15 mL
1 tsp	turmeric	5 mL
1 tsp	cracked black peppercorns	5 mL
2	bay leaves	2
1	can (14 oz/398 mL) diced tomatoes, including juice (see Tip, left)	1
2 cups	vegetable stock	500 mL
2 cups	frozen sliced green beans	500 mL
¼ tsp	cayenne, dissolved in 1 tbsp (15 mL) freshly squeezed lemon juice	1 mL
1 cup	coconut milk, optional	250 mL
½ cup	finely chopped cilantro leaves	125 mL

1. In a large saucepan, combine peas with 6 cups (1.5 L) cold water. Bring to a boil and boil rapidly for 3 minutes. Remove from heat and set aside for 1 hour. Rinse thoroughly under cold water, drain and set aside.

2. In a large dry skillet over medium heat, toast cumin and coriander seeds, stirring, until fragrant and cumin seeds just begin to brown, about 3 minutes. Immediately transfer to a mortar or a spice grinder and grind. Set aside.

3. In same skillet, heat oil over medium heat for 30 seconds. Add onions and cook, stirring, until softened, about 3 minutes. Add garlic, gingerroot, turmeric, peppercorns, bay leaves and reserved cumin and coriander and cook, stirring, for 1 minute.

Add tomatoes with juice and reserved split peas and bring to a boil. Transfer to slow cooker stoneware.

4. Add vegetable stock and green beans and stir well. Cover and cook on Low for 8 to 10 hours or on High for 4 to 5 hours, until peas are tender. Stir in cayenne solution and coconut milk, if using. Add cilantro and stir well. Cover and cook on High for 20 minutes, until heated through. Discard bay leaves.

Mindful Morsels

For centuries, many of the herbs used to season Indian food, such as curries, have been thought to have antibacterial qualities. As we learn more about the phytochemicals in food, it seems that many of them do.

Natural Wonders
TURMERIC

In culinary terms, turmeric is a modest spice. It has a slightly peppery flavor and works quietly in the background of a dish, adding a subtle hint of earthiness. But in terms of its nutraceutical ability turmeric packs a real wallop. Its anti-inflammatory abilities have been long recognized, and it appears to ease the symptoms of rheumatoid arthritis. One study suggests that it may be an effective treatment for inflammatory bowel diseases, such as Crohn's disease and ulcerative colitis. Turmeric contains curcumin, which has recently been identified as having the potential to prevent Alzheimer's disease. This powerful antioxidant seems to break up plaque and inhibit the formation of destructive protein fragments in the brain. So far, it's only been tested on mice but the Alzheimer's Disease Research Center at UCLA is beginning human trials. Researchers are also exploring turmeric as a possible cancer fighter.

Nutrients Per Serving	
Calories	193
Protein	10.4 g
Carbohydrates	33.1 g
Fat (Total)	3.3 g
Saturated Fat	0.4 g
Monounsaturated Fat	2.0 g
Polyunsaturated Fat	0.5 g
Dietary Fiber	5.8 g
Sodium	435 mg
Cholesterol	0 mg

Excellent source of folacin and potassium.

Good source of vitamin K, magnesium, iron and zinc.

Source of vitamins A, C and B6 and phosphorus.

Contains a high amount of dietary fiber.

Soy-Braised Tofu

It's amazing how tofu soaks up the mouth-watering Asian flavors in this recipe. Use this hot braised tofu as a centerpiece to a meal of vegetarian dishes that might include stir-fried bok choy or wilted greens garnished with toasted sesame seeds. Refrigerate any leftovers for use in other dishes, such as stir-fried mixed vegetables, or salads, such as an Asian-inspired coleslaw. You can also transform this flavorful tofu into a wrap. Place on lettuce leaves, garnish with shredded carrots and fold.

MAKES 4 SERVINGS

TIP

❖ To drain tofu, place a layer of paper towels on a plate. Set tofu in the middle. Cover with another layer of paper towel and a heavy plate. Set aside for 30 minutes. Peel off paper and cut into cubes.

• **Large (minimum 6 quart) slow cooker**

1 lb	firm tofu, drained and cut into 1-inch (2.5 cm) cubes (see Tip, left)	500 g
1/4 cup	light soy sauce	50 mL
1 tbsp	puréed gingerroot	15 mL
1 tbsp	pure maple syrup	15 mL
1 tbsp	toasted sesame oil	15 mL
1 tbsp	freshly squeezed lemon juice	15 mL
1 tsp	minced garlic	5 mL
1/2 tsp	cracked black peppercorns	2 mL

1. In slow cooker stoneware, combine soy sauce, gingerroot, maple syrup, toasted sesame oil, lemon juice, garlic and peppercorns. Add tofu and toss gently until coated on all sides. Cover and refrigerate for 1 hour.

2. Toss well. Cover and cook on Low for 5 hours or on High for 2½ hours, until tofu is hot and has absorbed the flavor.

Mindful Morsels

Soybeans, from which tofu is made, contain all nine essential amino acids, which means they are a complete protein.

Natural Wonders

TOFU

Tofu is a source of vitamins and minerals and disease-fighting phytonutrients, and there is evidence to suggest that adding soy to your diet is a healthful strategy. The U.S. Federal Drug Administration says that soy protein reduces blood cholesterol levels and may reduce the risk of coronary artery disease when it is part of a diet low in saturated fat and cholesterol. However, soy is not a panacea, and soy products, such as tofu, should be consumed as part of a varied and balanced diet. Since reducing the ratio of animal to plant protein in your diet helps to reduce intake of saturated fat and may reduce the risk of certain types of cancer, it makes sense to substitute tofu for animal protein as regularly as you can. One study, which followed more than half a million people, showed that those who ate the most red meat or processed meats had higher rates of colon cancer.

Nutrients Per Serving	
Calories	144
Protein	10.2 g
Carbohydrates	9.3 g
Fat (Total)	8.5 g
Saturated Fat	1.2 g
Monounsaturated Fat	2.5 g
Polyunsaturated Fat	4.3 g
Dietary Fiber	1.3 g
Sodium	610 mg
Cholesterol	0 mg

Good source of folacin, calcium, phosphorus, magnesium and iron.

Vegetable Curry with Lentils and Spinach

Serve this delicious curry for dinner with warm Indian bread such as naan. It's a meal in itself.

MAKES 8 SERVINGS

TIP

❖ If using fresh spinach, be sure to remove the stems, and if it has not been pre-washed, rinse it thoroughly in a basin of lukewarm water.

MAKE AHEAD

This dish can be partially prepared before it is cooked. Complete Steps 1 and 2. Cover and refrigerate overnight or for up to 2 days. When you're ready to cook, continue with Step 3.

● Large (minimum 5 quart) slow cooker

2 tsp	cumin seeds	10 mL
1 tsp	coriander seeds	5 mL
1 tbsp	olive oil or extra virgin coconut oil	15 mL
2	onions, finely chopped	2
4	carrots, peeled and thinly sliced (about 1 lb/500 g)	4
4	parsnips, peeled, tough core removed and thinly sliced (about 1 lb/500 g)	4
4	cloves garlic, minced	4
1 tbsp	minced gingerroot	15 mL
2 tsp	turmeric	10 mL
1	piece (2 inches/5 cm) cinnamon stick	1
1/2 tsp	cracked black peppercorns	2 mL
2 cups	vegetable stock	500 mL
	Salt, optional	
2	sweet potatoes, peeled and thinly sliced (about 1 lb/500 g)	2
1 cup	brown or green lentils, picked over and rinsed	250 mL
1	long red chile pepper, finely chopped, or 1/2 tsp (2 mL) cayenne pepper, dissolved in 1 tbsp (15 mL) lemon juice	1
1 lb	fresh spinach, stems removed, or 1 package (10 oz/300 g) spinach leaves, thawed and drained if frozen, coarsely chopped (see Tip, left)	500 g
1 cup	coconut milk, optional (see Mindful Morsels, right)	250 mL

1. In a dry skillet over medium heat, toast cumin and coriander seeds until fragrant and cumin seeds just begin to brown, about 3 minutes. Immediately transfer to a mortar or a spice grinder and grind. Set aside.

2. In same skillet, heat oil over medium heat for 30 seconds. Add onions, carrots and parsnips and cook, stirring, until vegetables are tender, about 6 minutes. Add garlic, gingerroot, turmeric, cinnamon stick, peppercorns and reserved cumin and coriander and cook, stirring, for 1 minute. Add vegetable stock and bring to a boil. Season to taste with salt, if using, and transfer to slow cooker stoneware. Add sweet potatoes and lentils and stir well.

3. Cover and cook on Low for 8 hours or on High for 4 hours, until lentils are tender. Add chile pepper and stir well. Add spinach, in batches, stirring after each batch until all the leaves are submerged in the liquid, then coconut milk, if using. Cover and cook on High for 20 minutes, until spinach is wilted and flavors have blended. Discard cinnamon stick.

Mindful Morsels

The coconut milk adds a pleasant nutty flavor and creaminess to the curry, but it is high in saturated fat. So if you're concerned about your intake of saturated fat, leave it out. The curry is very tasty on its own.

Natural Wonders
SPICY ANTIOXIDANTS

A curry is actually a spicy stew, not a dish seasoned with curry powder. In fact, most Indian cooks make their own curry seasoning (or powder) using a blend of spices that complements their recipe ingredients. Most include turmeric, which gives commercially blended curry powder its bright yellow color, and coriander seeds, which have a light lemon flavor. Cinnamon is often added for sweetness and cumin adds a pungent note. Chile peppers add heat. All these spices contain antioxidants, which have been linked with a range of health benefits. Moreover, when researchers in India studied the antioxidant ability of individual seasonings such as cinnamon, pepper, ginger, garlic and onion alone, and then together, they found the combination produced greater health benefits.

Nutrients Per Serving	
Calories	252
Protein	10 g
Carbohydrates	49.6 g
Fat (Total)	2.7 g
Saturated Fat	0.4 g
Monounsaturated Fat	1.5 g
Polyunsaturated Fat	0.5 g
Dietary Fiber	8.7 g
Sodium	308 mg
Cholesterol	0 mg

Excellent source of vitamins A, C, B6 and K, folacin, magnesium, potassium and iron.

Good source of phosphorus and zinc.

Source of calcium.

Contains a very high amount of dietary fiber.

See photo, page 246

Artichoke, Sun-Dried Tomato and Goat Cheese Strata

This is a great brunch dish. I like to serve it with a green salad tossed in walnut oil vinaigrette and sprinkled with toasted walnuts to add healthy omega-3 fatty acids to the meal.

MAKES 8 SERVINGS

TIPS

❖ **To toast bread cubes, place on a rimmed baking sheet in a 325°F (160°C) oven for 5 to 7 minutes, stirring twice.**

❖ **If you like the flavor of sun-dried tomatoes, you may wish to use the larger quantity.**

- **Large (minimum 5 quart) slow cooker**
- **Greased slow cooker stoneware**

8 cups	cubed (¹/₂ inch/1 cm) toasted sourdough or whole wheat bread (see Tips, left)	2 L
1 cup	sliced green onions, white part with just a bit of green	250 mL
4 to 6	oil-packed sun-dried tomatoes, drained and finely chopped (see Tips, left)	4 to 6
1	can (14 oz/398 mL) artichoke hearts, drained and chopped	1
8 oz	soft goat cheese, crumbled, divided	250 g
4	eggs	4
2 cups	2% evaporated milk	500 mL
1 tsp	salt	5 mL
¹/₂ tsp	cracked black peppercorns	2 mL

1. In prepared stoneware, combine bread, green onions, sun-dried tomatoes, artichokes and half of the goat cheese. Toss well.

2. In a bowl, whisk together eggs, milk, salt and peppercorns. Pour over bread mixture. Sprinkle remaining goat cheese evenly over top.

3. Place two clean tea towels, each folded in half (so you will have four layers) over top of stoneware to absorb moisture. Cover and cook on Low for 6 hours or on High for 3 hours, until strata is set and edges are browning.

See photo, page 247

Mindful Morsels

Think about using sea salt instead of refined varieties. Refined table salt, which is virtually pure sodium chloride, contains 2,325 milligrams of sodium per teaspoon (5 mL). Although unrefined sea salt is also high in sodium chloride, it contains a smattering of minerals such as magnesium and potassium, making it a positive alternative.

Nutrients Per Serving	
Calories	280
Protein	17.2 g
Carbohydrates	28.3 g
Fat (Total)	11.1 g
Saturated Fat	5.9 g
Monounsaturated Fat	3.3 g
Polyunsaturated Fat	0.9 g
Dietary Fiber	3.1 g
Sodium	790 mg
Cholesterol	111 mg

Natural Wonders

VITAMIN D

A serving of this recipe is an excellent source of calcium, an important mineral for bone health. But the calcium in foods is more readily absorbed and deposited in your bones if you have an adequate supply of vitamin D. The best food sources of vitamin D are egg yolks, fortified dairy products and oily fish, such as salmon and tuna. Some foods, such as soy and rice beverages are also fortified with the vitamin.

However, the best source of vitamin D is not food but sunlight. For years we've been told to avoid the sun because it increases the risk of skin cancer, but recent studies indicate that sunlight may actually improve outcomes in people with melanoma and reduce the risk of lymphatic and prostate cancers. A study conducted on 500 Connecticut residents diagnosed with melanoma found that the greater their exposure to sun, the less they were likely to die of the disease. Another study of 6,000 Scandinavian residents found the more participants were exposed to sunlight, the lower their risk of non-Hodgkin's lymphoma, and, to a lesser extent, Hodgkin's disease. A U.S. study of 450 white males found that by promoting vitamin-D production in the body, exposure to sunlight also lowered the risk of prostate cancer. Researchers stress the importance of avoiding sunburn, which does increase the risk of cancer. Moderate sunning, which creates a regular supply of vitamin D, seems to be the key.

Excellent source of vitamin K, calcium and phosphorus.

Good source of vitamin A, folacin, magnesium, potassium, iron and zinc.

Source of vitamin C.

Contains a moderate amount of dietary fiber.

Basic Beans

Loaded with nutrition and high in fiber, dried beans are one of our most healthful edibles. And the slow cooker excels at transforming them into potentially sublime fare. It is also extraordinarily convenient. Put presoaked beans into the slow cooker before you go to bed and in the morning they are ready for whatever recipe you intend to make.

**MAKES APPROX.
2 CUPS (500 mL)
COOKED BEANS, ABOUT
4 SERVINGS**

TIPS

❖ **This recipe may be doubled or tripled to suit the quantity of beans required for a recipe.**

❖ **Once cooked, legumes should be covered and stored in the refrigerator, where they will keep for 4 to 5 days. Cooked legumes can also be frozen in an airtight container. They will keep frozen for up to 6 months.**

• **Works in slow cookers from 3½ to 6 quarts**

1 cup	dried white beans (see Tips, left)	250 mL
3 cups	water	750 mL
	Bouquet garni, optional	

1. *Long soak:* In a bowl, combine beans and water. Soak for at least 6 hours or overnight. Drain and rinse thoroughly with cold water. Beans are now ready for cooking.

2. *Quick soak:* In a pot, combine beans and water. Cover and bring to a boil. Boil for 3 minutes. Turn off heat and soak for 1 hour. Drain and rinse thoroughly under cold water. Beans are now ready to cook.

3. *Cooking:* In slow cooker stoneware, combine 1 cup (250 mL) presoaked beans and 3 cups (750 mL) fresh cold water. If desired, season with garlic, bay leaves or a bouquet garni made from your favorite herbs tied together in a cheesecloth. Cover and cook on Low for 10 to 12 hours or overnight or on High for 5 to 6 hours, until beans are tender. Drain and rinse. If not using immediately, cover and refrigerate. The beans are now ready for use in your favorite recipe.

VARIATIONS

Substitute any dried bean (for instance, red kidney beans, pinto beans, white navy beans) chickpeas, or split yellow peas for the white beans. Soybeans and chickpeas take longer than other legumes to cook. They will likely take the full 12 hours on Low (about 6 hours on High).

Dried Lentils

These instructions also work for lentils, with the following changes: Do not presoak them and reduce the cooking time to about 6 hours on Low.

Mindful Morsels

If you are watching your sodium intake, it's a good idea to prepare dried beans from scratch. A half cup (125 mL) serving of regular canned beans is likely to contain about 300 milligrams of sodium.

Natural Wonders

LEGUMES

Although the benefits vary between different types, legumes share some common nutritional characteristics. All are an excellent source of many B vitamins, including folacin as well as iron, phosphorus, potassium and zinc. High in fiber, legumes are a source of calcium and low-cal, low-fat vegetable protein. They are also a natural appetite suppressant; because they are digested slowly and cause a low, sustained increase in blood sugar, eating legumes can delay the onset of hunger and make it easier to control appetite.

Nutrients Per ½ Cup (125 mL) Serving	
Calories	154
Protein	10.5 g
Carbohydrates	27.6 g
Fat (Total)	0.6 g
Saturated Fat	0.1 g
Monounsaturated Fat	0.0 g
Polyunsaturated Fat	0.3 g
Dietary Fiber	8.0 g
Sodium	2 mg
Cholesterol	0 mg

Excellent source of folacin and iron.

Good source of phosphorus, magnesium and potassium.

Source of vitamin K.

Contains a very high amount of dietary fiber.

Desserts

Gingery Pears Poached in Green Tea, see recipe overleaf

Gingery Pears Poached in Green Tea

I love the combination of ginger and pears in this light but delicious dessert. Sprinkle with toasted almonds and top with a dollop of vanilla yogurt for a perfect finish to a substantial meal.

MAKES 8 SERVINGS

TIPS

❖ **When poaching, use firmer pears, such as Bosc, for best results.**

❖ **I prefer a strong ginger taste in these pears, but some might feel it overpowers the taste of the pears. Vary the amount of ginger to suit your preference.**

MAKE AHEAD

This dessert should be made early in the day or the night before so it can be well chilled before serving.

• **Works best in a small (3½ quart) slow cooker**

4 cups	boiling water	1 L
2 tbsp	green tea leaves	25 mL
1 to 2 tbsp	grated gingerroot (see Tips, left)	15 to 25 mL
½ cup	liquid honey	125 mL
1 tsp	pure almond extract	5 mL
1 tsp	grated lemon zest	5 mL
8	firm pears, such as Bosc, peeled, cored and cut into quarters lengthwise	8
	Toasted sliced almonds, optional	
	Vanilla-flavored yogurt, optional	

1. In a pot, combine boiling water and green tea leaves. Cover and let steep for 5 minutes. Strain through a fine sieve into slow cooker stoneware.

2. Add gingerroot, honey, almond extract and lemon zest and stir well. Add pears. Cover and cook on Low for 6 hours or on High for 3 hours, until pears are tender. Transfer to a serving bowl, cover and chill thoroughly. Serve garnished with toasted almonds and a dollop of yogurt, if using.

Natural Wonders

TEA

In recent years, researchers have shown a great deal of interest in the health benefits of tea, especially the green variety. As the least processed tea, green tea is the richest in antioxidants. Among other benefits, people who drink green tea regularly appear to reduce their risk of infections and cardiovascular disease. Green tea contains an abundance of polyphenols. These antioxidants appear to inhibit the growth of early stage prostate cancer cells and may help prevent prostate cancer from spreading. But other varieties of tea may be good for you as well. Chinese studies found that male tea drinkers were about half as likely to develop stomach or esophageal cancer than men who didn't drink much tea. On the other side of the world, Harvard researchers concluded that all varieties of tea, when combined with soy, were even more effective in fighting prostate cancer than tea alone. Given all the positive news about tea, it makes sense to add the beverage to your diet, especially if it replaces less healthy drinks such as soda or fruit drinks loaded with added sugar.

Nutrients Per Serving	
Calories	131
Protein	0.5 g
Carbohydrates	34.5 g
Fat (Total)	0.5 g
Saturated Fat	0 g
Monounsaturated Fat	0.1 g
Polyunsaturated Fat	0.1 g
Dietary Fiber	2.4 g
Sodium	1 mg
Cholesterol	0 mg

Contains a moderate amount of dietary fiber.

VEGETARIAN FRIENDLY

Pumpkin Rice Pudding

The combination of flavors and the chewy but crunchy texture of this luscious pudding make it hard to resist.

MAKES 8 SERVINGS

TIPS

❖ If you prefer, use 1½ tsp (7 mL) pumpkin pie spice instead of the cinnamon, nutmeg and cloves.

❖ If you don't have evaporated cane juice sugar, use dark brown sugar instead.

❖ Cook 1 cup (250 mL) raw rice to get the 2 cups (500 mL) of cooked rice required for this recipe.

• **Works best in a small (3½ quart) slow cooker**
• **Greased slow cooker stoneware**

2 cups	cooked brown rice (see Tips, left)	500 mL
1½ cups	pumpkin purée (not pie filling)	375 mL
1 cup	dried cranberries or dried cherries	250 mL
1 cup	evaporated skim milk	250 mL
½ cup	packed muscovado or evaporated cane juice sugar (see Tips, left)	125 mL
2	eggs	2
1 tsp	ground cinnamon (see Tips, left)	5 mL
½ tsp	grated nutmeg	2 mL
¼ tsp	ground cloves	1 mL
	Toasted chopped pecans, optional	
	Vanilla-flavored yogurt or whipped cream, optional	

1. In prepared slow cooker stoneware, combine rice, pumpkin purée and cranberries.

2. In a bowl, whisk together milk, sugar, eggs, cinnamon, nutmeg and cloves until smooth and blended. Stir into pumpkin mixture. Cover and cook on High for 3 hours, until pudding is set. Serve warm, garnished with toasted pecans and a dollop of yogurt, if using.

Mindful Morsels

Finishing this pudding with a sprinkling of toasted pecans adds more than taste and texture to the dish. Pecans contain beneficial fats, fiber and iron, among other nutrients.

Natural Wonders

CINNAMON

A staple in North American kitchens, cinnamon is inextricably linked with fond memories of indulgent desserts. Now researchers are telling us that this delightful spice may actually be good for us. Long known to have benefits as a digestive, cinnamon bark contains essential oils that have been associated with a range of health benefits, from easing inflammation to inhibiting the growth of pathogens. Israeli research indicates that cinnamon extract stalls the growth of the ulcer-causing bacteria *Helicobacter pylori*, and other scientists found it dramatically undermined the power of the potentially life threatening *E. coli* bacteria. Cinnamon is also a powerful antioxidant. In fact, some research suggests it may have more antioxidant activity than almost any other spice. Other studies indicate that cinnamon may also have a role in controlling diabetes. One study showed that consuming less than ½ tsp (2 mL) of cinnamon a day reduced blood sugar levels, triglycerides and cholesterol in people with type-2 diabetes. And if that isn't enough, recent research found that just the smell of cinnamon may make you smarter. In one study, subjects who inhaled cinnamon or chewed cinnamon-flavored gum demonstrated improved cognitive function.

Nutrients Per Serving	
Calories	224
Protein	6.2 g
Carbohydrates	47.5 g
Fat (Total)	2.0 g
Saturated Fat	0.7 g
Monounsaturated Fat	0.7 g
Polyunsaturated Fat	0.4 g
Dietary Fiber	3.4 g
Sodium	68 mg
Cholesterol	48 mg

Excellent source of vitamin A.

Good source of vitamin K, magnesium and potassium.

Source of calcium, phosphorus and iron.

Contains a moderate amount of dietary fiber.

Coconut Cranberry Rice Pudding

This pudding is every bit as rich and satisfying as those your grandmother used to make.

MAKES 8 SERVINGS

TIP

❖ **Served hot, this pudding has a creamy consistency. If you prefer a more solid result, serve it chilled. It firms up considerably as it rests.**

- Works in slow cookers from 3½ to 6 quarts
- Greased slow cooker stoneware

³/₄ cup	Arborio rice	175 mL
2 cups	vanilla-flavored enriched rice milk	500 mL
1	can (14 oz/398 mL) coconut milk	1
½ cup	dried cranberries	125 mL
¼ cup	Demerara sugar	50 mL
2 tsp	ground cinnamon	10 mL
1 tsp	freshly ground nutmeg	5 mL
1 tsp	vanilla	5 mL
Pinch	salt	Pinch

1. In prepared slow cooker stoneware, combine rice, rice milk, coconut milk, cranberries, sugar, cinnamon, nutmeg, vanilla and salt. Cover and cook on High for 3 to 4 hours, until rice is tender. Uncover and stir well. Serve hot or transfer to a bowl, cover tightly and chill for up to 2 days.

Mindful Morsels

Each serving of this pudding provides 2.2 grams of iron, 1.6 grams of which is provided by the coconut milk, which also provides most of the fat (10.1 grams).

Natural Wonders
COCONUT OIL

Although research into the health benefits of coconut oil are in the preliminary stages, unless you are concerned about your blood cholesterol levels, adding a small amount to your diet may be beneficial to your health. Coconut oil is high in saturated fat, but it contains a number of fatty acids, which have anti-inflammatory properties and may help your body fight infections.

Nutrients Per Serving	
Calories	245
Protein	2.5 g
Carbohydrates	36.5 g
Fat (Total)	10.9 g
Saturated Fat	9.1 g
Monounsaturated Fat	0.9 g
Polyunsaturated Fat	0.3 g
Dietary Fiber	1.5 g
Sodium	29 mg
Cholesterol	0 mg

Good source of iron.

Source of calcium and phosphorus.

Basmati Rice Pudding

The cardamom in this pudding provides an irresistible Indian flavor. I like to serve it at room temperature, but it also works warm or cold. If you're feeling indulgent, add a little cream.

MAKES 8 SERVINGS

- Works best in a small (3½ quart) slow cooker
- Lightly greased slow cooker stoneware

4 cups	whole milk or enriched rice milk	1 L
⅓ cup	Demerara or evaporated cane juice sugar	75 mL
2 tsp	ground cardamom	10 mL
¾ cup	brown basmati rice, rinsed	175 mL
	Chopped unsalted pistachio nuts	

1. In a large saucepan over medium heat, bring milk to a boil, stirring often. Add sugar and cardamom. Remove from heat and stir in rice. Transfer to prepared slow cooker stoneware.

2. Place a tea towel folded in half (so you will have two layers) over top of stoneware to absorb moisture. Cover and cook on High for 3 hours, until rice is tender and pudding is creamy. Transfer to a serving bowl and cool to room temperature. Garnish with pistachios.

Mindful Morsels
Sprinkling the pudding with a handful of pistachios adds fiber, potassium and vitamin B6, among other nutrients.

Natural Wonders
EVAPORATED CANE JUICE SUGAR
I like to use sugar made from evaporated cane juice, such as Sucanat® or Rapadura®, because it is a healthier alternative to refined sugar. Although no sugar is a significant source of nutrients, these less processed versions have more nutrients than refined white or brown sugar. Evaporated cane juice retains complex sugars, minerals and molasses, which have some nutritive value. Also, studies suggest it is less likely to cause cavities than refined white sugar.

Nutrients Per Serving	
Calories	173
Protein	5.6 g
Carbohydrates	27.5 g
Fat (Total)	4.6 g
Saturated Fat	2.6 g
Monounsaturated Fat	1.2 g
Polyunsaturated Fat	0.3 g
Dietary Fiber	1.0 g
Sodium	63 mg
Cholesterol	17 mg

Good source of phosphorus and magnesium.

Source of calcium.

See photo, page 260

Cranberry Pear Brown Betty

I love the combination of textures and flavors in this old-fashioned favorite. When cranberries are in season, I always freeze a bag or two so I can make this wholesome dessert year round. It's a great way to use up day-old bread.

MAKES 6 SERVINGS

TIPS

❖ **To make dried bread crumbs for this recipe, toast 4 slices of whole wheat bread. Tear into pieces and process in a food processor fitted with a metal blade until finely ground.**

❖ **Use a light whole wheat loaf for this recipe. Those with heavy molasses content will overpower the fruit.**

❖ **If you don't have stevia, use ¼ cup (50 mL) brown sugar, such as Demerara, or evaporated cane juice sugar, such as Sucanat®, instead.**

- **Works best in a small (3½ quart) slow cooker**
- **Greased slow cooker stoneware**

2 cups	dry whole wheat bread crumbs	500 mL
2 tbsp	butter, melted, or extra virgin olive oil	25 mL
6	pears, peeled, cored and sliced	6
1 tbsp	freshly squeezed lemon juice	15 mL
1 cup	fresh or frozen cranberries	250 mL
2 tbsp	stevia extract (see Tips, left)	25 mL
½ cup	cranberry juice	125 mL

1. In a bowl, combine bread crumbs and butter. Set aside.

2. In a separate bowl, combine pears, lemon juice, cranberries and stevia.

3. In prepared slow cooker stoneware, spread one-third of the bread crumb mixture. Layer half of the pear mixture over top. Repeat. Finish with a layer of crumbs and pour cranberry juice over top. Cover and cook on High for 4 hours, until fruit is tender and mixture is hot and bubbly.

See photo, page 261

Mindful Morsels

Pears are a good source of fiber. Over half the fiber in a serving of this dessert (2.3 grams) is provided by the pears.

Natural Wonders

STEVIA

Stevia is a herb with a mild licorice flavor that is native to parts of South America. A member of the Chrysanthemum family, it is almost 300 times sweeter than ordinary table sugar and is used extensively as a sweetener in Japan. Stevia contains virtually no calories and some nutrients and can be used to replace all or some of the sugar in many recipes. Although it has not received approval from the FDA or Argriculture Canada as a sweetener, it does seem to be a healthy alternative to refined sugar and artificial sweeteners. There is some evidence to suggest that stevia may reduce the bacteria that cause dental cavities and gum disease.

Nutrients Per Serving	
Calories	168
Protein	2.3 g
Carbohydrates	32.6 g
Fat (Total)	5.1 g
Saturated Fat	2.6 g
Monounsaturated Fat	1.5 g
Polyunsaturated Fat	0.4 g
Dietary Fiber	4.1 g
Sodium	137 mg
Cholesterol	12 mg

Source of vitamin C.

Contains a high amount of dietary fiber.

Apple Oatmeal Pudding

This tasty pudding, which combines luscious apples with hearty oatmeal, is an adaptation of a traditional Irish recipe. If you feel like a splurge, add a dollop of freshly whipped cream.

MAKES 6 SERVINGS

TIP

❖ **I prefer to use rice milk in this recipe because it has a milder flavor than soy milk.**

❖ **I like to use stevia to sweeten the apples because its mild licorice flavor complements the fruit and adds a pleasant hint of complexity. But evaporated cane juice or brown sugar works well, too.**

- **Works best in a small (3½ quart) slow cooker**
- **Greased slow cooker stoneware**

2 tbsp	melted butter	25 mL
1 cup	rolled oats (not quick-cooking)	250 mL
⅓ cup	Demerara or evaporated cane juice sugar	75 mL
½ cup	all-purpose flour	125 mL
1 tsp	baking soda	5 mL
Pinch	salt	Pinch
2	eggs, beaten	2
1 cup	rice or soy milk or 2% evaporated milk	250 mL
6	apples, peeled, cored and thinly sliced	6
1 tbsp	freshly squeezed lemon juice	15 mL
1 tsp	ground cinnamon	5 mL
½ tsp	stevia extract or 1 tbsp (15 mL) Demerara or evaporated cane juice sugar	2 mL
	Whipped cream, optional	

1. In a bowl, mix together butter, oats and sugar. Stir in flour, baking soda and salt. Gradually add eggs and rice milk, mixing until blended. Spoon into prepared slow cooker stoneware.

2. In a separate bowl, combine apples, lemon juice, cinnamon and stevia. Spread evenly over oatmeal mixture. Cover and cook on High for 3½ to 4 hours, until apples are tender.

Nutrients Per Serving	
Calories	217
Protein	4.2 g
Carbohydrates	39.8 g
Fat (Total)	5.4 g
Saturated Fat	2.4 g
Monounsaturated Fat	1.7 g
Polyunsaturated Fat	0.8 g
Dietary Fiber	3.8 g
Sodium	205 mg
Cholesterol	56 mg

Natural Wonders

ROLLED OATS

Using old-fashioned rolled oats rather than the quick-cooking variety adds nutrients to this dessert. Rolled (and steel-cut) oats contain the bran layer of the grain, which contains minerals, antioxidants, plant lignans and fiber. Among other benefits, the fiber in oatmeal helps keep cholesterol under control. Oatmeal also contains unique compounds called avenanthramides, which work synergistically with vitamin C to prevent oxidation of LDL ("bad") cholesterol, thus lowering the risk of cardiovascular disease. The plant lignans that it is rich in appear to protect against breast cancer. Enjoying oatmeal in a dessert is one way to increase your intake of healthy whole grains.

Source of phosphorus.

Contains a moderate amount of dietary fiber.

Peach Raspberry Betty

The combination of peaches and raspberries is a personal favorite. Although I enjoy making this dessert in summer when fresh fruit is in season, it is also delicious made with canned and/or frozen fruit, making it a year-round treat.

MAKES 6 SERVINGS

TIPS

❖ **To make dried bread crumbs for this recipe, toast 4 slices of whole wheat bread. Tear into pieces and process in a food processor fitted with a metal blade until finely ground.**

❖ **Use a light whole wheat loaf for this recipe. Those with heavy molasses content will overpower the fruit.**

- **Works in slow cookers from 3½ to 6 quarts**
- **Lightly greased slow cooker stoneware**

2 cups	dry whole wheat bread crumbs	500 mL
¼ cup	chopped toasted almonds	50 mL
2 tbsp	extra virgin olive or coconut oil or almond butter	25 mL
5 cups	sliced peaches (about 4 or 5)	1.25 L
2 cups	raspberries	500 mL
½ cup	Demerara or evaporated cane juice sugar	125 mL
1 tbsp	all-purpose flour	15 mL
½ tsp	almond extract	2 mL
¼ cup	cranberry-raspberry or cranberry juice (see Tips, page 270)	50 mL

1. In a bowl, combine bread crumbs, almonds and oil. Set aside.

2. In a separate bowl, combine peaches, raspberries, sugar, flour and almond extract.

3. In prepared slow cooker stoneware, layer one-third of the bread crumb mixture, then one-half of the peach mixture. Repeat layers of bread crumbs and fruit, then finish with a layer of bread crumbs on top. Drizzle cranberry juice over the top. Cover and cook on High for 2½ to 3 hours, until hot and bubbly.

Mindful Morsels

Virtually all the fat in this recipe comes from the almonds and the olive oil and is the healthy unsaturated kind.

Natural Wonders

RASPBERRIES

Like all berries, raspberries are extremely nutritious. Not only are they high in fiber, they are also loaded with vitamin C and provide a smattering of other nutrients such as folacin, iron and potassium. All berries are a rich source of antioxidants, which help to prevent degenerative diseases, among other benefits. Raspberries are particularly high in ellagic acid, which has been identified as a cancer fighter. Don't just limit berries to dessert. Increase your consumption of these healthful fruits by sprinkling them over breakfast cereal, adding them to smoothies or just enjoying a handful as a healthy snack.

Nutrients Per Serving	
Calories	267
Protein	4.1 g
Carbohydrates	48.7 g
Fat (Total)	8.1 g
Saturated Fat	1.0 g
Monounsaturated Fat	5.3 g
Polyunsaturated Fat	1.4 g
Dietary Fiber	6.3 g
Sodium	87 mg
Cholesterol	0 mg

Excellent source of magnesium.

Good source of potassium.

Source of vitamins A and C.

Contains a very high amount of dietary fiber.

See photo, page 268

VEGAN FRIENDLY

The Ultimate Baked Apples

These luscious apples, simple to make yet delicious, are the definitive autumn dessert. I like to serve these with a dollop of whipped cream, but they are equally delicious (and healthier) accompanied by yogurt or on their own.

MAKES 8 SERVINGS

TIPS

❖ I like the rich molasses taste and the more favorable nutritional profile of muscovado sugar but, in this recipe, light or dark brown sugar makes an acceptable substitute.

❖ When buying nuts be sure to source them from a purveyor with high turnover. Because nuts are high in fat (but healthy fat) they tend to become rancid very quickly. This is especially true of walnuts. In my experience the vast percentage of walnuts sold in supermarkets have already passed their peak. Taste before you buy. If they are not sweet, substitute an equal quantity of pecans.

❖ The nutritional analysis on this recipe was done using sweetened cranberry cocktail, which adds calories and carbohydrates to every serving of this dessert. If you prefer, use unsweetened cranberry juice from a natural foods store.

• Large (minimum 5 quart) oval slow cooker

1/2 cup	chopped toasted walnuts (see Tips, left)	125 mL
1/2 cup	dried cranberries	125 mL
2 tbsp	packed muscovado or evaporated cane juice sugar (see Tips, left)	25 mL
1 tsp	grated orange zest	5 mL
8	apples, cored	8
1 cup	cranberry juice (see Tips, left)	250 mL
	Vanilla-flavored yogurt or whipped cream, optional	

1. In a bowl, combine walnuts, cranberries, sugar and orange zest. To stuff the apples, hold your hand over the bottom of the apple and, using your fingers, tightly pack core space with filling. One at a time, place filled apples in slow cooker stoneware. Drizzle cranberry juice evenly over tops.

2. Cover and cook on Low for 8 hours or on High for 4 hours, until apples are tender. Transfer to a serving dish and spoon cooking juices over them. Serve hot with a dollop of yogurt or whipped cream, if using.

See photo, page 269

Mindful Morsels

The walnuts in this recipe are a source of omega-3 fatty acids. They also contribute 0.5 grams of fiber per serving.

Natural Wonders

APPLES

Most of us grew up taking it on faith that an apple a day keeps the doctor away. Now scientists are confirming the truth of this maxim and explaining the reasons why. We've long known that apples contain nutrients such as vitamin C and fiber, but it's the range of phytochemicals, such as the flavonoid quercetin, that most interests researchers today. Quercetin is a potent antioxidant that works to strengthen the body's immune system. The consumption of quercetin has been linked with a reduced risk of heart disease, and it has also shown promise as a cancer fighter in laboratory situations. The phytonutrient combination in apples has also been shown to prevent breast cancer in animals and inhibit the growth of colon cancer cells in laboratories. In fact, a review of 85 studies, published in *Nutrition Journal*, linked eating apples, in comparison with other fruits, with a reduced risk of heart disease, cancer and type-2 diabetes.

Nutrients Per Serving	
Calories	184
Protein	1.4 g
Carbohydrates	36.3 g
Fat (Total)	5.5 g
Saturated Fat	0.6 g
Monounsaturated Fat	0.7 g
Polyunsaturated Fat	3.7 g
Dietary Fiber	4.0 g
Sodium	2 mg
Cholesterol	0 mg

Source of vitamin C.

Contains a high amount of dietary fiber.

Cornmeal Pudding

Not only is this old-fashioned dessert great comfort food, it is also very versatile. It is delicious served with fresh berries, a dollop of whipped cream or a scoop of vanilla ice cream.

**MAKES
6 TO 8 SERVINGS**

TIP

❖ The nutrient analysis on this recipe was done using 2% milk. If you are concerned about your fat intake, use skim milk instead.

- Works best in a small (3½ quart) slow cooker
- Greased slow cooker stoneware

4 cups	milk (see Tip, left)	1 L
½ cup	yellow cornmeal, preferably stone-ground	125 mL
2	eggs, beaten	2
1 tbsp	extra virgin olive oil	15 mL
½ cup	fancy molasses	125 mL
½ tsp	ground ginger	2 mL
½ tsp	ground cinnamon	2 mL
½ tsp	freshly grated nutmeg	2 mL
½ tsp	salt	2 mL
	Fresh berries, optional	
	Vanilla ice cream, optional	
	Whipped cream, optional	

1. In a saucepan, heat milk over medium-high heat, stirring often to prevent scorching, until boiling. Gradually whisk in cornmeal in a steady stream. Cook, stirring, until mixture begins to thicken and bubbles like lava, about 5 minutes. Remove from heat.

2. In a small bowl, combine beaten eggs with about ½ cup (125 mL) of the hot cornmeal, beating until combined. Gradually return to pot, mixing well. Stir in olive oil, molasses, ginger, cinnamon, nutmeg and salt. Transfer to prepared slow cooker stoneware.

3. Cover and cook on High for 3 hours, until set. Spoon into individual serving bowls and top with fresh berries, vanilla ice cream or a dollop of whipped cream, if using.

Natural Wonders

MILK

Although milk is high in saturated fat, it is one of the best food sources of calcium and a good source of protein. The milk in one serving of this pudding provides 4.1 grams of protein. Milk is often derided in contemporary society, but there is little doubt that drinking milk can have significant health benefits beyond the contribution that calcium makes to preventing osteoporosis. For instance, a recent study published in *The New England Journal of Medicine* linked the consumption of milk with a reduced risk of gout, a type of arthritis. Drinking milk may also play a role in weight control and in controlling diabetes. One study found that women who consumed at least three daily servings of dairy reduced their risk of becoming obese by 80 percent, and another, published in the *Journal of the American Medical Association*, linked young adults' consumption of milk with a significant reduction in insulin resistance. Milk is also a major food source of conjugated linoleic acid (CLA), which has been identified as a nutraceutical with bioactive properties. Studies done on animals suggest that CLA may be anticarcinogenic and reduce fat to lean body mass ratio, among other benefits.

Nutrients Per Serving	
Calories	181
Protein	6.4 g
Carbohydrates	27.0 g
Fat (Total)	5.5 g
Saturated Fat	2.1 g
Monounsaturated Fat	2.4 g
Polyunsaturated Fat	0.5 g
Dietary Fiber	0.5 g
Sodium	227 mg
Cholesterol	56 mg

Good source of calcium, potassium and magnesium.

Source of vitamin B6 and phosphorus.

Indian Banana Pudding

This traditional Indian pudding has an unusual thickener: dried split peas. Exotic and delicious, it has a light banana flavor enhanced with sweet dates and the texture of crunchy toasted almonds.

MAKES 8 SERVINGS

TIP

❖ **To toast almonds: Spread in a single layer on an ungreased baking sheet. Bake at 350°F (180°C), stirring once, until lightly browned, about 5 minutes.**

- **Works best in a small (3½ quart) slow cooker**
- **Greased slow cooker stoneware**

½ cup	yellow split peas, soaked according to Quick Soak method (see Basic Beans, page 250) and drained	125 mL
1 tbsp	minced gingerroot	15 mL
¼ cup	Demerara or evaporated cane juice sugar	50 mL
1	can (14 oz/398 mL) coconut milk	1
½ tsp	almond extract	2 mL
1 tsp	ground cardamom	5 mL
2	ripe bananas, peeled and chopped	2
¼ cup	finely chopped pitted soft dates, preferably Medjool	50 mL
½ cup	toasted slivered almonds, divided	125 mL
	Whipped cream, optional	

1. In a blender or food processor, combine soaked peas, ginger, sugar and ½ cup (125 mL) of the coconut milk. Process until puréed. Add remaining coconut milk, almond extract and cardamom and blend. Pour into prepared slow cooker stoneware.

2. Place a tea towel folded in half (so you will have two layers) over top of stoneware to absorb moisture. Cover and cook on High for 3 hours, until peas are tender and mixture begins to thicken. Stir in bananas. Replace folded towel and cook on High for 30 minutes.

3. Remove stoneware from casing and, using a wooden spoon, beat mixture vigorously. Fold in dates and half the almonds. Transfer to a serving bowl. Cover and refrigerate until thoroughly chilled, about 1½ hours. Garnish with remaining almonds and serve with a dollop of whipped cream, if using.

Natural Wonders

ALMONDS

The almonds in this recipe deliver more than flavor and texture; they also provide significant health benefits. Almonds are one of the best food sources of vitamin E, an antioxidant that protects cells against free radical damage and helps prevent some chronic diseases. They also contain magnesium, folacin, iron and several important phytonutrients. Almonds are high in healthy monounsaturated fat, which helps keep cholesterol under control. Studies have linked eating almonds with improved cholesterol levels, and one study published in 2002 showed that people with elevated cholesterol could significantly reduce their levels of LDL ("bad") cholesterol by consuming almonds.

Nutrients Per Serving	
Calories	252
Protein	6.2 g
Carbohydrates	28.6 g
Fat (Total)	14.4 g
Saturated Fat	9.4 g
Monounsaturated Fat	3.0 g
Polyunsaturated Fat	1.1 g
Dietary Fiber	3.0 g
Sodium	12 mg
Cholesterol	0 mg

Good source of magnesium, potassium and iron.

Source of vitamin B6 and phosphorus.

Contains a moderate amount of dietary fiber.

Diabetic Food Values

The diabetic food values for all the recipes were prepared by Info Access (1988) Inc.

Info Access is a Canadian firm of registered dietitians and computer experts specializing in computer-assisted nutrient analysis, assessing more than 4,000 recipes annually for a broad range of international clients. The Nutritional Accounting System component of the CBORD Menu Management System is used, as well as the Canadian Nutrient File, augmented as necessary with data from other reliable sources.

Info Access has also been involved with the assignment of food choice values in Canada, acting as the consulting firm assigning values for the Canadian Diabetes Association. The U.S. determinations were based on Exchange List Guidelines for Recipe/Food Label Calculations, Page 174, *Diabetes Medical Nutrition Therapy*, The American Dietetic Association/American Diabetes Association, 1997.

While the U.S. and Canadian diabetes assignment methodologies are similar, there are some variations in the approaches taken and the base values used that account for the observed differences. In the U.S. System, dietary fiber is generally not deducted from total carbohydrate (except for high fiber cereals); thus carbohydrate choices may be higher with the U.S. assignments. Vegetables (up to 5 g carbohydrate) are considered "free" in Canada, whereas vegetable assignments are made in the U.S. In the U.S., the Starch Exchange assumes 1 g fat per choice; in Canada the same assignment assumes no fat. Consequently fat assignments may be higher in Canada. In the U.S., half meat and fat exchanges are not allowed; in Canada, half values may be assigned for these choices. Thus, there may be some rounding changes introduced.

Recipes	Page No.	Canadian Diabetes Association Values	American Diabetes Association Values
Apple Cranberry Bread (1/8 of recipe)	14	3 Carbohydrates, 2 Fats	2 Starches, 1/2 Fruit, 1 Other, 1 1/2 Fat
Apple Oatmeal Pudding (1/8 of recipe)	264	2 1/2 Carbohydrates, 1 Fat	1 1/2 Starches, 1 Fruit, 1 Fat
Apple Oatmeal with Wheat Berries (1/6 of recipe)	28	2 Carbohydrates, 1/2 Fat	1 1/2 Starches, 1 Fruit
Artichoke, Sun-Dried Tomato and Goat Cheese Strata (1/8 of recipe)	248	1 1/2 Carbohydrates, 1 Meat, 1 Fat	1/2 Low Fat, 1 Starch, 1 Vegetable, 1 Low Fat Meat, 1 Fat
Banana Walnut Oat Bread (1/8 of recipe)	18	2 1/2 Carbohydrates, 1/2 Meat, 2 1/2 Fat	1 Starch, 1 Fruit, 1 Other, 3 Fats
Barley and Sweet Potato Chili (1/6 of recipe)	202	2 Carbohydrates, 1/2 Fat	2 Starches, 2 Vegetables
Barley and Wild Rice Pilaf (1/6 of recipe)	178	1 1/2 Carbohydrates, 1 1/2 Fat	1 1/2 Starches, 1 Vegetable, 1 Fat
Basic Beans (1/4 of recipe)	250	1 Carbohydrate, 1 Meat	1 1/2 Starches, 1 Very Low Fat Meat
Basic Polenta (1/6 of recipe)	182	1 1/2 Carbohydrates	1 1/2 Starches
Basic Tomato Sauce (1/4 of recipe)	212	1 Carbohydrate, 1 Fat	1 1/2 Carbohydrates, 1 Fat

Recipes	Page No.	Canadian Diabetes Association Values	American Diabetes Association Values
Basic Vegetable Stock ($1/12$ of recipe=1 cup)	34	1 Extra	1 Free
Basmati Rice Pudding ($1/8$ of recipe)	259	2 Carbohydrates	$1/2$ Whole Milk, 1 Starch, $1/2$ Other Carbohydrate
Beef and Barley with Rosemary and Orange ($1/8$ of recipe)	140	$1\frac{1}{2}$ Carbohydrates, 3 Meats	$1\frac{1}{2}$ Starches, 2 Vegetables, 3 Lean Meats
Beef and Chickpea Curry with Spinach ($1/4$ of recipe)	174	1 Carbohydrate, 4 Meats	1 Starch, Vegetable, 4 Lean Meats
Beef Carbonnade with Collards ($1/8$ of recipe)	172	3 Meats, 1 Extra	$1/2$ Starch, 1 Vegetable, 4 Lean Meats
Beet Soup with Lemongrass and Lime ($1/8$ of recipe)	44	$1/2$ Carbohydrate, $1/2$ Fat	1 Carbohydrate, $1/2$ Fat
Bistro Fish Soup ($1/10$ of recipe)	126	1 Carbohydrate, $1/2$ Meat, $1\frac{1}{2}$ Fat	1 Starch, 2 Vegetables, 2 Fat
Breakfast Rice ($1/4$ of recipe)	25	$4\frac{1}{2}$ Carbohydrates, $1/2$ Fat	$2\frac{1}{2}$ Starches, 1 Fruit, $1\frac{1}{2}$ Other
Buckwheat Meatballs in Tomato Sauce ($1/8$ of recipe)	162	$1/2$ Carbohydrate, 2 Meats, $1/2$ Fat	$1/2$ Starch, 1 Vegetable, 2 Medium Fat Meats
Cabbage Borscht ($1/8$ of recipe)	68	$1/2$ Carbohydrate, $1/2$ Fat	1 Starch, 1 Vegetable
Caldo Verde ($1/8$ of recipe)	58	$1\frac{1}{2}$ Carbohydrates, $1/2$ Meat	$1\frac{1}{2}$ Starch, 2 Vegetables, $1/2$ Fat
Caramelized Onion Sauce with Whole Wheat Pasta ($1/6$ of recipe)	188	3 Carbohydrates, 1 Fat	2 Starches, $1\frac{1}{2}$ Carbohydrates, 1 Fat
Caraway Soda Bread ($1/8$ of recipe)	24	$1\frac{1}{2}$ Carbohydrates, 1 Fat	$1\frac{1}{2}$ Starches, $1/2$ Fat
Caribbean Fish Stew ($1/8$ of recipe)	84	3 Meats	2 Vegetables, 3 Very Lean Meats
Celery Root and Mushroom Lasagna ($1/8$ of recipe)	180	2 Carbohydrates, 2 Meats, $1\frac{1}{2}$ Fat	2 Starches, 2 Vegetables, 2 Medium Fat Meats, 1 Fat
Chestnut Soup ($1/6$ of recipe)	78	1 Carbohydrate, 1 Fat	1 Starch, 1 Vegetable, 1 Fat
Chicken Cacciatore with Broccoli ($1/6$ of recipe)	90	$4\frac{1}{2}$ Meats, 1 Extra	1 Carbohydrate, 4 Lean Meats, $1/2$ Fat
Chicken Cassoulet ($1/8$ of recipe)	86	1 Carbohydrate, 3 Meats	1 Starch, 1 Carbohydrate, 2 Lean Meats
Chicken Chili and Barley Casserole ($1/8$ of recipe)	100	2 Carbohydrates, $2\frac{1}{2}$ Meats, 1 Fat	2 Starches, 2 Vegetables, 2 Lean Meats, $1\frac{1}{2}$ Fat
Chicken with Leeks in Walnut Sauce ($1/8$ of recipe)	96	4 Meats	2 Vegetables, 3 Lean Meats, 2 Fat

Recipes	Page No.	Canadian Diabetes Association Values	American Diabetes Association Values
Chili con Carne ($^1/_8$ of recipe)	170	1 Carbohydrate, 4 Meats	1 Starch, 1 Vegetable, 4 Lean Meats
Cioppino ($^1/_8$ of recipe)	118	$3^1/_2$ Meats	2 Vegetables, 4 Very Lean Meat
Cockaleekie ($^1/_8$ of recipe)	76	$1^1/_2$ Carbohydrates, 3 Meats	$1^1/_2$ Starches, 2 Vegetables, 3 Very Low Fat Meat, $^1/_2$ Fat
Coconut Cranberry Rice Pudding ($^1/_8$ of recipe)	258	2 Carbohydrates, 2 Fat	$1^1/_2$ Starches, 1 Other Carbohydrate, 2 Fat
Cornmeal Pudding ($^1/_8$ of recipe)	272	2 Carbohydrates, $^1/_2$ Fat	1 Starch, 1 Other Carbohydrate, 1 Fat
Cranberry Pear Brown Betty ($^1/_6$ of recipe)	262	2 Carbohydrates, 1 Fat	2 Fruit, 1 Fat
Creamy Morning Millet with Apples ($^1/_6$ of recipe)	24	3 Carbohydrates	2 Starches, 1 Other
Creamy Polenta with Corn and Chiles ($^1/_6$ of recipe)	184	$1^1/_2$ Carbohydrates, 1 Meat, 1 Fat	$^1/_2$ Skim Milk, 1 Starch, 1 Lean Meat, 1 Fat
Creamy Tuna Casserole ($^1/_6$ of recipe)	116	2 Carbohydrates, 2 Meats	2 Starches, 1 Vegetable, 1 Lean Meat 1 Fat
Curried Parsnip Soup with Green Peas ($^1/_8$ of recipe)	66	1 Carbohydrate, 1 Fat	1 Starch, 1 Vegetable, 1 Fat
French Basil Chicken ($^1/_8$ of recipe)	94	$3^1/_2$ Meats	2 Vegetables, 3 Lean Meats
Gingery Carrot Soup with Orange and Parsley ($^1/_8$ of recipe)	46	$^1/_2$ Carbohydrate, $^1/_2$ Fat	$^1/_2$ Fruit, 2 Vegetables, $^1/_2$ Fat
Gingery Pears Poached in Green Tea ($^1/_8$ of recipe)	254	2 Carbohydrates	1 Fruit, 1 Other Carbohydrate
Greek-Style Beans and Barley ($^1/_6$ of recipe)	200	2 Carbohydrates, 1 Fat	2 Starches, 2 Vegetables, $^1/_2$ Fat
Greek-Style Beef with Eggplant ($^1/_8$ of recipe)	142	$^1/_2$ Carbohydrate, $1^1/_2$ Meats, 1 Fat	1 Carbohydrate, 1 Lean Meat, 2 Fat
Greek-Style Split Pea Soup ($^1/_8$ of recipe)	80	2 Carbohydrates, 1 Meat	2 Starches, 1 Vegetable, 1 Very Low Fat Meat
Greek-Style Veal Shanks with Caper and Feta Gremolata ($^1/_6$ of recipe)	148	$^1/_2$ Carbohydrate, $4^1/_2$ Meats	$^1/_2$ Starch, 1 Vegetable, 5 Lean Meats
Harira ($^1/_8$ of recipe)	72	$1^1/_2$ Carbohydrates, 1 Meat	$1^1/_2$ Starches, 1 Vegetable, 1 Low Fat Meat
Homemade Chicken Stock ($^1/_{12}$ of recipe=1 cup)	35	1 Extra	1 Free
Indian Banana Pudding ($^1/_8$ of recipe)	274	$1^1/_2$ Carbohydrates, $^1/_2$ Meat, $2^1/_2$ Fat	1 Starch, 1 Fruit, $2^1/_2$ Fat

Recipes	Page No.	Canadian Diabetes Association Values	American Diabetes Association Values
Indian Beef with Cauliflower and Peppers ($1/8$ of recipe)	164	$3\frac{1}{2}$ Meats	1 Vegetable, 4 Lean Meats
Indian Peas and Beans ($1/6$ of recipe)	240	$1\frac{1}{2}$ Carbohydrates, 1 Meat	$1\frac{1}{2}$ Starches, 2 Vegetables
Indian-Style Chicken with Puréed Spinach ($1/8$ of recipe)	88	$4\frac{1}{2}$ Meats	2 Vegetables, 4 Lean Meats
Irish Oatmeal ($1/4$ of recipe)	29	1 Carbohydrate	1 Starch
Lamb with Lentils and Chard ($1/10$ of recipe)	150	$1\frac{1}{2}$ Carbohydrates, $3\frac{1}{2}$ Meats	$1\frac{1}{2}$ Starches, 2 Vegetables, 3 Lean Meats
Leafy Greens Soup ($1/8$ of recipe)	42	$1/2$ Carbohydrate, $1/2$ Fat	$1/2$ Starch, 2 Vegetables, $1/2$ Fat
Louisiana Seafood Stew with Chicken and Sausage ($1/8$ of recipe)	134	$3\frac{1}{2}$ Meats	2 Vegetables, 3 Lean Meats
Mediterranean Beef Ragout ($1/8$ of recipe)	168	3 Meats	2 Vegetables, 3 Lean Meats, 1 Fat
Mixed Vegetables in Spicy Peanut Sauce ($1/8$ of recipe)	216	$1/2$ Carbohydrate, 1 Meat, 2 Fat	$1/2$ Starch, 1 Carbohydrate, 1 High Fat Meat, 1 Fat
Moroccan-Style Chicken with Prunes and Quinoa ($1/8$ of recipe)	106	$2\frac{1}{2}$ Carbohydrates, 2 Meats	$1\frac{1}{2}$ Starches, 1 Fruit, 2 Lean Meats
Moroccan-Style Lamb with Apricots and Raisins ($1/8$ of recipe)	154	1 Carbohydrate, $2\frac{1}{2}$ Meats	$1\frac{1}{2}$ Fruit, 3 Lean Meats
Multigrain Cereal with Fruit ($1/6$ of recipe)	26	3 Carbohydrates, $1/2$ Fat	2 Starches, $1\frac{1}{2}$ Fruit
Mushroom Lentil Soup ($1/8$ of recipe)	36	$1\frac{1}{2}$ Carbohydrates, 1 Meat	$1\frac{1}{2}$ Starches, 2 Vegetables, 1 Very Low Fat Meat
Mushroom Soup with Millet ($1/8$ of recipe)	38	$1/2$ Carbohydrate, $1/2$ Fat	$1/2$ Starch, 2 Vegetables, $1/2$ Fat
Mushroom Tomato Sauce ($1/6$ of recipe)	210	$1/2$ Fat	2 Vegetables, $1/2$ Fat
Mushrooms and Chickpea Stew with Roasted Red Pepper Coulis ($1/6$ of recipe)	236	1 Carbohydrate, $1/2$ Meat, 1 Fat	1 Starch, 2 Vegetables, $1\frac{1}{2}$ Fat
New Age Succotash ($1/8$ of recipe)	226	2 Carbohydrates, 2 Meats	2 Starches, 2 Vegetables, 2 Medium Fat Meats
New World Leek and Potato Soup ($1/8$ of recipe)	62	$1\frac{1}{2}$ Carbohydrates, $1\frac{1}{2}$ Fat	$1\frac{1}{2}$ Starches, 2 Vegetables, $1\frac{1}{2}$ Fat
Onion-Braised Shrimp ($1/4$ of recipe)	124	$1/2$ Carbohydrate, 3 Meats	1 Carbohydrate, 3 Lean Meats
Pasta with Syracuse Sauce ($1/6$ of recipe)	198	$1/2$ Carbohydrate, 1 Fat	1 Carbohydrate, 1 Fat

Recipes	Page No.	Canadian Diabetes Association Values	American Diabetes Association Values
Peach Raspberry Betty (1/6 of recipe)	266	3 Carbohydrates, 1 1/2 Fat	1 Starch, 1 Fruit, 1 Other Carbohydrate, 1 1/2 Fat
Peppery Turkey Casserole (1/8 of recipe)	110	1 1/2 Carbohydrates, 2 Meats	1 1/2 Starches, 1 Vegetable, 2 Lean Meats
Pumpkin and Rice Casserole with Mushrooms (1/6 of recipe)	192	3 1/2 Carbohydrates, 1 Fat	3 1/2 Starches, 2 Vegetables
Pumpkin Date Loaf (1/8 of recipe)	16	2 Carbohydrates, 2 Fat	1 1/2 Starches, 1 Other, 1 1/2 Fat
Pumpkin Rice Pudding (1/8 of recipe)	256	3 Carbohydrates	1 Starch, 1 Fruit, 1 Other Carbohydrate
Ratatouille (1/8 of recipe)	218	1/2 Carbohydrate, 1 Fat	1 Carbohydrate, 1 Fat
Ratatouille (1/2 Portion – 1/16 of recipe)	218	1/2 Fat	1/2 Fat
Ribs 'n' Greens with Wheat Berries (1/8 of recipe)	160	2 Carbohydrates, 2 Meats, 1 Fat	2 Starches, 1 Vegetable, 2 High Fat Meats
Ribs with Hominy and Kale (1/8 of recipe)	158	1 Carbohydrate, 2 1/2 Meats, 1 Fat	1 Starch, 2 Vegetables, 2 High Fat Meats
Salmon Loaf (1/6 of recipe)	120	1/2 Carbohydrate, 2 Meats, 1 Fat	Starch, 1 Vegetable, 2 Lean Meats, 1 1/2 Fat
Scotch Broth (1/10 of recipe)	64	1 1/2 Carbohydrates, 1 Meat	1 Starch, 1 Carbohydrate, 1 Low Fat Meat
Shrimp 'n' Grits (1/4 of recipe)	192	2 Carbohydrates, 2 Meats, 1/2 Fat	2 Starches, 2 Vegetables, 2 Lean Meats
Soy-Braised Tofu (1/4 of recipe)	242	1/2 Carbohydrate, 1 Meat, 1/2 Fat	1/2 Starch, 1 Low Fat Meat, 1 Fat
Spanish-Style Pork and Beans (1/10 of recipe)	152	1/2 Carbohydrate, 3 Meats	1/2 Starch, 1 Carbohydrate, 3 Lean Meats
Spicy Peanut Chicken (1/8 of recipe)	98	1/2 Carbohydrate, 4 1/2 Meats	1/2 Starch, 1 Vegetable, 4 Lean Meats, 1 Fat
Spinach Dal With Millet (1/8 of recipe)	230	2 Carbohydrates, 1 Meat	2 Starches, 2 Vegetables, 1/2 Fat
Spinach, Sun-Dried Tomato and Cheddar Cheesecake (1/6 of recipe)	222	1 Carbohydrate, 1 Meat, 2 Fat	1 Starch, 1 Low Fat Meat, 3 Fats
Squash and Black Bean Chili (1/6 of recipe)	228	1 1/2 Carbohydrates, 1 Meat	1 1/2 Starches, 2 Vegetables
Squash with Quinoa and Apricots (1/8 of recipe)	208	2 1/2 Carbohydrates, 1 Fat	2 Starches, 1 Fruit
Stuffed Onions (1/6 of recipe)	144	1 1/2 Carbohydrates, 2 Meats	1 Starch, 1 1/2 Carbohydrates, 1 Medium Fat Meat, 1 Fat

Recipes	Page No.	Canadian Diabetes Association Values	American Diabetes Association Values
Sweet Potato Coconut Curry with Shrimp ($1/4$ of recipe)	132	$1\frac{1}{2}$ Carbohydrates, 3 Meats	2 Starches, 1 Vegetable, 3 Lean Meats
Sweet Potato Shepherd's Pie ($1/8$ of recipe)	220	$3\frac{1}{2}$ Carbohydrates, 1 Fat	$3\frac{1}{2}$ Starches, 2 Vegetables
Tamale Pie with Chili Millet Crust ($1/8$ of recipe)	204	2 Carbohydrates, 1 Meat	2 Starches, 2 Vegetables, 1 Medium Fat Meat
Thai-Style Coconut Fish Curry ($1/8$ of recipe)	128	3 Meats	$1/2$ Starch, 1 Vegetable, 3 Lean Meats
Thai-Style Pumpkin Soup ($1/8$ of recipe)	54	$1/2$ Carbohydrate, $1\frac{1}{2}$ Fat	$1/2$ Starch, 1 Vegetable, $1\frac{1}{2}$ Fat
The Ultimate Baked Apples ($1/8$ of recipe)	270	2 Carbohydrates, 1 Fat	$2\frac{1}{2}$ Fruit, 1 Fat
Turkey and Black Bean Soup ($1/8$ of recipe)	48	$1/2$ Carbohydrate, 3 Meats	1 Starch, 2 Vegetables, 3 Very Low Fat Meats
Turkey and Corn Chowder with Barley ($1/10$ of recipe)	32	1 Carbohydrate, 2 Meats	1 Starch, 1 Vegetable, 2 Low Fat Meats
Turkey in Cranberry Leek Sauce ($1/6$ of recipe)	104	$1/2$ Carbohydrate, 3 Meats	$1/2$ Fruit, 1 Vegetable, 3 Lean Meats
Turkey, Mushroom and Chickpea Sauce ($1/6$ of recipe)	108	1 Carbohydrate, 2 Meats	1 Starch, 2 Vegetables, 2 Lean Meats, $1/2$ Fat
Two-Bean Soup with Pistou ($1/8$ of recipe)	52	$1\frac{1}{2}$ Carbohydrates, 1 Meat, 1 Fat	2 Starches, 1 Low Fat Meat, 1 Fat
Two-Bean Turkey Chili ($1/8$ of recipe)	114	1 Carbohydrate, 3 Meats	1 Starch, 1 Carbohydrate, 3 Very Lean Meats
Veal Goulash ($1/8$ of recipe)	138	3 Meats	2 Vegetables, 3 Lean Meats
Vegetable Chili ($1/8$ of recipe)	232	$1\frac{1}{2}$ Carbohydrates, 1 Fat	$1\frac{1}{2}$ Starches, 2 Vegetables, $1/2$ Fat
Vegetable Cobbler with Millet Crust ($1/8$ of recipe)	190	$1\frac{1}{2}$ Carbohydrates, 1 Meat, 1 Fat	2 Starches, 2 Vegetables, $1\frac{1}{2}$ Fat
Vegetable Curry with Lentils and Spinach ($1/8$ of recipe)	244	2 Carbohydrates, $1/2$ Meat	$2\frac{1}{2}$ Starches, 2 Vegetables
Vegetable Gumbo ($1/6$ of recipe)	74	1 Carbohydrate, $1/2$ Fat	1 Starch, 2 Vegetables, $1/2$ Fat
Vichyssoise with Celery Root and Watercress ($1/10$ of recipe)	56	$1\frac{1}{2}$ Fat	1 Vegetable, $1\frac{1}{2}$ Fat
Winter Vegetable Casserole ($1/6$ of recipe)	238	$2\frac{1}{2}$ Carbohydrates, $1/2$ Fat	2 Starches, $1\frac{1}{2}$ Carbohydrates

Selected Bibliography

Books

McCullough, Fran. *The Good Fat Cookbook* (Scribner, 2003)

Pratt, Steven, M.D. and Matthews, Kathy. *Superfoods: Fourteen Foods That Will Change Your Life* (HarperCollins, 2004)

Reader's Digest. *Foods That Harm, Foods That Heal: An A-Z Guide to Safe and Healthy Eating* (Revised Edition, The Reader's Digest Association, 2004)

Willett, Walter C. M.D. *Eat, Drink and Be Healthy: The Harvard Medical School Guide to Healthy Eating* (Free Press, 2001)

Wood, Rebecca. *The New Whole Foods Encyclopedia: A Comprehensive Resource for Healthy Eating* (Penguin Books, 1999)

Yeager, Selene and the Editors of Prevention. *The Doctor's Book of Food Remedies* (Rodale, 1998)

Websites

American Institute for Cancer Research (www.aicr.org)

Harvard School of Public Health, Department of Nutrition (www.hsph.harvard.edu/nutritionsource)

HealthierUS.gov (www.healthierus.gov)

Health Canada (www.hc-sc.gc.ca)

National Agricultural Library, U.S. Department of Agriculture (www.nutrition.gov)

National Cancer Institute (www.nci.nih.gov)

National Institutes of Health (www.nih.gov)

U.S. Department of Agriculture: Dietary Guidelines for Americans 2005 (www.health.gov/dietaryguidelines/dga2005/document)

The World's Healthiest Foods (www.whfoods.com)

Library and Archives Canada Cataloguing in Publication

Finlayson, Judith
    The healthy slow cooker : more than 100 recipes for health and wellness / Judith Finlayson.

Includes index.
ISBN-13: 978-0-7788-0133-0
ISBN-10: 0-7788-0133-0

1. Electric cookery, Slow. I. Title.

TX827.F555 2005   641.5'884   C2005-906130-8

Index